EMINENT AMERICANS

Namesakes of the Polaris Submarine Fleet

The author inspecting the first nuclear powered submarine, USS NAUTILUS, *in September 1964. Other books by Admiral Rickover include* Education and Freedom; Swiss Schools and Ours: Why Theirs Are Better; *and* American Education—A National Failure.

EMINENT AMERICANS

NAMESAKES
of the
POLARIS SUBMARINE FLEET

H. G. RICKOVER

L.C. CARD NO. 72-90503

© *Copyright 1972, H. G. Rickover*

For sale by the Superintendent of Documents, U.S. Government Printing Office
Washington, D.C. 20402 - Price $1.25 (paper cover)
Stock Number 5271-00315

This book is a memorial to my wife, Ruth Masters Rickover, who gave me unmeasurable assistance in preparing the text. She was at once the most human and intelligent person I ever knew, the greatest influence on my life and work.

To borrow from Tibullus: *"Tu mihi curarum requies, tu nocte vel atra lumen, et in solis tu mihi turba locis."*

PREFACE

IN 1957, the United States embarked upon a program of the highest priority to build a fleet of nuclear powered submarines to carry the Polaris missile. Ultimately, 41 of these ships were built, each capable of launching 16 missiles. The Polaris submarines were the largest ever built, displacing over 9,000 tons — as much as or more than many cruisers. Their purpose was to provide a powerful force that would serve as a deterrent to a nuclear attack upon the United States. Hidden in the vast reaches of the Atlantic and Pacific, these submarines would be invulnerable to attack. The enemy must know—so it was reasoned—that were he to launch a nuclear attack on the United States he must inevitably be destroyed. Because these ships would be so important to our defense, it was decided to name them after well-known figures in American history who had won and defended our freedom. The men for whom these submarines were named are the subject of this book.

Ever since the first nuclear submarine—the USS *Nautilus*— went to sea in January 1955, I have been responsible for directing the initial sea trials of each of our nuclear ships so as to make sure that their nuclear propulsion plants functioned properly and that the officers and men had been well trained. Because many members of Congress had given strong support in getting the *Nautilus* built, I decided that it would be no more than proper for me to send each of them a letter reporting what the ship had done. I remember writing some 80 letters in longhand during that first voyage. Soon I expanded the list of recipients to include all members of Congress and appropriate officials in the executive branch.

When it came time to test our first Polaris submarine, the USS *George Washington* in 1960, I thought it would be appropriate to include in my letter a brief biography of the man for whom the ship was named, and I continued this practice for each of the 40 Polaris submarines which followed. These letters were well received, and most of them were printed in the *Congressional Record*. Frequently I was urged to publish them in book form. This I agreed to do and Congress, in 1968, passed a resolution authorizing the printing of this book.

Because these letters had been written aboard ship, they had been necessarily limited to two or three pages. For the purposes of a book, I wanted to expand the original brief sketches of these figures into more complete essays. During the past 4 years I have devoted virtually all of my spare time to this task. Had it not been for the devoted efforts of my dear wife, who did most of the research for these essays, I could not possibly have completed this task while carrying out my official duties as a naval officer.

The careers of the men for whom the Polaris submarines are named span the full range of American history from the time of the Revolution to the present century. The preparation of these essays therefore required me to explore many aspects of our national history. In the process I learned a great deal, particularly about the origins of our Government and the events that led to the Civil War. Although I had read a good deal of ancient and modern history, I had never fully realized the fragile base upon which our system of National Government was established, the extent of the struggle it took to make us a Nation, and the part played in this struggle by nationalism, sectionalism, and the conflict over slavery. I was fascinated by the role of large corporations, Populist movements, and interest groups during the period after the Civil War in molding our Federal system of government to meet the needs of a modern, industrial nation.

This broader interest in the history of the United States led me to the conclusion that I should try to reflect in these biographical essays some of those historical themes which seem to me to have particular relevance for the kinds of problems our Nation faces today. Since I can lay no claim to being a professional historian, I would not want to suggest that these essays contain anything really new and original. But as a lifetime student of history and as one who has spent many years in intimate contact with virtually every aspect of our Federal Government, I thought my observations on these matters might be of some interest. I therefore decided to use the careers of the men for whom the Polaris submarines were named as the focus for essays which would be broad enough to include some of the significant events which occurred during their lifetimes.

The order in which these essays are printed, therefore, is not necessarily the order in which the submarines were commissioned. For example, the essays on Clay, Webster and Calhoun follow each other because the lives and actions of these men encompassed the great and divisive issues of States' rights and slavery.

To keep the size of this book within reasonable bounds, I was forced merely to suggest rather than fully develop many important themes in our history. Yet these essays will have served their purpose if they reveal something of the amazing diversity of principles and ideals which our forebears had to reconcile in building a Nation out of 13 suspicious and jealous Colonies.

All great contributions to political science were answers to challenges arising from political reality. Men of the ancient world, such as Plato, Aristotle and St. Augustine, down to the modern times of *The Federalist* and Calhoun, did not pursue theoretical concerns for their own sake. Facing political problems and experiences they could not understand, they accepted a great intellectual task. They delved into their cultural heritage, separating that which was the legacy of history from that which was true regardless of time and place. They had to reframe the age-old truths of politics in the light of contemporary experience.

Those men who are properly honored by the title "Founding Fathers" valued freedom and culture more than wealth. Nevertheless, they did not lose contact with political reality. Steeped in the principles of the Enlightenment, they could have easily constructed an artificial system of government so theoretical as to have failed to meet the needs of a people living in an unformed nation. These men however were practical politicians: none of them was content with a private life, no matter how successful. Based upon their own experience they built a government and endowed it with a flexibility so that each generation would have the chance to measure its own means against the age-old truth of political reality.

Perhaps a major reason for their success was the fundamental honesty they brought to the business of government. Their words were their own; there was substantiality in their writings. Not for them the imagery and public relations that pervade modern political life; they dealt with their countrymen on frank and open terms.

It was a galaxy of statesmen never again equalled in our Nation, seldom found anywhere else, that forged a political revolt into successful independence. Their great and contagious ideals have inspired other peoples to imitate the American struggle for liberty and independence.

The Declaration of Independence was no idle statement for these men, for in signing that document they pledged . . . "our lives, our fortunes and our sacred honor." Had the Revolution failed, they would have lost everything. That power-seeking individuals and base principles cluster around good men with lofty motives is a commonplace observation about revolutionary movements. But the human material, the intense drama, the ideas—these are the essence of the American political achievement. This was what Lafayette meant when he observed years later to Napoleon: "Great events were decided by a small number of men."

The adoption of the Federal Constitution did create a political union of 13 States, but it did not automatically create a nation in the sense that Great Britain, France or Spain were nations. These European powers each had a common language and strong national traditions going back several centuries. The citizens of these countries felt a sense of personal loyalty to the nation, as represented by the king. They also had a national history which recorded in fact or in legend the moments of victory or defeat from which their nation had emerged. The common sacrifices and achievements of their ancestors bound the people of these European states into something approaching our modern conception of a nation.

In the fledgling United States of America, most of these elements of nationhood were missing. Although Americans were still predominantly English in their political and cultural traditions, many of them retained the dress, language, and customs of their German, Dutch, or Scandinavian ancestors. Those of English background had, by the act of revolution, repudiated much of their political heritage, while those from other national stocks brought diversity rather than a common tradition to American life. Having won independence as citizens of the several States, most Americans did not at once develop a feeling of national loyalty, at least not in the sense that most Europeans had. Only the Revolution itself, and especially as it began to fade into legend, provided the common experience in which the seeds of nationalism would grow.

In addition to the Revolutionary tradition, Americans at the beginning of the 19th century found the cement of nationalism in the common threat posed to the young Nation's existence by continuing conflict in Europe. By the time the Napoleonic wars and the War of 1812 had ended, the nationalist sentiments of the American people had reached a level of fervor seldom, if ever, again attained in our history. The great leaders on the American political scene in those years—from Madison, Marshall and Monroe, to Clay, Webster, Calhoun and Andrew Jackson—based their policies and actions upon the premise that the welfare of the American people rested upon the creation of a strong nation-state.

At the very same time, other influences in American life were nurturing ideas which ran directly counter to the spirit of nationalism. The idea of State sovereignty, which had in reality died with the adoption of the Constitution, lived on as a myth in the minds of many Americans, North and South. The rapidly growing dimensions of the Nation and its rural character bred a reliance on local self-government which de Tocqueville had found so refreshing. Americans were proud of their new Nation even to the point that chauvinism became a common failing; but when national commitments conflicted with local interests, they could quickly reassert their presumed rights as citizens of the States, much as their fathers had done during the Revolution. Thus during the War of 1812 sturdy New Englanders who had played a part in establishing the Nation did not hesitate to undermine the war effort and talk privately about secession. When the Tariff of 1828 threatened to destroy the cotton economy of South Carolina, Calhoun, once a strident nationalist, formulated the doctrine of nullification and began building an elaborate political theory which would protect the minority interests of the South even at the cost of the Union.

Just as Americans struggled on the political scene to reconcile their conflicting loyalties to the Nation and their States, so too they faced deeply troubling moral issues which went to the very heart of their civilization. The two fundamental political documents of the Nation epitomized this moral dilemma. On the one hand there was the Declaration of Independence, with its ringing idealism of personal freedom from the tyranny of government—which provided the inspiration in later years for many revolutions in other lands. On the other hand, the Constitution, with its emphasis on the protection of property rights, provided a firm institutional structure for slavery, guaranteeing its existence in the United States long after it had been abolished by most European nations.

These profound contradictions, which were beyond the capacity of any individual American to resolve, fed the flames of moral and sectional conflict in the middle decades of the last century. The brilliant compromises of Henry Clay, the sophisticated disquisitions of John C. Calhoun, and the stirring appeals to nationalism by Daniel Webster could not turn the Nation from the course of disaster. Only the Civil War, one of the bloodiest conflicts in history, and the extraordinary leadership of Abraham Lincoln made possible the slow and painful restoration of the national tradition in the years after 1861.

Had we remained, after the Civil War, a country of small farms and factories, we might have grown into a true Nation in which all of our people could have been joined together by common interests. But at this point, the Industrial Revolution reached our shores along with swarms of immigrants from the poverty-stricken and oppressed nations of Europe. These new forces in American life made possible the exploitation of a vast continent in a matter of decades, extraordinary advances in technology, and the formation of huge business organizations and corporations. These same forces also produced working conditions which rivaled the horrors of the English Midlands, unprecedented wealth among the privileged few, and blatant corruption in government. These national scandals in turn fostered strong sentiments for reform. By the turn of the century, farmers in the West and South were organizing themselves in what became the Populist movement and workers in our cities had embarked on the bloody path of the labor union movement. From this national reform effort also came the Federal regulatory agencies, beginning with the Interstate Commerce Commission of 1887, Theodore Roosevelt's denunciation of "malefactors of great wealth," and finally the election of Woodrow Wilson in 1912.

Within the great sweep of American history fall the careers of those men for whom the Polaris submarines have been named. They left a lasting imprint on the political, cultural and military life of our Nation. Their lives show the great impact that a single individual can make upon his Nation and his time if he has the ability, the energy, and above all the determination to see his ideas become reality.

A nation happens when people, as a result of common experience, sense a unity of interest among themselves and a common pattern in their relationship, their ideas, and their institutions.

Historically, in many countries, the sense of nationhood has been set by a class who felt responsible for their government. In turn, the government being largely recruited from this group, depended on and felt responsible for it. For much of their existence, this was true of Rome and Byzantium. When this group became weakened, the foundation for support of these empires likewise weakened and deterioration set in.

The middle class has in modern times set the national standard and tone for all Western countries. During most of the

19th century our middle class had faith in the Government and its leaders. Their quality of honesty, dignity and identity with the Nation made that class the focal point for the deep feeling of our people for the Republic.

Today, it is more important than ever that high officials and the institutions in their charge set the moral tone for our people. Contributing to this need is the lessening in religious convictions—many seeing the world as fulfilling today what in the past was promised for Heaven—and decline of the Protestant Ethic of work. If the present trend is to be arrested and corrected we must have more leaders who set the moral tone and example for our people as did men such as Washington, Adams, Jefferson, Madison, Clay, Webster, Lincoln, Theodore Roosevelt and Woodrow Wilson. Unless this takes place, we will increasingly become a fragmented Nation, each interest group attempting to use the national patrimony for its own good rather than for the Nation as a whole.

The lives of the Americans described in these essays may offer insights into how we may once again feel a sense of unity of interest.

H. G. RICKOVER

October, 1972
Washington, D.C.

CONTENTS

House Concurrent Resolution No. 213

IN THE SENATE OF THE UNITED STATES

July 27, 1968

Referred to the Committee on Rules and Administration

Resolved by the House of Representatives (the Senate concurring), That there be printed as a House document the letters of Vice Admiral Hyman G. Rickover, United States Navy, to the Speaker of the House of Representatives relating to the distinguished Americans in whose honor the United States Navy Polaris nuclear submarines were named. The copy for such House document shall be prepared under the supervision of the Joint Committee on Printing.

SEC. 2. In addition to the usual number, there shall be printed twelve thousand additional copies of such House document, of which four thousand copies shall be for the use of the Senate, and eight thousand copies shall be for the use of the House of Representatives.

SEC. 3. That, notwithstanding any provision of the copyright laws and regulations with respect to publications in public domain, the letters shall be subject to copyright by the author thereof, Vice Admiral Hyman G. Rickover, United States Navy.

SEC. 4. Copies of such document shall be prorated to Members of the Senate and House of Representatives for a period of sixty days, after which the unused balance shall revert to the respective Senate and House document rooms.

Passed the House of Representatives July 26, 1968.

Attest:

W. PAT JENNINGS,
Clerk.

EXCERPT FROM CONGRESSIONAL RECORD—SENATE, AUGUST 1, 1968, P. S. 9928:

Letters of Vice Adm. Hyman G. Rickover

The concurrent resolution (H. Con. Res. 213) authorizing the printing as a House document of the letters of Vice Adm. Hyman G. Rickover relating to the distinguished Americans in whose honor the U.S. Navy Polaris nuclear submarines were named was considered and agreed to.

xvii

USS GEORGE WASHINGTON
(SSBN 598)

THIS SHIP has been given the most illustrious name in America. Rarely does history confirm contemporary judgment in pronouncing a man "indispensable" to his country. But there is general agreement that on three occasions, when the fate of our Nation hung in balance, one man was decisive in resolving the crisis. This man was George Washington (1732–99), affectionately known in life as the "Father of his Country," eulogized after death (by Henry Lee) as "first in war, first in peace, and first in the hearts of his countrymen."

When the 13 Colonies (numbering but a fraction over 1 percent of today's American population) took on the mighty British Empire in 1775, they chose Washington to command the first American Army ever to take the field. With skill, patience, devotion, and fortitude he wrested independence from an enemy enormously superior in warmaking resources. "The success of America," wrote Lord Russell, "was owing, next to the errors of their adversaries, to the conduct and character of General Washington." When, after repeated failure, the now independent States made a final supreme effort in 1787 to establish a viable Federal Union, Washington presided over the Philadelphia Convention which drew up the first plan ever to have been devised for a "compound republic." Though silent at the meetings, he was immensely persuasive in private conversation. That the delegates reached near-unanimous agreement is

The first Polaris submarine USS GEORGE WASHINGTON (SSBN 598)
on sea trials in 1959.

credited largely to his influence. During the often fierce campaign over ratification of the Constitution, his signature on the document reassured many Americans with serious misgivings but who trusted Washington's judgment implicitly. In 1789, no other name was even considered for the Presidency. Men who differed in almost everything else (Jefferson and Hamilton, for example) were united in the conviction that to succeed, the new experiment must be inaugurated by Washington. Moving with his usual careful deliberation, Washington gave the country, at the very start of national life, one of its strongest, most competent administrations. It is a measure of the greatness of this man who never sought high public office, yet was always chosen unanimously, that so many of the precedents he set, in going about his duties, have stood the test of time. A few might be mentioned.

Though a disciplinarian, he took a deep personal interest in the welfare of his troops. With him, "to share a common lot and participate in the inconveniences wch. the army . . . are oblig'd to undergo," was a "fundamental principle." The first general to insist that military decorations be given not only to officers, but to soldiers as well, he founded the Order of the Purple Heart (revived in 1932 as a mark of distinction for servicemen wounded in action). If all this now seems no more than elementary justice, it was an innovation in his time. For centuries, armies had been thought of exclusively in terms of their officers. There is a scene in Act IV of Shakespeare's *Henry V* that illustrates the point. When the herald bringing news of England's victory in the Battle of Agincourt is asked "the number of our English dead," he hands over a paper listing "Edward the Duke of York, the Earl of Suffolk, Sir Richard Ketly, David Gam, esquire: *None else of name*" (my italics). Ordinary soldiers counted for so little, they remained anonymous even when they died for their country.

Politically of greatest importance was Washington's refusal to serve more than two terms as President. From this tradition we deviated but once, only to return hastily to the old practice by making Washington's precedent binding through the 22nd amendment (1951). This limitation on presidential power assumes ever greater importance as the complexities of life in modern society lead to the growth of large and powerful bureaucracies within the Executive Department, thus inevitably shifting power from the legislature to the executive and upsetting the system of checks and balances, planned with such care by the founders of our Nation in order that government might be kept responsive to the public will.

Equally important was Washington's precedent in foreign policy. Down to very recent times we followed him in holding aloof from the quarrels of other nations. His Farewell Address, widely read throughout the world, has doubtless influenced many another young nation. He was the first head of state to set his Nation deliberately on a course of steering "clear of permanent alliances," the operative word here being "permanent." (It was Jefferson, not Washington, who used the term "entangling" alliances.) Washington believed that if we kept ourselves "by suitable establishments on a respectable defensive posture," we might "safely trust occasional alliances for extraordinary war emergencies." He was, however, inflexible in condemning "permanent, inveterate antipathies against particular nations and passionate attachments for others." This is not easy during periods of worldwide revolutionary upheavals. Americans have at times disregarded his warning that "a Nation which indulges toward another an habitual hatred or an habitual fondness is in some degree a slave. It is a slave to its animosity or to its affection, either of which is sufficient to lead it astray from its duty and its interest."

Washington had hoped to establish the National Executive on a nonpartisan basis, carefully balancing his Cabinet appointments between strong supporters of the Constitution (Hamilton in the Treasury, and Knox, Secretary of War) and men who mistrusted central power (Jefferson in the State Department, and Randolph, Attorney General). The joint task of setting up the new government did not lead to a merging of these "factions" but rather crystallized them into formal parties (Jefferson's Republicans and Hamilton's Federalists). That this was inevitable, indeed that parties are an essential part of the "democratic process," seems not to have occurred to anyone, not even to the leaders of the two parties. Each evidently thought that on any public issue only one view was correct and patriotic, and that view his own. How else can one explain the passionate sense of outrage which led Jeffersonians to look for Royalists, aristocrats, and Anglicans under every Federalist bed, and Hamiltonians to see the shadow of the guillotine behind every Republican protest against extension of Federal power?

What Washington rightly deplored was that one party allowed its affection for revolutionary France, and the other for the former mother country Great Britain, to influence positions taken on domestic issues. Not only was party strife thereby exacerbated but foreign intervention invited at a time when the country was weak and might have been crushed by the two

European giants locked in mortal combat. This, Washington saw clearly; he did not allow his justifiable pride in American political ideas and practices to nurture delusions of grandeur in other respects.

America now holds premier rank in the world; all of us in some degree have a sense of enhanced status because of it. We find it difficult to conceive that our country ever held a position below that of the leading powers. We find it even more difficult to believe that there was ever a time when, in the eyes of the world, individual Americans, so to speak, "outranked" the United States. Yet that is how things stood at the start of our national existence. America did not possess great economic or military power, but a few American citizens—notably Washington—commanded such universal admiration that their country gained in status thereby. America stood higher in world esteem than its actual power warranted because she had produced these men, and because the American people embraced their lofty ideals and followed their lead. On hearing of Washington's death, England honored her old enemy and Napoleon said, "Washington is dead. That great man fought against tyranny. He consolidated the liberty of his country. His memory will always be dear to the French people and to all free men of the two worlds—especially to the French soldiers who, like him and the American soldiers, have fought for equality and liberty. Consequently, the First Consul orders that for ten days black crepe be hung on all the flags and pennants of the Republic." The tribute was paid the man, not the office of President of the United States.

Many of the Revolutionary leaders were more brilliant than Washington; most were better educated; all made important contributions. Yet to his contemporaries here and abroad Washington was the indispensable man of his time. They saw the essence of his greatness more clearly than we who must search for evidence in the record. His life may perhaps give us a clue. It will at least reveal some of the factors that went into the shaping of this man.

He was a fourth generation Virginian with deep roots in the land. Little Creek Plantation (Westmoreland County) where he was born, and Mount Vernon on the Potomac where he grew to manhood, had been in his family since great-grandfather John (son of the Anglican rector at Purleigh, England) first settled in Virginia in 1657. When his father, a moderately well-to-do planter, died, Washington was 11. Since he was a younger son (fifth of 10 children by two marriages), none of the land came to him; it went, as customary, to the two eldest sons, Lawrence and Augustine. Fortunately, the father's will made Lawrence his guardian. Theirs was an unusually close and affectionate relationship, resembling more nearly that of father to son (Lawrence was 15 years his senior) than older to younger brother.

The year Lawrence inherited Mount Vernon, he married Ann Fairfax and built for her the manor house that still stands as a national shrine. It became young Washington's second home and, when his older brother died without living issue, it passed to him as residuary heir (after the death of Lawrence's widow in 1761). No spot on earth was dearer to Washington than this plantation, nor any work more congenial than that of managing it. When a Jeffersonian newspaper once accused him of Royalist ambitions, he said angrily that he would rather live at Mount Vernon than be emperor of the universe. Doubtless, he loved it all the more since he grew up with no expectations of ever owning any part of his family's land.

Of Washington's education we know little except that it probably did not exceed 6 or 7 years. His father and brother Lawrence (both educated in England) seem to have been his teachers. Of our first six Presidents he was the only one without a college education. Nevertheless, he appreciated the value of books and of education in general. Disturbed that many Americans went abroad for their higher education, thus exposing themselves to ideas "not congenial to republicanism," he left a sum of money in his will to found at Washington a "national university." But his wish was disregarded and the money disappeared, no one knows how or where.

Washington's mind and character were formed chiefly by association with the cultivated and civic minded Tidewater society into whose circle he was drawn through his brother's Fairfax connections, and by his early familiarity with wilderness life as surveyor, explorer, militia leader, and Indian fighter. He had the best of two worlds: Tidewater Virginia and the western frontier. Life in the first gave him his stately bearing, poise, and dignity, his deep sense of public responsibility and duty to country, a natural ease in the company of the great of this world. Life in the second hardened him physically and endowed him with the stamina that stood him in good stead during the grim years of the Revolutionary War when he seldom had more than 3 or 4 hours of consecutive sleep in any 24. He also gained firsthand knowledge of the nature and extent of the American West and of its pioneering people, many of whom later served under him.

With no prospects of owning land, he chose surveying as his

career. At 15, he was earning small sums; at 16, Lord Fairfax entrusted a major surveying job to him; at 17, he became official surveyor of Culpeper County. He was 20 when his brother died. Besides the management of Mount Vernon, the office of District Adjutant now devolved upon him, including responsibility for training the militia in that sector of Virginia. Two years later, he was sent on an important mission into the Great Lakes region by Governor Dinwiddie who published his report as *The Journal of Major George Washington* (1754). It made quite an impact in America and England.

In 1754, he fought against the French in and around Fort Duquesne (now Pittsburgh), building a fortified camp he called Fort Necessity, from which he inflicted considerable damage on the enemy. He was with Braddock in the ill-fated expedition of 1755, and with Forbes in 1758 when the French were forced to evacuate Fort Duquesne. At 23 he had been given command of all of Virginia's forces and for the next 3 years he was responsible for defending the Colony's 300-mile western frontier (with 300 men). Over this vast territory, he fought an average of two military engagements a month against the French and Indians—excellent preparation for the difficult situation in which he found himself during the Revolutionary War.

Resigning from the militia at 27, he married and settled down to the busy life of a planter, interrupted by attendance at the brief annual sessions of the House of Burgesses to which he was periodically elected. An early adherent of the Revolutionary cause, he moved with the Burgesses to Raleigh's Tavern in 1770 when the Governor dissolved the House; he chaired the Richmond Convention which adopted George Mason's famous Virginia Resolves, and was one of the more radical delegates at the First and Second Continental Congresses. His conviction that the colonial relationship could no longer be tolerated was an outgrowth of personal experience and observation, and was based on practical common-sensical considerations, not ideology. Witness his blunt comment that Parliament "hath no more right to put their hands into my pocket without my consent, than I have to put my hands into yours for money." Britain's shabby treatment of the colonial veterans of the French and Indian Wars and various other frustrating experiences had gradually eroded his loyalty to the Crown.

Though political considerations played a part in his appointment as Commander in Chief of the Continental Army (notably the wish to unite the North and South), Congress would have been hard put to find a better man. He was not, of course, a professional soldier. There were none in the Colonies. But few had fought in so many frontier skirmishes or were temperamentally so well-fitted to command an army of citizen soldiers. At his request, he served without pay, accepting reimbursement only for expenses (a practice he followed in the Presidency as well).

His biggest problem was a chronic shortage of men, rations, and military equipment. To secure for herself a cheap supply of forest and farm products and a market where English manufactures faced no domestic competition, Britain had deliberately kept the Colonies agricultural. They could not suddenly turn out war materiel. Nor could they easily spare men for military service. Everyone in America was employed; no one produced much above his own needs. If inferiority in numbers and equipment thus was unavoidable, inferiority in training was not. But Congress and the States feared a disciplined professional army (preferring a loose association of State militias) and were dogmatically committed to short-term enlistments. Washington had moments when he feared "short enlistments and a dependence upon militia" would prove "the downfall of our cause." He had to fight a superior enemy while his army was in constant flux, trained men leaving in the midst of battle when their enlistments were up, green recruits taking their place. The militia, he wrote, "come in you cannot tell where, consume your Provisions, exhaust your Stores, & leave you at last in a critical moment." It took all his steadfastness and skill to maintain a body of trained men in the field large enough to keep the enemy off balance until time seasoned his citizen army and French help arrived.

Such help, Washington realized, would be contingent on French conviction that the Americans would neither be decisively defeated nor induced to compromise with Britain. This, his victories at Boston, Trenton, and Princeton, and the decisive defeat of Burgoyne by Gates at Saratoga, accomplished. Though we did not know it for almost a year, even Washington's unsuccessful attack at Germantown had impressed the French who were present as observers. John Adams wrote from Paris in 1778, some months after conclusion of the alliance with France: "I do not know, indeed, whether this last affair (Germantown) had not more influence upon the European mind than that of Saratoga. Although the attempt was unsuccessful, the military gentlemen in Europe considered it as the most decisive proof that America would finally succeed."

In the now classic pattern of wars between inadequately

equipped local defenders and superior invading forces, the British soon found themselves holding the towns while Washington's troops roamed the countryside. In 1778, Parliament was ready to grant almost every demand the colonists had made 3 years earlier. But with the French alliance concluded, Congress now felt strong enough to reject negotiations unless "as a preliminary thereto," Britain would "either withdraw their fleets and armies, or else in positive and express terms, acknowledge the independence of the United States."

The Revolutionary War was a thoughtful, organized revolution which grew out of a philosophy of the highest order. It was directed toward specific, defined goals. It was fought not for power but for ideas; not for occupying buildings and guerrilla warfare as an end in itself, but to establish, as Washington said, "a Government by which our lives, liberties, and properties shall be secured."

Peace finally came in 1783. Washington fixed on the eighth anniversary of the Battle of Lexington as the date on which he bade farewell to his troops and resigned his commission. To the end, Congress never lost its fear that he might emulate Cromwell and make himself military dictator. Nothing was more alien to his character and sense of honor. He showed this in 1782 when the Army, grimly observing civilian speculation and irresponsibility while their basic needs were neglected, showed symptoms of incipient mutiny. Mistrusting congressional promises of payments of arrears in their pay (meager enough at 1 shilling per day for ordinary soldiers) and veterans' benefits, they proposed to make Washington king. He furiously rejected the proposal.

Washington served as a beacon to which "the wise and honest" repaired. "The simple thought," one of his officers recalled at the close of the Revolution, "that we were then about to part from the man who had conducted us victoriously through a long and bloody war, and that we should see his face no more in this world, seemed utterly insupportable. But the time of separation had come and we watched in mournful silence the departure of the man who, under God, had been the great agent in establishing the glory and independence of these United States."

A letter to General Greene stands as an epitaph to the men of the American Continental Army and, though not intended, to their commander as well. Wondering how the history of the war would be received by future generations, Washington wrote: "It will not be believed, that such a force as Great

Britain has employed for eight years in this country could be baffled in their plan of subjugating it, by numbers infinitely less, composed of men often times half starved, always in rags, without pay, and experiencing every species of distress which human nature is capable of undergoing."

USS JOHN ADAMS (SSBN 620)

NAMED FOR John Adams (1735–1826), greatest constitutional thinker of the Revolutionary period, foremost parliamentarian in the Congress of the confederated 13 Colonies and their able representative on difficult diplomatic missions abroad, first Vice President and second President of the United States; a man of powerful intellect, transparent honesty, and unflinching moral courage and integrity.

Born at Braintree, Mass., eldest son of a farmer and cordwainer, John married the daughter of a country parson and together they founded one of America's most illustrious families, their son John Quincy becoming the sixth American President (the only such instance in our history), and succeeding generations of Adamses making distinguished careers in various areas of human endeavor.

John and Abigail came of English Puritan stock, their ancestors having arrived here within 5 years of each other (1638 and 1633). Until these two married and broke the pattern, their families had not in a century differed much from the majority of their neighbors—hard-working, thrifty farmers, enlarging their land holdings bit by bit, often adding to their income by working winters at a skilled trade; pillars of the Congregational Church, active members of the town meeting. But these plain folk had a tradition that whenever possible one son, as part of his patrimony, should be given a Harvard education and thus entree into one of the professions, usually the ministry; to his brothers would go the farm. It was so with John Adams.

Even before John was born, his father began to accumulate pieces of land that were to pay the heavy cost of college (£45 per annum). These careful plans came close to foundering on the obtuseness of the local Latin schoolteacher. Not recognizing the boy's quick mind, this pedant held him to the slow pace and routine of the rest of the class. John was so bored he played truant and did no homework; the very idea of schooling disgusted him. Not yet 15, he made up his mind to become a farmer. Fortunately, he had a father who, despite his own limited schooling (6 years in all), understood better than the boy or his learned teacher both the value of a Harvard education and the capacities and temperament of his gifted son. Ordinarily a mild man, he proceeded to administer a painful but salutary lesson. Taking John along with him on his daily rounds, he demonstrated what farming meant—full-time farming—not the part-time chores expected of young boys, which John enjoyed. After several weeks of dawn-to-dusk work of the hardest, most disagreeable kind, and long evenings of cleaning and oiling harness, John gave in. This was not what he had envisaged as the life of a farmer. Having proved his point, the father agreed that the boy should quit school and be tutored, though this meant added expense. A year later Harvard accepted him. Even for a bright boy, it was an astonishing feat of making up for wasted time.

He did well, received his bachelor's degree before he was 20, and found a position teaching school which he combined with the study of law. At 23, he was admitted to the bar. The recently published *Legal Papers of John Adams* (three volumes), based on his voluminous trial notes, give a vivid picture of day-to-day life in New England on the eve of the Revolution, and of the busy life of circuit riding colonial lawyers. Adams acquired a large and varied clientele, appearing in several hundred cases a year, some of historic importance, none more so than the criminal trials arising out of the "Boston Massacre" (1770). The story is well-known, as is John's successful defense of Captain Preston and his British soldiers. But worth repeating is his remark when he, an acknowledged Revolutionary leader, was asked to undertake this unpopular task. He accepted at once, saying: "Counsel ought to be the very last thing that an accused person should want in a free country." To Adams and his friend and associate in the defense, Josiah Quincy, Jr., we owe a glorious moment in our history, for it was they who made sure that in a town infuriated beyond endurance by the acts of Britain and her soldiery, the hated Redcoats received a fair trial.

As was true of most of our Revolutionary leaders, John Adams had grown to manhood a loyal and contented English subject, taking the colonial relationship for granted. He did not begin to think seriously about the nature of this relationship until it was drastically altered by Britain, following victory in the Seven Years' War (1763). She had previously ruled with a light hand, leaving management of their own affairs to the colonists. True, the Royal Governors had power to veto laws and to call and dissolve the locally elected legislatures, but since they depended for their salaries on annual appropriations by these legislatures, they usually exercised these powers with circumspection. It has been said that under Britain's policy of "salutary neglect," the colonists enjoyed a larger measure of liberty and self-government than their English cousins. Certainly, there was a tremendous difference in the tax burden: the colonists averaging 1 shilling per capita per annum against 26 shillings for Englishmen.

Victory over France left Britain with a vastly enlarged North American empire and a huge war debt. Doubtless it seemed reasonable to her that the colonists should share in the cost of administering and defending this empire since they would be its chief beneficiaries (indeed all the land ceded in 1763, except Canada, eventually came to us). Parliament, accordingly, passed a series of statutes designed to tighten enforcement of existing laws which had been laxly administered and widely disobeyed—a thoroughly unpopular move. Worse, it enacted the Stamp Act (1765) which for the first time imposed a direct tax on the colonists. The tax, in force in England since 1694, required revenue stamps for newspapers, commercial bills and various other documents. If any single British act can be said to have lost her the Colonies, it was this tax. It brought to light a conflict of opinion concerning the nature of the relation of mother country to colony that in the end proved irreconcilable.

John Adams was well on the way to becoming a luminary of the Massachusetts bar when for him, as for so many others, the Revolution put an end to a promising private career and launched him on a life of public service. He was 39 when he left to sit in the First Continental Congress (1774) and 66 when he finally returned to private life to farm a little, write a lot. Publication of his diaries, correspondence, and documents was begun in 1961 when the first volume of the Adams Papers appeared. There is a homely notation penned in his diary 3 years after the end of his Presidential term (Vol. VI): "We ploughed a ditch and brought the earth into the yard and 32 loads of mud from the cove." It takes us back to the 14-year-old, firmly declaring he would be a farmer. Much happened to John, to Braintree, to Massachusetts, and to the 13 rebellious Colonies in the intervening years.

One is hard put to convey in a few pages the fullness of his life or to pick out his most significant contributions, for there were many. Adams was as resolute a man of action as he was a profound thinker. His capacity for intense concentration on whatever task lay at hand made him highly effective whether he acted or thought. He saw earlier than most of his colleagues in the Continental Congress (which he served from its tentative beginning in 1774 to its dissolution in 1788) that petitions and lists of "grievances" would not alter Britain's determination to incorporate the Colonies in her Imperial Scheme; that she would by force of arms seek to bend to her will the "subjects" whose allegiance she had lost by infringing their traditional liberties. To accept this did not come easy to him. "I go mourning in my Heart all Day long," he wrote. But once it was obvious that Britain would not compromise, it made no sense to him for Congress to indulge in "talk of harmony, accommodation, loyalty, allegiance, love" until the Colonies had made themselves strong enough to *assert* their rights. This was the objective to which he bent every effort. He urged creation of a Continental Army, manned and supplied by Congress, and proposed that Washington be appointed its Commander in Chief; he advocated arming merchantmen as privateers (this was the beginning of our Navy; as President, he established the Navy Department). He pressed for an alliance with France or Spain or Holland "with any European power that cares to listen." He worked mightily to steer the Declaration of Independence through Congress. A "colossus on the floor," wrote Jefferson in 1824, "he came out with a power of thought and expression that moves us from our seats."

As early as June 1775, Adams urged that independent, republican state governments be formed. "Let Congress recommend to every colony," he wrote, "that it begin at once to call conventions and set up governments under the people, who are the authority of all power." This became an urgent necessity when the King formally proclaimed the Colonies to be "in a state of rebellion" (August 22, 1775). Governors and their advisory councils fled and the courts were dissolved. Had the colonists not acted promptly, anarchy might have resulted. A number of them sought Adams' advice for he was by now an acknowledged authority on matters of government. How should they go about creating popular governments? It had never been done; there were no precedents. Adams, who as early as 1765 had insisted that government "was a plain, simple, intelligible thing, founded in nature and reason and intelligible by common

sociological and psychological dogmas may establish a new type of "twin tyranny." The mere assertion that they are "scientific" gives these dogmas an "authority" in the eyes of modern man as absolute as once was the divine right of kings. The most autocratic regimes today are sociologically based. Marxism cannot be debated in the U.S.S.R.; by government fiat it is "scientific truth." All other philosophies are officially declared in error and their adherents are granted no rights. Even in the Free World, allegedly "scientific" sociological and psychological dogma are held to justify extraordinary infringements of individual liberty.

Not even our right to free speech and our vast system of public education have entirely prevented such infringements. New forms of censorship—covert, private, commercial—at times impede "easy, cheap and safe" communication of ideas. So also does the modern tendency to regard freedom of speech not so much as a right possessed by every citizen, but as pertaining chiefly to the business of publication and communications media. Public education fails its purpose (diffusion of knowledge through the whole body politic) when the child's need for the kind of schooling that will best develop *his* mind is subordinated to extraneous objectives, reflecting adult aims, in particular, to a dogmatic egalitarianism that cannot bring itself to come to terms with natural inequalities of talent, and uses the power of government to try to level them out. We would do well to recall Adams' views on equality. He wrote, "that all men are born to equal rights is true. Every being has a right to his own, as clear, as moral, as sacred, as any other being has . . . But to teach that all men are born with equal powers and faculties, to equal influence in society, to equal property and advantages through life, is as gross a fraud, as glaring an imposition on the credulity of the people, as was ever practiced . . . Let American philosophers and politicians despise it."

Equally pertinent today, when the expectations of men tend to outrun their capabilities, was Adams' recognition that the upward march of civilization is a matter of generations. "I must study politics and war," he wrote, "that my sons may have liberty to study mathematics and philosophy, geography, natural history and naval architecture, navigation, commerce and agriculture, in order to give their children a right to study painting, poetry, music . . ." This indeed was the pattern of his posterity. I think he would have felt that he had laid good foundations, had he lived to hear what his eldest son said in 1825, that America should be "the well-wisher to the freedom

16

and independence of all" but the "champion and vindicator only of her own." And when he was asked whether it was not degrading for an ex-President to serve as Congressman, John Quincy, who at 64 began a distinguished career in the House, replied that no person could be degraded by serving the people as a Representative in Congress or, for that matter, as a Selectman of his town.

USS THOMAS JEFFERSON (SSBN 618)

Named FOR Thomas Jefferson (1743–1826), foremost exponent of the American Enlightenment, a philosopher-statesman whose lofty ideas of the dignity of free men and the proper function of government provide the philosophical foundation on which our political system rests.

In some 30 years of public service, Jefferson held nearly every office the people could bestow. He was twice Governor of Virginia and for many years a member of the legislature. As delegate to the Continental Congress, he headed some of the most important committees; he was instrumental in the cession by Virginia of her vast territories northwest of the Ohio; for 5 years he represented the Confederation in Paris. He was Washington's first Secretary of State, Adams' Vice President, and third President of the United States.

His contributions were both practical and philosophical. We owe him our decimal coinage and the geometric shape of our Western States. He bought us half a continent at the bargain price of $15 million (Louisiana Purchase, 1803), and relieved us of the tribute exacted by the pirate State of Tripoli for immunity from raids on shipping (1805), the first head of a Western nation to challenge this ancient practice. He drafted one of our three basic charters of liberty (the Declaration of Independence) and laid the basis for the second (the Northwest Ordinance of 1787 which incorporated Jefferson's Ordinance of 1784). Its importance to national unity was immense, notably the provision that slavery should not exist after 1800; a step which set the precedent for Federal control of slavery in the territories. Like Adams, he was abroad when the third (the Constitution) was written and ratified, but present, as it were by proxy, in the person of his close friend and political disciple, James Madison, "Father of the Constitution."

Without doubt the most versatile of the galaxy of brilliant men who led the 13 Colonies out of the British Empire and into a political experiment never before attempted, Jefferson was not only preeminent as legislator, diplomat, lawyer, but pioneered in such diverse fields as ethnology, geography, botany, and paleontology. A gifted amateur architect, he introduced Palladian neoclassicism and founded an American School of Architecture. He was among the first to practice "scientific" agriculture, importing new ideas and new seeds from abroad and designing the mould plow (for which the French gave him a gold medal). A notable inventor of ingenious and useful devices, he was also first in establishing legal protection of inventions as U.S. Commissioner of Patents and Patent Examiner. A universal man of politics, and scholarship and art, he could have said with Francis Bacon, "I have taken all knowledge to be my province." As James Parton, America's first professional biographer described him, he was "a gentleman of thirty-two who could calculate an eclipse, survey an estate, tie an artery, plan an edifice, try a cause, break a horse, dance a minuet, and play a violin."

Jefferson was born at Shadwell Plantation (Albemarle County, Va.), in a house his father built when he settled there in 1737, the third or fourth to take up land in what was then still a frontier wilderness in the Blue Ridge. When Shadwell burned down, Jefferson built Monticello on a hilltop close by (1770). According to family tradition, the Jeffersons came originally from Wales, records showing them established in Virginia by 1677. They were a "rising" family of modest origins, cast in a pattern we see repeated in the lives of nearly all the great leaders of our early history. Land was then the basis of wealth and land was still plentiful and cheap, though less so along the coast than in the interior. To turn the land into flourishing farms or plantations, required but industry and ability. These Thomas Jefferson's father had in abundance, and they made up for lack of formal schooling.

The son was to write years later, "my father's education had been quite neglected; but being of a strong mind, sound judgment, and eager after information, he read much and improved himself," becoming not only a prosperous tobacco planter, but also a land surveyor entrusted with some of the most important boundary demarcation tasks, including that between Virginia and North Carolina, which led to his making the first map of Virginia. A "coming" man, he married into a prominent Virginian planter family and in due time assumed the offices of public trust that were expected of men of substance: Justice of the Peace, Colonel of the Militia, Member of the House of Burgesses.

Though he died when Thomas was only 14, Jefferson's father deeply influenced his son. Their close association accounts in part for Jefferson's dislike of pomp and circumstance and his faith in the common man. From his father he learned horseback riding, canoeing, carpentry; how to shoot, manage a farm, build a house. These were skills needed by everyone in a region which retained its frontier character, though it was rapidly filling up with people. There were no longer Indians, but wolf bounties were still being granted.

Thomas' formal schooling began at age 5 in a small tutorial group; at 9 he started Latin. Unlearned himself, his father was determined the boy should receive the best possible education, which then meant in America—as it still does in Europe—a rigorous course in Latin, Greek, and one or two modern foreign languages; in literature, history, mathematics, and science. He specified in his will that his son's classical education be completed. Thomas Jefferson inherited much property and, through his mother, Jane, the daughter of the lordly Randolphs on the James River, good family connections, but it was the education his father secured for him that he appreciated most. At 57, he wrote: "I thank on my knees, Him who directed my early education, for having put into my possession this rich source of delight; and I would not exchange it for anything which I could then have acquired."

He entered William and Mary at 17 and graduated 2 years later, having set himself a study program that would stamp him a "compulsory over-achiever" in today's educational jargon. He had the good fortune to be taught by men outstanding in their field who took a personal interest in him and made him their friend. From Dr. William Small, a Scotsman who held the chair of mathematics and natural history at William and Mary, he acquired his interest in the natural sciences. Through Small he was accepted, after graduation, as a law student by George Wythe, Virginia's foremost legal practitioner—"my most faithful and beloved mentor," wrote Jefferson, "and my most affectionate friend through life." Small and Wythe introduced their young friend to Fauquier, the Royal Governor, a man of charm and culture, the ablest man ever to fill that office, in Jefferson's opinion. He was often invited to the Palace to join these three in good conversation and amateur musicales (he played both violin and cello), profiting greatly from interchange of ideas with these intelligent and accomplished men. But he was also part of a gay social circle of young people, as fond of parties, dancing, theater, as any of them. Despite a grueling work schedule, Jefferson always found time for stimulating sociability.

Already a well-organized, highly disciplined person when he came to Williamsburg in 1760, he enjoyed nothing so much as using his capable mind and exercising his strong body. The program of alternating studies, physical exercise, and social relaxation he set himself while a student of law is awe-inspiring. All his life he urged young friends to pursue similar programs, outlining them in detail. He recommended rising at dawn and reading in the natural sciences, ethics, religion, and philosophy until eight; in law until noon. The afternoon should be devoted to history, reading the classics (in the original Greek and Latin), and political science. For the evenings, he suggested literature and practice in speaking and writing, with emphasis on a graceful style. He was still busy drawing up curricula for the University of Virginia when he died. "I was a hard student," he wrote, "until I entered on the business of life the duties of which leave no idle time to those disposed to fulfill them; and now, retired, and at the age of seventy-six, I am again a hard student." It must have been a healthy scheme, for Jefferson remained vigorous into old age, reading, writing, and horseback riding almost to the day of his death. As everyone knows, he died on the 50th anniversary of the Declaration of Independence, a few hours before his old friend and sometime political opponent, John Adams.

There was a curious parallelism in the lives of these two men, despite different beginnings, different backgrounds, different temperaments. Loyal British subjects, neither questioned the constitutional basis of the relationship with the mother country until Britain began to infringe traditional colonial liberties. For Jefferson, the decisive moment came when, still a law student, he listened to a "most bloody" debate in the House of Burgesses (1765) over a series of resolutions introduced by Patrick Henry declaring the Stamp Act null and void. When the harshest of these had passed by one vote, he overheard Peyton Randolph muttering: "By God, I would have given one hundred guineas for a single vote."

Both Jefferson and Adams were chosen to represent their Colonies in the First Continental Congress. The year 1774 marked for each the end of a lucrative law practice and the beginning of a long public career which saw them taking turns filling the same public offices. Jefferson's first major political document, *A Summary View of the Rights of British America*, was written that year. Intended to serve as a policy paper for the Virginia delegation to the Congress, it was then considered too radical. But printed as a pamphlet, it established Jefferson at once as a powerful thinker and polished writer. Largely on the strength of having written the *Summary*, he was chosen 2 years later to draft the Declaration of Independence.

The impetus for the Declaration came from the Virginia delegation. On June 7, 1776, Richard Henry Lee called on Congress to proclaim "that these United Colonies are, and of right ought to be, free and independent States." A lively debate ensued during which the *timing* was the chief point at issue. Some members urged deferral until the Colonies had formally united in a Confederation, or until they had become firmly allied to France. Others believed an open declaration of independence would clarify our international status and hasten the French alliance. In actual fact, the Colonies had been acting as "independent" States for over a year. They had been at war since April 19, 1775. George III had proclaimed them "in rebellion" on August 22, 1775 and, unbeknown to Congress, France had already decided to come to their aid.

Postponing action on the Virginia resolution until July 1st, Congress appointed a committee (Jefferson, John Adams, Franklin, Livingstone, and Sherman) to "prepare a declaration" in support of the resolution. The committee selected Jefferson to write the draft. Most members of Congress had nothing more in mind than a sort of final listing of "grievances," a statement that these absolved us from our allegiance to Britain, and a proclamation of independent statehood. The larger part of the Declaration does just that. As evidence of the King's desire to establish "an absolute Tyranny" over the Colonies, 27 specific "injuries and usurpations" are listed (four having to do with Britain's manner of waging war with the colonists). Note is taken of the King's rejection of numerous petitions for redress, submitted "in the most humble terms." Having proved him a tyrant, the Declaration judges him "unfit to be the Ruler of a free People." As for our "British Brethren," having ignored all our appeals to their sense of justice and "the Ties of our common Kindred," they are henceforth to be held, "as we hold the rest of Mankind, Enemies in War, in Peace, Friends." The severance of all bonds could not have been stated in more categorical terms. This part of the Declaration is generally thought to have only historic interest. But since it indicates what 18th century Americans considered unacceptable infringements of liberty, it may still serve as a useful yardstick for measuring *any* government's respect for the rights of a "free people."

Jefferson was not content to rest the American case on particular instances of British violation of colonial rights; he lifted it to the higher plane of a general violation of the rights of all mankind. Postulating in a few terse sentences a concept of government which at that time existed nowhere abroad except in the minds of Enlightenment philosophers, he nevertheless held Britain to account for having failed to live up to this concept. He did so because the ideas underlying the concept were "self-evident" to most Americans, had indeed been realized in good part during the era of "salutary neglect" when England left the Colonies free to manage their own affairs. They were not new, not original, Jefferson said, but "an expression of the American mind." His intent was merely to place "before mankind the common sense of the subject, in terms so plain and firm as to command their assent, and to justify ourselves in the independent stand that we are compelled to take."

The Declaration posits government squarely on the *free* citizen. Observe the order in which the following basic axioms appear: *First,* all men are born equally endowed with certain "unalienable" rights. Some are listed in the Declaration—life, liberty, and the pursuit of happiness—others were almost at once so declared by bills of rights in the State constitutions and later in the first nine amendments of the U.S. Constitution (the 10th amendment belongs properly to the body of the Constitution). *Second,* governments "are instituted among Men" *in order* "to secure" these rights. We were the first people to make the preservation of certain human rights—rights deemed essential to the liberty and dignity of man—an express function, indeed *the main function of government,* a notion we now take for granted but which at the time turned existing concepts of government upside down. *Third,* government derives its "just powers from the consent of the governed." *Fourth,* "whenever any Form of Government becomes destructive of these Ends, it is the Right of the People to alter or to abolish it, and to institute new Government, laying its Foundation on such Principles, and organizing its Powers in such Form, as to them shall seem most likely to effect their Safety and Happiness."

These words still move us, though Americans have lived almost two centuries in a society based upon them. It has been said, and rightly, that the ideas and even some of the words are Locke's. This only shows that this philosopher of England's "Glorious Revolution" (1688) left so deep an impact on the colonists that his ideas became "the common sense of the subject." Jefferson arranged them better, condensed them, and thereby gave them a power they had not previously had.

In his absence, Virginia had adopted a republican constitution and begun to revise her laws to bring them into harmony with republican principles. Jefferson resigned from Congress, resumed his place in the State legislature, and took part in a program of thoroughgoing law revision (he drafted 126 bills). It was obvious to him that when government is based on the will of the people, they must be *free* to think and *able* to think for themselves. Liberty of conscience and an opportunity for all to become educated were to him prerequisites of a free society; for these he worked assiduously till the end of his life, succeeding in the first but failing in the second. His bill disestablishing the Anglican Church and granting religious freedom (adopted 1786) reflects in its broad and generous terms Jefferson's personal commitment: "I have sworn on the altar of God eternal hostility against every form of tyranny over the mind of man." Of his comprehensive education scheme in three stages—elementary, college-preparatory, university—only the last was achieved in his lifetime when the University of Virginia opened its doors (1824), Jefferson becoming its first rector. He had envisaged giving elementary schooling to all children and providing State scholarships for able but poor scholars at the higher levels. It is probable he knew of the educational provision of the 1812 Spanish Constitution: "From the year of one thousand eight hundred thirty those who shall enter into the exercise of the rights of citizenship must know how to read and write." "If a nation expects to be ignorant and free, in a state of civilization," he warned, "it expects what never was and never will be." But at the time, the dispersed population made the cost prohibitive in the eyes of Virginia's legislators.

In his national role subsequent to the establishment of our government under the Constitution, Jefferson became the leader and philosopher of the Virginia school. Its creed was stated in the Virginia and Kentucky Resolves, wherein the art of politics was reduced to an enumeration of powers reserved from exercise. Yet nothing was so little suited to Jefferson's intellectual temper. His instincts led him to widen rather than narrow the bounds of every intellectual exercise; and when vested with political authority, he could no more resist the temptation to stretch his powers than he could abstain from using his mind on any object merely because he might be drawn upon ground supposed to be dangerous.

The history of Jefferson's administration (1801–09), so largely an extension of his personality, bore out this view. The awkward Virginia principles were dropped, powers were stretched beyond the limits of federalism, nationalism went forward. The turning-point away from the Republican landmarks and along the path of democracy took place at Jefferson's second inauguration. Although it lacked the flourishes that had made his First Inaugural Address the quintessential expression of Virginia ideals, it did indicate the creed of a powerful political party and the standard by which the future would be measured.

In the Second Inaugural, Jefferson broached the idea, and Gallatin soon developed it into a comprehensive plan of a Federal system of internal improvements ranging from roads and canals to arts and education. His proposal put to naught every principle of the Republican Party, Adams declared. "At no time since the Declaration of Independence had the prospects of nationality seemed so promising as in the spring of 1805." They were doomed in Jefferson's administration, as the sequel showed, and Jefferson still later reverted to his Virginia principles; but America's *democratic* direction was fixed.

The moral drama of Jefferson's administration revolved around the eternal problem of ideals versus realities in the conduct of government. The ideals and doctrines of the Jeffersonians were defeated, deflected, diluted by realities of power— its responsibilities with its temptations—and force of circumstances. Historian Artemas Muzzy has summed it up well:

"This advocate of strict economy had spent on his own executive authority an amount equal to almost three fourths of the debt which Hamilton had assumed for the States with the sanction of Congress. This champion of the letter of the Constitution had exercised the power of acquiring foreign territory and promising foreigners admission to the citizenship of the United States for which no clause could be found among the 'enumerated powers.' This opponent of the extension of the 'general Government' had stretched its power beyond any point the Federalists had reached."

Looking back in the serenity of old age on a life of great and varied achievements, Jefferson picked three for inscription on his grave: "Author of the Declaration of Independence, of the Statute of Virginia for Religious Freedom, and Father of the

University of Virginia." By these, he said, "as testimonials that I have lived, I wish most to be remembered." And he is right. In them is distilled the essence of the man and his philosophy. They are his most lasting bequests to us (except for the Louisiana Purchase). If we know what he wished to accomplish in each case, we may understand this complex, subtle man and what he meant and always will mean to America.

USS JAMES MADISON (SSBN 627)

NAMED FOR James Madison (1751–1836) fourth President of the United States, Secretary of State under Jefferson, one of the most distinguished legislators of his time, and a member of the group of gifted and patriotic men we call the Founding Fathers. Like most of these men, Madison made his own specific contribution to the building of our Nation: he was principal architect of the Constitution.

An early advocate of a strong central government, Madison actively promoted the series of interstate conferences on navigation and commerce (Alexandria and Mount Vernon, 1785; Annapolis, 1786) which led to the Philadelphia Convention of 1787. He played a prominent part in the decision of this Convention to exceed its narrow mandate (revision of the Articles of Confederation) and to substitute for mere amendment of the old form of union a wholly new scheme of government. The "Randolph Plan," adopted by the delegates as a basis for discussion, incorporated many of his ideas. He was principal guide and recorder of their deliberations and, next to Hamilton, did more than anyone else to propound and defend the Constitution when its acceptance by State ratification conventions hung in balance. Keenly aware that a major factor in public mistrust of the Constitution was the absence of a Federal Bill of Rights, he worked assiduously to remedy this defect and succeeded in obtaining adoption of the Bill of Rights amendments in the first session of the Congress (1791). Assuredly, Madison deserves his title of "Father of the Constitution."

Washington, who presided over the Philadelphia Convention, later remarked that it seemed to him "little short of a miracle" that the delegates were able to agree on a common plan of government, given the fact that they represented States so different "in their manners, circumstances, and prejudices." They were driven by a sense of urgency. Better than ordinary Americans, better than the State legislatures, they knew that the Union was in grave danger. "The situation of the general government, if it can be called a government," wrote Washington, "is shaken to its foundation, and liable to be overturned by every blast." Self-willed and heedless of each other's rights, the States were destroying the Union; there was talk that it might break into two or more independent confederacies or even splinter into something resembling the Germanic Confederation.

The delegates at Philadelphia representing 12 States (as usual, obstreperous, irresponsible Rhode Island absented herself), were agreed that a federal republic strong enough to act as a sovereign power *must* be established. Apart from this there was little agreement. Some wished to set up an Executive, elected for life, with power to coerce recalcitrant States, others had no Executive at all in mind; the large States wanted a national legislature based upon population, the small ones wanted equal representation for each State. These were but two of the controversies that had to be mediated.

For Madison, the part he played in the final success was something of a "personal" miracle. No one could have foreseen even a few years back that he would be capable of the sustained effort he put forth during the 4 months it took to hammer out the Constitution—4 months of an exceptionally hot and humid Philadelphia summer when acute physical discomfort was added to all the other difficulties the delegates had to surmount.

Madison was born to many advantages but good health was not one of them. His family, which he described as of "respectable, though not the most opulent class" of planters, had been settled in Virginia since the first ancestor, a ship carpenter, arrived from England in 1653. Madison's birthplace was Port Conway, but he lived all his life at Montpelier, on land patented by his grandfather in 1723 (inherited by his father in 1732 and by himself in 1801). Over the generations, the plantation was enlarged to some 4,000 acres, worked by a hundred or more slaves. At first, his home was a modest wooden house built by grandfather Ambrose, but around 1761 the family moved into a large and elegant mansion half a mile distant. In early childhood, Madison knew the terror that gripped the Piedmont when Braddock's defeat (1755) left the region helplessly exposed to French and Indian attack. Virginia's frontier guard was too small to afford protection to outlying districts.

Only after Britain defeated France in 1763 and took over her American empire, did peace come to Montpelier and other Orange County plantations.

In the sparsely settled Virginia of Madison's youth, education was a private responsibility, there being virtually no schools. Madison was taught at home, receiving the customary classical education. He went to Princeton at 18 and graduated at 20. Uncertain whether to choose the ministry or the law as his profession, indeed doubtful whether he would live long enough to have a career, he returned home to read widely and tutor his younger brothers and sisters. In a manner of speaking, the Revolution gave him a purpose and thus a new lease on life. So intensively did he become involved in the cause of freedom and self-government that he rose above his weak constitution and his frequent illnesses to live a long and active life. He died at 85.

Military service was beyond his capacity; his experiences during exercises of a militia company showed this conclusively. But, elected to the Virginia Constitutional Convention (1776) he soon proved himself a highly effective legislator. He served in this capacity for a quarter century, including 3 years in the Continental Congress (1780–83) and 8 as a United States Congressman (1789–97). Jefferson appointed him Secretary of State, a post he held through both terms (1801–09), thereafter succeeding to the Presidency (1809–17).

He was by all odds the best prepared member of the Philadelphia Convention which drew up the Constitution. Jefferson had been sending him books from Paris on government, political philosophy, constitutional and international law, which Madison devoured as fast as they arrived. Having learned all there was then known of the history and constitution of confederacies he quietly took charge. His special talent was the ability to use superior expertise as means of persuasion, appealing not to the emotions of men but to their reasoning capacity. He had "a gift of creative compromise," as one historian put it. Though a man of principle, he was never dogmatic. Courteous by nature, his respect for the opinions of those who differed with him made him all the more effective in persuading them to accept solutions based on mutual concessions. Nowhere was this more essential than in this assemblage of able men of strong and diverse opinions where nothing could be achieved unless everyone sacrificed *some* cherished conviction; where, as Madison later remarked, "every step was a contest between power and liberty."

One of his colleagues (William Pierce of Georgia) said that Madison blended together "the profound politician with the Scholar. In the management of every great question he evidently took the lead in the convention . . . He always comes forward the best informed man of any point of debate. The affairs of the United States, he perhaps has the most correct knowledge of, of any man in the Union." Pierce might have added that Madison was influential not only because he was informed and persuasive, but perhaps most of all because his devotion to the good of the country was transparent.

He knew history was being made. That *we* know *how* it was made we owe entirely to the full record Madison kept of the proceedings of the Convention. In collaboration with Hamilton and Jay, he also gave us the best exposition of the political system under which we live—the essays later published as *The Federalist*.

The ink was hardly dry on the signatures to the Constitution before Madison was in the thick of the battle over ratification. The defenders of the Constitution had no easy time, especially in Virginia, New York, and Massachusetts. The old Confederation suited many, perhaps most Americans; the proposed new government looked suspiciously like a replica of the British government from which they had just managed to free themselves. One had to be engaged in foreign trade, represent the American government abroad, or try to negotiate a foreign loan to experience *personally* and unmistakably the disadvantages of life under a powerless government. Ordinary people did not readily see the connection between worthless paper money, rising prices, diminishing land values, and the fact that the Articles of Confederation gave Congress no authority to regulate commerce or raise taxes.

Weakness in government seemed desirable to 18th century Americans. They identified strong government with autocratic government and were particularly mistrustful of "distant" government which was thought to have no "common feelings and common interests with the governed." Having obtained republican constitutions in their States, and thus an effective means of keeping the men who ruled them responsive to their wishes, they feared the Constitution, by usurping the power of the States, might rob them of these hard-won political gains. Who is to say their instincts were wholly wrong?

It was to calm these fears and misgivings that the *Federalist* essays were written. They exposed the defects of The Confederation and explained exactly and in detail what the Constitution said and how it could be expected to work. The articles went out over the signature "Publius" and there is still some dispute concerning the authorship of individual pieces. Hamilton, who originated the idea, probably wrote 50, Madison 30, and Jay 5 of the essays. Hamilton and Jay later became political enemies of Madison, but in 1788 all three were united in the belief that the country needed a strong central government and that the Constitution would provide it.

Hastily written—sometimes as many as four a week—the *Federalist* articles have been praised ever since their first appearance both for their literary quality and for the cogency of their arguments. As campaign literature designed to win the support of State ratifying conventions, they deserve particular praise for their calm and judicious tone and their fairness to the opposition. Every point brought up against the Constitution is dealt with honestly and reasonably. Never before or since have Americans thought so hard about the nature and structure of their political system or received such frank answers to their questions from their leaders. The fine art of drenching the public with mixtures of fact and fiction, attractively packaged by experts in "public relations," had not yet been invented.

In Hamilton's felicitous phrase, the Constitution achieved a happy mean between "the energy of government and the security of private rights." Far from contradicting the Declaration of Independence, as is sometimes claimed, it provided the machinery through which the maxims of the Declaration were translated into political reality. Supplementing each other, these great political charters stand as a monument to the Enlightenment under whose aegis they came into being. All the Founding Fathers—in differing degrees—were influenced by the ideas of that remarkable age when throughout the Western World philosophers and political thinkers mounted an attack upon every custom and institution that shackles the mind of man or arbitrarily restrains his actions—from superstition to class privilege, from tyranny by an established church to tyranny by an absolute monarch.

Madison, who died in 1836, was the last luminary of the American phase of the Enlightenment; Franklin, born in 1706, was the first. It seems fitting that these two, meeting for the first time at Philadelphia, should have become close friends while they worked together on the document that was to establish here, in this vast and rich land, just such a Utopia as had been dreamed about for more than a century by the philosophers of the European Enlightenment but which no one in that

31

old and crowded continent knew how to bring into concrete existence.

The problem that seemingly defied solution was *how to limit power so that men might be free*. It was thought to arise out of an inherent conflict between civilization and liberty. Primitive men living in a "state of nature" (about whom the Enlightenment knew little and romanticized a lot), supposedly knew how to remain free, but when men entered civilized society their social needs generated power which in the end suppressed their liberties. The problem thus posed by European thinkers was resolved by Americans who were both thinkers and men with much practical experience in self-government, if only at the local level permitted "colonials." Their solution — the "American formula" — may be summarized as popular government plus division of power plus "unalienable" rights. To this day, Madison remains its best expositor.

Could anyone improve on the classical simplicity of his definition of popular government (*Federalist* #39) as one: "which derives all its powers directly or indirectly from the great body of the people, and is administered by persons holding their offices during pleasure, for a limited period, or during good behavior"? Or on his description of the system of division of power which makes ours a "compound republic," as he called it (*Federalist* #51)? "The power surrendered by the people is first divided between two distinct governments, and then the portion allotted to each is subdivided among distinct and separate departments. Hence a double security arises to the rights of the people. The different governments will control each other at the same time that each will be controlled by itself."

Reporting to Jefferson, our envoy in Paris at the time the Constitution was being drafted, Madison wrote that the most difficult problem had been "to draw a line of demarcation which would give to the General Government every power requisite for general purposes, and leave to the States every power which might be most beneficially administered by them." State loyalties were running deep, yet even those most jealous of State power realized that much of it would have to be relinquished, for the country obviously needed a viable central government. Those, who like Hamilton wished to make provinces out of the States and establish a strong unitary government, knew the people would never accept this. Under the circumstances, it is not surprising that nobody was entirely satisfied with the line as it was finally drawn and that for decades to come most political controversies involved attempts to tinker with it.

32

Thirty-four years later, Madison was still not certain that the
Constitution would prove an effective safeguard against either
                                          ement" of the Federal Government,
                                          ndence" of the State governments.
                                          rote a friend in 1821. He had no doubt,
                                          , power were shifted from the States
                                          ent, this would inevitably upset the
                                          of checks and balances within the
                                          of all power in the general govern-
                                          ly lead to a dangerous accumulation
                                          s how he put it.
                                          nature of "unalienable rights," per-
                                          od part of the "American formula,"
                                          t informant. He was on the committee
                                          ; the Virginia Declaration of Rights
                                          as model for the Federal Bill of Rights
                                          st State bills. It is more explicit than
                                          ependence (which it antedated by 4
                                          rase being that all men "have certain
inherent natural rights of which they cannot, by any compact,
deprive or divest their posterity." In his *Memorial and Remonstrance Against Religious Assessments* (1783), Madison
explained that these unalienable rights are not lost because a
man "enters civil society." They are "not abridged by the institution of civil society," but constitute permanent limits on
government action designed to guarantee the individual
certain rights that are basic to man as a human being and
indispensable to citizens of a self-governing society. One category holds government to prescribed standards of behavior
(as in the administration of justice); another category recog-
nizes the existence of a private realm from which government
is categorically excluded (as in the matter of liberty of conscience). The latter was of special interest to Madison who
wrote in 1822: "We are teaching the world the great truth that
Gov'ts. do better without Kings & Nobles than with them. The
merit will be doubled by the other lesson that Religion flourishes in greater purity, without than with the aid of Gov'."

The idea of charters permanently protecting specified individual rights was of course not new, but in combination with
the principle of popular sovereignty it made for a stronger
injunction than anything previously known. In the Magna
Carta, the King promises he "will not" do certain things; the
English Bill of Rights of 1689 says the King "ought not" to do
them; but our Federal Bill uses the words "shall" and "shall

not." It is a *command* addressed by the people to their government: by a principal to his agent. How well the people are obeyed depends—as in corresponding private relationships—on whether they fully understand their position (on their having read, so to speak, the fine print in the contract) and on whether they keep at all times an eye on the activities of their agent, the government.

Madison's brief message "to his country," written near the end of his life, has often been quoted. He hoped it might carry some weight as coming from one "who had espoused in his youth and adhered through his life to the cause of liberty," serving 40 years in a variety of public offices. "The advice nearest to my heart and deepest to my convictions," he wrote, "is that the Union of the States be cherished and perpetuated. Let the open enemy to it be regarded as a Pandora with her box opened; and the disguised one, as the Serpent creeping with his deadly wiles into Paradise."

USS BENJAMIN FRANKLIN
(SSBN 640)

NAMED FOR Benjamin Franklin (1706–90), one of the most illustrious of our Founding Fathers. A plain man of the people, his life was the American success story writ large. In his autobiography he speaks of his "lowly beginnings" and notes with quiet pride that he "emerged from the poverty and obscurity" of his birth to "a state of affluence and some degree of reputation in the world." He did so purely on merit for he was, in every sense of the word, a self-made man, owing little if anything to luck or the assistance of others, never pushing ahead at the expense of a fellow man.

Franklin was the youngest son of a poor tallow chandler who had migrated to Boston from England and married, as his second wife, the daughter of a former indentured serving maid. With 17 children to raise, he could give Benjamin only 2 to 3 years of schooling, but he encouraged him to study on his own, a habit which was to remain with Franklin all his life. At 10 the boy went to work in the family shop; at 12 he was apprenticed to his half brother to learn the printing trade, this being considered a suitable vocation for one whose love of books was already manifest.

In later life Franklin often remarked that he could not remember a time when he did not read. Books were his teachers. Through them he made himself a well-educated man. Taking the best authors as his models, he worked hard at perfecting his writing, eventually achieving a simple, lucid style. His thirst for knowledge never ceased. Since he wanted to read foreign books, he decided at 27 – a busy young merchant – to teach himself to do so. "I soon made myself so much the master of the French," he remarked, "as to be able to read the books with ease, I then undertook the Italian." Later on, "with a little painstaking, acquired as much of the Spanish as to read their books also." He read not only for instruction but for enjoyment. His taste was catholic. All his life, men of learning and position, who would ordinarily not bother with an artisan, sought Franklin's company. He supposed it was because "reading had so improved my mind that my conversation was valued."

Franklin by age 17 had learned all his brother could teach him and was ready to make his own way in the world. He went to New York but could find no work there, so continued on to Philadelphia. This is how he describes his arrival there after a long and uncomfortable trip — walking 50 miles, getting nearly shipwrecked, and helping to row a boat part of the way: "I was dirty from my journey; my pockets were stuffed out with shirts and stockings; I knew no soul, nor where to look for lodging. I was fatigued with traveling, rowing, and want of rest. I was very hungry and my whole stock of cash consisted of a Dutch Dollar . . ." He bought three large bread rolls. Wandering about town, munching, he met a fellow traveler. He gave her and her child two of his rolls. Thus did Franklin enter the town that was to become his permanent home, where he would rise to wealth and fame.

Seven years later he owned his own print shop, a stationery store, and a newspaper. He had in the meantime perfected his art by working for 18 months in England and could do the most intricate and difficult print jobs. At 26 he began the highly profitable annual publication of *Poor Richard's Almanac.* He managed his affairs so ably that at 42 he retired with an income equivalent to that of a royal governor. Though he was good at it, money-making never interested him, except as a means to obtain leisure for the things he really enjoyed: reading, study, scientific experimentation, social discourse and correspondence with men of similar interests.

While still a journeyman printer, he had founded a club for sociability and self-improvement, called the Junto, of which he later said that it was "the best school of philosophy, morals and politics" then existing in Pennsylvania. Its membership of about 12 consisted of alert, intelligent young artisans, tradesmen and clerks who liked to read and debate. They met Friday evenings to discuss history, ethics, poetry, travels, mechanic arts and science (then called "natural philosophy"). It has been said of this group that it "brought the Enlightenment in a leather apron to Philadelphia."

Franklin, who was full of ideas for improving life in Philadelphia and the Colonies in general, submitted all his proposals to the Junto where they were debated. Once accepted, members worked hard to get them put into effect. As a result, improvements were made in paving, lighting and policing the town; a volunteer fire department and militia were formed; a municipal hospital was established; the foundations were laid for what became the University of Pennsylvania and the American Philosophical Society. Of most lasting importance, perhaps, was Franklin's plan for a subscription library, the first in the Colonies. Access to books, he felt, meant that "the doors to wisdom were never shut." The idea caught on. He noted with satisfaction that the numerous libraries springing up everywhere "have improved the general conversation of Americans, made the common tradesmen and farmers as intelligent as most gentlemen from other countries, and perhaps have contributed in some degree to the stand so generally made throughout the colonies in defense of their privileges." The value of knowledge to man and society has never been put more succinctly.

When he was 40, Franklin discovered electricity. It was then a sort of magic, a parlor trick. Franklin—ably supported by his Junto—threw himself into experimentations and developed a workable theory which he proved in his famous kite experiment. In the 6 years between 1746 and 1752 his contributions to electricity changed it from a curiosity to a science, and in the process made him world famous. His writings on electricity were compared with Newton's *Optics;* he became the friend of most contemporary scientists, was made a member of virtually every scientific society and received honorary degrees from 20 universities. He was the first American scientist to win universal acclaim; the first American author to have his books translated and read as widely in Europe as in America. When he was sent to Paris, as America's first ambassador to a major power, the admiration of France for Franklin's scientific achievement in catching lightning and putting it to man's use contributed not a little to the success of his mission: winning the help of France to the Revolutionary cause.

As a man of leisure, Franklin found himself more and more drawn into public service, this being expected of anyone who had the time and ability to serve. He became a member of the Pennsylvania Legislature, the Committee of Five charged with drafting the Declaration of Independence, the Second Continental Congress and the Constitutional Convention. In one way or another, he represented America abroad a total of 25 years, becoming an exceedingly skillful diplomat. His statement, in hearings before Parliament, of the case of the Colonies against the hated Stamp Act was masterly and helped bring about the repeal of this Act. He was among the first to recognize that not merely "taxation" but "legislation in general" without representation could not be borne by Englishmen, whether they lived at home or abroad. The bond uniting England and its Colonies, he argued, was the King, not Parliament. Had his "dominion status theory" been accepted, the war might have been prevented but, as he sadly remarked, "there was not enough wisdom."

At 65, Franklin began his autobiography, intending it for his son. When pressure of public duties interrupted work on the book, one of his friends pleaded with him to complete it. All that had happened to Franklin, he urged, was of great historic interest since it was "connected with the detail of the manners and situation of a rising people." Moreover, the way he had planned and conducted his life was "a sort of key and explained many things that all men ought to have once explained to them, to give them a chance of becoming wise by foresight."

His philosophy of life, the virtues he cultivated—competent workmanship, honesty, industry and frugality—are within everyone's grasp; they are as important to a good and successful life today as in his time. No American child ought to grow to adulthood without having read the autobiography of this talented, wise and good man who personified all that is best in America. "Merely by being himself," wrote Mark van Doren, "he dignified and glorified his country."

USS ALEXANDER HAMILTON
(SSBN 617)

Named FOR Alexander Hamilton (1757–1804), brilliant statesman, lawyer, and political writer. No one, in his time, could equal him in the instancy of his grasp of complicated issues, whether relating to government and political economy, or law and organization; nor in the skill with which he put forth well-organized, systematic programs of action to remedy the problems besetting the newly emerging United States. For him, to see a defect was to put every ounce of energy into correcting it; to glimpse an opportunity was to seize it with both hands. His plans were bold and often at odds with prevailing opinion. He was as bitterly hated by his political opponents as he was extravagantly admired by his friends.

Political feuds were taken more seriously then and often led to vituperation and violence. His eldest son, a youth of 20, died in a duel defending his father's honor. Hamilton himself was mortally wounded on the very same spot 3 years later (at 47), called out by Aaron Burr whose political ambitions he had thwarted. Yet for all its brevity and tragic ending, Hamilton's life was a remarkable success story. No other Founding Father had so inauspicious a start or rose so quickly to influence, position, and wealth.

Born on the tiny island of Nevis in the British West Indies, he was the son of James Hamilton, a Scottish merchant, and Rachel Fawcett, daughter of a French Huguenot physician and planter. These two could not marry because Rachel's husband, despite long separation, would not grant her a divorce. The union of Alexander Hamilton's parents, though socially accepted, was therefore never legitimized. Nor did it otherwise prosper. His father was one of those younger sons of good family who seek their fortunes in the outposts of Empire but succeed in nothing they undertake. When he went bankrupt, the destitute family broke up; wife and son moved in with her relations on St. Croix; the father for a time was lost from sight.

Well-educated herself, Rachel obtained for her son as good an education as could be procured on the island. She first taught him herself, then had him tutored by a Presbyterian minister. But all this came to an end when she died, leaving Hamilton at 11 a virtual orphan. The following year he started to earn his living as clerk in the general store of Nicholas Cruger in Christiansted. In a letter to a friend written at that time, he confided his ambition to raise himself from "the grov'ling . . . condition of a Clerk or the like, to which my Fortune &c. condemns me." Though well aware that no prospects for advancement were in sight, he vowed, "I mean to prepare the way for futurity . . . Im no Philosopher you see and may be justly said to Build Castles in the Air . . . yet we have seen such Schemes successfull when the Projector is Constant." Something of the indomitable spirit of the penniless, lonely boy comes through to us across the barrier of archaic style and 18th century spelling. He seems to have continued his reading, meanwhile doing so well on his job that when Cruger went on a trip abroad, he left the business in the hands of young Hamilton, then in his early teens. Letters of that period show him to have been unusually mature and a writer of uncommon skill. It was his facile pen that ultimately won him release from a position and an environment too narrow for the unfolding of his talents. A description of the disastrous hurricane of 1772 which he wrote for the local newspaper won much acclaim. His mother's relations appear to have realized suddenly that this brilliant youth deserved the chance of a college education. Funds were provided and in 1772 Hamilton set sail for the mainland Colonies.

On arrival, he was found to have such serious gaps in knowledge that admission to college was out of the question. To the surprise of his teachers, he made up the deficiencies in a single year and entered King's College (now Columbia University) at 17. Throughout life he absorbed knowledge with incredible rapidity. Born with a quick mind, he acquired habits of systematic study at an early age. "Having always had a strong propensity to literary pursuits," he wrote in a brief autobiographical note (1797), "I was able, by the age of nineteen to qualify myself for the degree of Bachelor of Arts . . . and to lay the foundation by preparatory study for the future profession of the law. The American Revolution supervened. My principles led me to take part in it; at nineteen, I entered into the American army."

Hamilton committed himself to the Revolutionary cause when he was 17 and had lived in this country but one year. He joined one of the militias preparing for the coming struggle, spoke at protest meetings, wrote regularly for the press, and contributed two essays to the anonymous pamphlet "War of the Day" in which he brilliantly defended the actions of the First Continental Congress. These showed such knowledge and reasoning power, such a grasp of the issues, that when Dr. Myles Cooper of King's College was told they had been written by one of his own undergraduate students, he was incredulous; they had been attributed to John Jay.

Eager to get into the war, Hamilton organized an artillery company, was examined and awarded its captaincy, and distinguished himself in the campaigns around New York City and in New Jersey. His skill as a drillmaster, his competent military leadership, and outstanding personal bravery were noted, and on March 1, 1777, Washington asked him to become his secretary and aide-de-camp with the rank of lieutenant colonel, an unusually responsible position for one so young. Since Washington was in effect his own Secretary of War, much of his time was taken up with administrative matters. Of these, Hamilton relieved the general at once. Only 20, he already showed great skill as an administrator, bringing system and order into the mass of business passing through headquarters, handling all of Washington's correspondence, acting for him on various important missions. He drew up a complete set of military regulations and a plan for the Inspector General's Office (adopted by Congress). His fluent command of French proved invaluable. Common enough in the West Indies, it was as rare an accomplishment in America in those days as it still is today. Even Jefferson, Adams, and Franklin, our envoys to France, though able to read and understand French, did not speak it well. The position as confidant and right-hand man to the general eminently suited Hamilton's special talents, but he grew restless and tried many times to exchange it for a field command. It took him 4 years and a contrived quarrel to get back into the fighting, but he managed it just in time to win laurels at Yorktown (Oct. 14, 1781), where he led the American column in Lafayette's corps which stormed the first redoubt of the British works.

Returning at the end of hostilities to his interrupted law studies, he completed them in 5 months, passed his bar examinations, and embarked on a spectacularly successful legal career. Talent, energy, and luck all played a part in his rapid rise to eminence in the New York bar. The most important and remunerative cases soon came to him partly, no doubt, because he had allied himself in marriage (1780) to one of the wealthiest and most influential families in the city; his marriage—an unusually happy one—gave him entree into the best social circles. He commanded fees that earned him one of the highest incomes in the profession. Before he was 30, he had achieved everything he ever dreamed of as an obscure young clerk in a West Indian backwater, building "castles in the air," and preparing for "futurity."

But, happily situated though he now was in private life and determined, as he wrote Lafayette, to "retire a simple citizen and good paterfamilias," Hamilton could no more forego immersion in public affairs than any of our other great Revolutionary leaders. None of them would have been content with a purely private life, no matter how successful. Their sense of duty would not have permitted them to stand apart when their talents were needed. Nor could they have resisted the challenge of the times. John Adams spoke for them all when he wrote George Wythe of Virginia (1776): "You and I my dear friend, have been sent into life at a time when the greatest lawgivers of antiquity would have wished to live. How few of the human race have ever enjoyed an opportunity of making an election of government . . . for themselves or their children! When, before the present epocha, had three millions of people full power and a fair opportunity to form and establish the wisest and happiest government that human wisdom can contrive?"

Sociological dogmas attributing historic events and human actions exclusively to class interests and economic motives may easily lead us astray in evaluating the contributions of the Founding Fathers. Their political aims were in accord with those of the mass of their compatriots to a degree rarely found in the history of social upheavals. They sacrificed as much if not more than the rest of the population to see these aims realized. This surely is one reason why our Revolution did not "devour its children," and why we fought for independence in a civilized manner—more civilized at times than the enemy, as the English historian Lecky admits.

Indeed, seldom before or since has a revolution been led by men who had so much to lose, so little to gain. Their lives, fortunes, and honor would have been forfeit had the Revolution failed; that it succeeded brought them no special advantages.

Successful men for the most part, public office meant sacrifice, not profit. Those in the professions gave up lucrative careers it had taken years to build; well-to-do landowners neglected plantations which deteriorated without their personal care and supervision. Jefferson, Madison, even Washington might have lost their properties had they lived a few years longer. John Adams often worried over the economies his family had to practice that he might serve in the Congress (Massachusetts paid its delegate no salary, only expenses). Hamilton took a 70 percent cut to enter Washington's Cabinet. In a letter to a relative in Scotland he wrote that "public office in this country has few attractions"; that "the opportunity of doing good" is small, the pay "so inconsiderable as to amount to a sacrifice" for any professional man. Nevertheless he had given half his adult life to public service when he was cut down in his prime and would have given more had he been permitted a normal span of life.

Among the founders of our Nation, he was of the minority that thought in "continental" terms from the very start. A foreigner, he had no close attachment to any particular State. "My country" to him never meant Massachusetts or Virginia or even New York but always the larger unit emerging out of the wartime alliance of the 13 former Colonies. He shared Washington's distress that so many of the ablest men in the country served in their States rather than in the Congress during the war years. In letters to the speaker of the Virginia House of Delegates (1778), Washington warned that the "common interests of America are mouldering and sinking into irretrievable ruin . . . the great and important concerns of the Nation are horribly conducted, for want of either abilities or application of the members" of the Continental Congress. He pointedly asked: "Where is Mason—Wythe—Jefferson—Nicholas—Pendleton—Nelson?" He begged Virginia to send her ablest and best men to the body entrusted with the conduct of the war.

More competent members alone would, of course, not have made Congress an effective agency of government. It needed more power; above all, it needed dependable revenues. It was weak because it was desperately poor. So poor that when news was brought of the victory at Yorktown, there was not enough petty cash on hand to pay the messenger. Members of Congress had to dig into their own pockets for a dollar each. The States would not permit Congress to levy taxes to pay for the war, nor would they raise sufficient taxes themselves to pay the requisitions their own members in Congress had voted. "America is not used to great taxes," said John Adams. Costs were met, in a fashion, by printing worthless paper money and by domestic and foreign loans (on which interest payments were always in arrears). A year after the end of the war, Washington, contemplating the bankrupt country, warned that "the disinclination of the individual States to yield competent powers to Congress for the Federal Government, their unreasonable jealousy of that body and of one another, and the disposition, which seems to pervade each, of being all-wise and all-powerful within itself, will, if there is not a change in the system, be our downfall as a Nation."

Hamilton was as vividly aware as Washington that the country's independence, won at so great a price, might be lost for "want of power in Congress." As early as 1780, when he was but 23, he wrote eloquently of this danger and urged remedial action. He had practiced law only a short time when, to quote him, "the derangement of our public affairs, by the feebleness of the general confederation, drew me again reluctantly into public life." Next to Madison, he deserves chief credit for the calling of the Philadelphia Convention which drafted the Constitution (1787). It was his idea to publish a series of essays (later published as *The Federalist*) explaining the proposed new Federal Union. Not only did they help win popular acceptance of the Constitution but, to this day, *The Federalist* essays remain the best source of information on the American political system.

Years later, Madison praised Hamilton for having cooperated "faithfully in maturing and supporting a system which was not his choice" (1830). Hamilton would have preferred a stronger central government but knew it was unobtainable. He fought hard and effectively for adoption of the Constitution in New York, where the men elected to the ratifying convention at first stood 47 to 19 against it. Almost single-handedly, he won a slim majority of five (30 to 25) for ratification—a rare instance of one man's reasoned argument and sheer intellectual power causing a strongly committed assembly to reverse itself; Hamilton's last great speech is said to have brought tears to many convention delegates.

Appointed Secretary of the Treasury by Washington, he assumed his post in the fall of 1789, becoming almost at once the focus of a factional dispute over the principal issue of the time: how to put the country economically on its feet. Ten days after he took office, Congress asked him to submit a plan for "adequate support of public credit." He promptly came up with a four-point program that was simple, practical, and highly effective, but daring for the time. His first report (Jan. 14, 1790) proposed funding the domestic and foreign debt at par and assumption of the war debts of the States by the Federal Government. It has been estimated that nine out of ten members of Congress were prepared to scale down the debts but, as Jefferson once remarked of Hamilton, "without number, he is an host within himself"; his arguments proved irresistible.

Without credit, he pointed out, American economic development must lag. Future credit depended on whether current obligations were met. *Ergo*, there was no choice but to pay up. Moreover, the Revolutionary War debt "was the price of liberty. The faith of America has been repeatedly pledged to it. There is, indeed, reason to regret that it has not hitherto been kept." Honest discharge of the debt would, *inter alia* "promote the increasing respectability of the American name . . . cement more closely the Union of the States"; and increase "their security against foreign attack."

Hamilton added an urgent plea that there be incorporated "in the system of public credit of the United States," a fundamental maxim "that the creation of a debt should always be accompanied with the means of extinguishment." His second report (Dec. 13, 1790) proposed an excise tax to supplement the 5 percent import duty imposed by Congress in 1789 (before Hamilton took office), the additional revenue to be applied to service the debt. In his third report, issued the same day, he proposed a National Bank to assist the Government in its funding operations, provide a depository for Government funds, and issue notes that would give the country a sound currency. The report was attacked on the grounds that the Constitution does not empower Congress to create a bank or even a corporation. Hamilton countered with a famous passage, subsequently quoted almost verbatim by Chief Justice Marshall in *McCulloch* v. *The State of Maryland* (1819): "If the end be clearly comprehended within any of the specified powers, and if the measure have an obvious relation to that *end*, and is not forbidden by any particular provision of the Constitution, it may safely be deemed to come within the compass of the national authority" (doctrine of "implied powers.")

His fourth report (Dec. 5, 1791) *Report On Manufactures* caps the system that was henceforth to carry his name. He recommended protective tariffs for industry, bounties for agriculture, and federally sponsored internal improvements, citing the "general welfare" clause as justification.

By 1792, the recommendations of the first three reports and part of the fourth had become law. The results were spec-

eralists, with the tables turned, resorting to threats of nullification.

Once in power, what had divided the opponents proved less significant than what they had in common. They had in common commitment to popular government and a federal republic based upon the Constitution; they differed in their vision of America. Hamilton and the Federalists wanted America to be great, prosperous, secure in its vast domain. They believed a balanced economy to be the *sine qua non* of political independence since it would free Americans from dependence on foreign products and markets. The Republicans, on the other hand, and especially Jefferson, dreamed not of a powerful, self-sufficient country but rather of a country so organized as to preserve forever what they considered the most priceless heritage of the Revolution – the change in the status of the ordinary human being that comes with self-government. Almost the last thing Jefferson wrote before he died was a letter expressing the fervent hope that all men might be aroused "to assume the blessings and security of self-government." Paraphrasing the words spoken from the scaffold by Richard Rumbold (1685), erstwhile soldier in Cromwell's army, Jefferson declared it "palpable truth, that the mass of mankind has not been born with saddles on their backs, nor a favored few booted and spurred, ready to ride them."

Jefferson's overriding concern was ever the fitness of the people to govern themselves. No other advantages counted with him if they produced a society in which the common man lacked either the *power* or the *capability* to control his government. He felt strongly, as he wrote Madison in 1787, that our governments "will remain virtuous only as long as they are chiefly agricultural." His *Notes on Virginia*, published the same year, contain this oft-quoted paean to the farmer: "Those who labour in the earth are the chosen people of God . . . whose breasts he has made his peculiar deposit for substantial and genuine virtue. . . . While we have land to labour then, let us never wish to see our citizens occupied at a work-bench, or twirling a distaff." He mistrusted commerce and industry because he saw them creating inequalities of wealth and status. Commerce, he said in his First Inaugural Address, should be the "handmaid" of agriculture; of industry he would have nothing – "let our workshops remain in Europe." The sight of Europe's slums so horrified him that he determined then and there we should have no great cities in our fair land. "Great cities add just so much to the support of pure government, as sores do to the strength of the human body. It is the manner and spirit of a people which preserve the republic in vigour." He fought Federalist measures encouraging nonagricultural pursuits because he feared an industrialized America. Insistence on strict construction of the Constitution was the means he used to stop them. "It is unconstitutional," became the stock response of his followers to virtually every Federalist motion. Complained Fisher Ames, "I scarce know a point which has not produced this cry, not excepting a motion for adjournment . . . the fishery bill was unconstitutional . . . it was unconstitutional to give bounties; to make the militia worth having; order is unconstitutional; credit is ten fold worse."

Hamilton lost out in the short run; in the long run his was the more prophetic vision. The United States today resembles more nearly the kind of country Hamilton wanted it to be, though the national creed it professes is more closely akin to that of Jefferson. Most people veer instinctively toward the one or the other of these two men; unbiased judgment suggests that both were needed to shape our destiny.

Senator Arthur H. Vandenberg, a political statesman deeply interested in our history, said of Hamilton: "He was ever the subject of white-heat controversy—in death even as in life. But for myself, summing it all up, I say that five words might be his epitaph, 'The Republic Is His Monument.' "

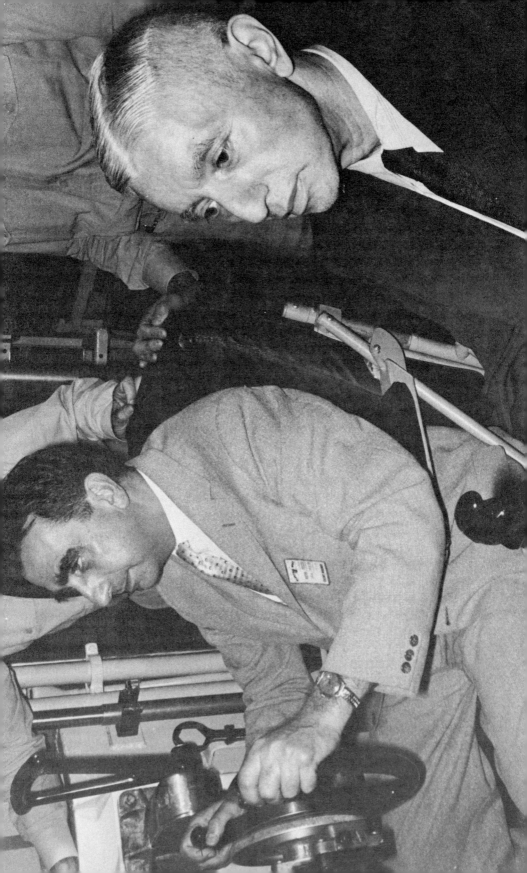

USS PATRICK HENRY (SSBN 599)

NAMED FOR Patrick Henry (1736–99), the foremost orator of the American Revolution. His stirring words swept like wildfire from Georgia to Massachusetts, arousing the patriotic fervor of the colonists, hastening their ultimate decision to separate from the mother country. He deserves to be remembered and more highly honored than he has been. In those days of slow communication, vivid phrases, easily remembered and retold, were needed to electrify public opinion. Some will doubtless live on long after it has been forgotten when and why he said them. Three made a special impact.

There was the dramatic conclusion to his fiery speech introducing a series of resolutions declaring the Stamp Act illegal (Virginia, House of Burgesses, May 1765), on the grounds that "the right and power to lay taxes and impositions upon the inhabitants of this colony" were vested exclusively in the legislative assembly. In a solemn tone he warned that "Caesar had his Brutus, Charles the First his Cromwell, and George the Third" – here he was interrupted by cries of "treason" – "and George the Third may profit by their example! If this be treason, make the most of it." The swerving of the thought from the expected parallelism is a thing of beauty. There was also Henry's eloquent plea for unity in the First Continental Congress (May 1774): "Throughout the continent, government is dissolved. Landmarks are dissolved! Where are now your boundaries? The distinction between Virginians, Pennsylvanians, New Yorkers, New Englanders are no more. I am not a Virginian but an American." This was treason and the Colonies made the most of it. He was not very learned, but he had a powerful and persuasive mind and a forensic skill to express

Nuclear physicist Dr. Edward Teller and the author at the controls of the USS PATRICK HENRY (SSBN 599).

51

it. People not only listened when he spoke, they obeyed him, too. And, there was his urgent plea for immediate arming of the Virginia militia (addressed to the Revolutionary convention assembled in Richmond, March 1775): "I know not what course others may take, but as for me, give me liberty, or give me death."

We have no accurate record of Henry's speeches, only recollections of men who heard them and were deeply moved. To John Adams, his voice "was like an angel's; it went through to the bone." Jefferson wrote of Henry's "sublime imagination, his lofty and overwhelming diction," of his talents as a popular orator which "were great indeed; such as I have never heard from any other man. He appeared to me to speak as Homer wrote."

Henry did not so much innovate ideas as clothe the thoughts then occupying the minds of Americans in words as persuasive to a backwoods jury of his old neighbors as to the sophisticated and more critical gentlemen of the Virginia Legislature or the Continental Congress. Years later, in a conversation with Daniel Webster (1824), Jefferson put his finger on the flaw that—great orator though he was—prevented Henry from attaining top level either as a statesman or as a political thinker. It was the *manner* of his speaking that bedazzled audiences, not the *substance* of what he said. His words were audacious when they were spoken, but it is the rhetoric rather than the man that sustains them. "While he was speaking, it always seemed directly to the point," remarked Jefferson, but when he ceased to speak "I asked myself what the d - - - l has he said?"; and to this query he never found an answer.

These two Virginians, usually friends working for a common end, but sometimes political opponents, were curious opposites. Jefferson, so it is said, never made a speech, but he left us a mass of writings that will influence Americans and others for generations to come. Henry, too busy with practical affairs, private and public, wrote nothing; his words, once so influential, are gone with the wind. Oratory is an evanescent trait, something later generations have to take on trust. Both had splendid minds but Jefferson's had been developed to its fullest power by the best education then available, while Henry's schooling had been brief. Jefferson read profusely and widely; Henry did not and so remained a genius *manqué*.

Born in upcountry Virginia, at Studley, Hanover County, he was tutored by his father who, with 11 children and but a small plantation, could not afford the high fees of boarding school, the only educational institutions then available above elementary level. Himself a well-educated Scotsman, he could have given Patrick a fine classical education had the boy not been an indifferent scholar. Efforts to set him up in a trade also failed. In 7 years, Henry managed to go bankrupt twice as a storekeeper, once as a farmer. He simply could not make a living. He married at 18, and ultimately had 17 children. With no prospects he lived aimlessly in the backwoods. Neither he himself nor anyone else suspected that he had a superior mind.

Suddenly, at 24, he took himself in hand. Since he seemed to have no gift other than an ability to talk, he decided to become a lawyer. With some few textbooks and entirely on his own, he proceeded to cram enough law to pass the bar examinations. His ignorance of the law was preposterous but the examiners recognized an extraordinary, if undeveloped, talent. Their estimate proved correct. Two years later, already well established and with a fast growing practice, he took on a seemingly lost case which turned into a *cause celebre* and made him famous overnight as a skillful advocate, compelling orator, and courageous defender of the rights of the colonists in matters of local self-government.

Known as "Parson's Cause," (1764) this was a suit for back pay brought by the Anglican minister Reverend James Maury against his vestry. It had its origin in the conflict of two Virginia statutes dealing with ministerial salaries. The law of 1748 fixed these at 16,000 pounds of tobacco per annum. As a temporary relief measure, during a severe shortage of tobacco, the legislature passed the so-called Two Penny Act (1755, reenacted 1758) permitting payment in specie at 2 pence per pound of tobacco, well below the current market price. The clergy petitioned the King for redress and, on the advice of the Privy Council, he declared the Two Penny Act void, thus reinstating the earlier law. The court had already upheld the plea of Reverend Maury and all that remained was to call a jury to consider the amount of damages.

Patrick Henry, acting for the defense, made a sensation when he argued with passionate eloquence that the Two Penny Act "ought to be considered as the law of the land, and the only legitimate measure of the claims of the clergy," the King's action in voiding this act being "an instance of royal misrule" which "dissolved the political compact, and left the people at liberty to consult their own safety." Basing his argument on Locke's theory that government is a mutual contract between ruler and ruled whose "violation by one party discharged the other," he declared that the King's action had been in disregard of the pressing needs of the colonists. "By annulling or disallowing laws of this salutary nature," the King had become a tyrant, thus forfeiting "all rights to his subject's obedience."

Henry bolstered this argument with a violent attack on the clergy which fell on sympathetic ears among the dissenters on the jury (and among the spectators) who bitterly resented having to maintain the ministers of a church professing doctrines they deemed erroneous. In colonial Virginia, the Anglican Church was "established"; that is, its support was laid on all the people at a rate fixed by law, but it had long since become a minority church and the tax was widely considered unjust. It was also a heavy burden, especially for the poorer farmers in Hanover County where the case was being tried. Henry had no difficulty persuading the jury to award total damages of 1 penny!

The clergy with some justification called the whole proceeding treasonous. Henry did indeed win the case by defying Virginia's charter. As in all the "royal" Colonies, the right of the legislature to enact laws was subject to the "royal" prerogative; that is, the King could void colonial laws if advised by the Privy Council that they were contrary to British law or to the colonial charter in question. During the period of British rule, some 5 percent of all the laws passed by colonial legislatures were so voided. Though much disliked by the colonists, no court had ever questioned the practice which was based on the long-established principle that a lower law contravening a higher law is invalid — a principle that was incorporated into our Constitution (Art. VI).

In British eyes, the legal position of colonial legislatures was equivalent to that of municipal corporations or county councils existing by virtue of a grant or charter (Lord Mansfield). They were therefore subordinate to Parliament. Basic to the Revolutionary conflict was the eventual rejection of this view by most of the colonists and their insistence that the constitutional relationship between mother country and colony was one of equality and separateness, the two being linked only through the Crown. Colonial legislatures were therefore held to be independent of Parliament. As Jefferson put it, Parliament was "a body of men foreign to our constitutions and unacknowledged by our laws."

Patrick Henry put himself into the vanguard of the Revolution by attacking not a new kind of English law, such as the Stamp Act which violated traditional colonial rights, but the very substance of the colonial relationship itself. He made revolution in the King's court, which, incidentally, was presided over by his own father. Good Anglican and loyal subject though father John had been all his life, he too was carried away by the eloquence of his son.

Parson's Cause made Henry the idol of the backcountry people who thenceforth sent him regularly to the legislature and elected him Governor five times. The case procured him an enormous clientele (if only a 15 shilling fee!) and made him rich enough to afford giving 25 years to the service of his State.

Throughout his life Virginia remained the principal arena of Henry's political activities. Even his considerable services to the Revolutionary cause proceeded from this center of his political being. From there, as Jefferson said, he started "the ball of the Revolution rolling." Speaking as a delegate of his State he gave the ball a mighty push in the First and Second Continental Congresses. As wartime Governor, he loyally supported Washington, Virginia supplying proportionately more than her share in men and resources. In 1778, he sent George Rogers Clark with 175 men into the territories north of the Ohio where British and Loyalist troops under Colonel Hamilton held a number of forts. From these forts Hamilton (the "Hair Buyer," so-called because he paid Indians for every American scalp) directed his Indian allies in depredations against isolated settlements.

A gifted military leader, Clark captured the forts and took Hamilton prisoner, besides winning over the French *habitants* and even some Indian tribes. The Old Northwest was thus in American hands when peace negotiations began. It may well be that this fact helped bolster our claim to this vast territory which Britain ceded in 1783 (and out of which were formed Michigan. ᵀllinois, Ohio, Indiana, Wisconsin and a part of Minnesota).

This successful military venture has been called Virginia's own small war. Although it was undertaken to secure territories Virginia claimed under her charter, she ceded them all to the Confederation, as did six other States with similar western claims. This was done to allay the fear of smaller States, notably Maryland, which held up ratification of the Articles of Confederation until assured of cession. Surely history has no parallel of so great a sacrifice for the sake of harmony among confederated States. Although nearly all of the leaders of the Colonies acted out of sectional interests, they usually took a national view, too. Henry was more regional than most; he did not participate in framing the Constitution, nor in the administrations that grew out of it.

Though he was urged to take important posts outside Virginia (Senator (1794), Secretary of State or Chief Justice of the Supreme Court (1795), envoy to France (1799)), he declined them all. Although he took a lofty view of public affairs, his vision did not see much beyond the boundaries of Virginia. At the start of the Revolution, he had, in youthful fervor, declared himself "an American, not a Virginian," but he never fully made that transition. Like many Americans of the time, he had no political aims beyond independence from Britain, establishment of popular or republican government in the States and their union in the Confederation. With all this accomplished, he saw no need for the Constitution.

Virginia, largest and richest of the States — larger than Great Britain — was economically self-sufficient. Under the Confederation, she had negotiated with foreign governments, obtained loans, signed treaties. To give this up was not easy. Indeed, for the three largest States (Virginia, New York, Massachusetts), the step from loose Confederation to firm Federal Union was difficult. In all three a majority were at first opposed to the Constitution; the debates on ratification were bitter and protracted; acceptance was by small margins (89 to 79, 30 to 27, and 187 to 168, respectively). Deeply mistrustful of the power of the central government, Patrick Henry led a spirited opposition in the Virginia ratifying convention. He was on his feet for hours every day warning that this new government would in time obliterate the States and encroach on hard-won individual liberties. Once it was adopted, however, he loyally accepted the Constitution, even consenting in the last year of his life to become once more a member of the Virginia Assembly, and on the Federalist ticket at that, in order to defeat the Kentucky and Virginia Resolves (1798) which he feared might dissolve the Union. He died before taking office.

Jefferson said of him that "he was as well suited to the times as any man ever was, and it is not now easy to say what we should have done without Patrick Henry. He was far above all in maintaining the spirit of Revolution."

USS NATHAN HALE (SSBN 623)

Named FOR Nathan Hale (1755–76), a young schoolmaster who, by the manner of his dying in the cause of liberty, taught Americans the true meaning of love of country.

The soldiers of the Revolution under Washington's command were engaged in the first enterprise jointly undertaken by all of their 13 home States. They had need of a hero who would symbolize the Union they were bringing forth by their common effort, their common suffering; a hero who would put into words their still inchoate sense of devotion to this Union that was slowly and painfully evolving out of their shared experience. Nathan Hale was their first *national* hero. His story was simple; his life brief. There was time only for a single heroic act. But it was enough.

Nathan Hale was born in Coventry, Conn., a descendant of Robert Hale who arrived in Cambridge, Mass., from England in 1632. His father was a well-to-do farmer. Both parents were much concerned with public affairs. Of their 12 children, nine were sons. Six took part in the Revolution. Nathan received an excellent classical education from the village pastor, entered Yale at 14 and graduated at 18. An omnivorous reader, he was noted for his literary and oratorical powers. No less remarkable was his physical prowess. The marks he left in a tremendous broad jump were long preserved on the New Haven Green. His statue on the Yale Campus shows him to have been a handsome young man. Indeed, he was a child of good fortune, well-liked

The USS Nathan Hale (SSBN 623)
on sea trials in October 1963.

by everyone for his athletic skills, intelligence, good looks, and pleasant manners. He was successful and popular in his chosen career as a teacher.

At the outbreak of hostilities, he at once joined up and was commissioned a lieutenant by the legislature of his State (July 1, 1775) 2 days before Washington assumed command of the Continental Army in Cambridge. A capable and resourceful officer, he was selected by Lt. Col. Thomas Knowlton to a captaincy in the famed "Knowlton's Rangers" (early in 1776). Hale took part both in Washington's successful siege of Boston, ending March 1776 when General Howe evacuated Boston, and in his unsuccessful attempt to hold New York against the British 6 months later.

Anticipating the enemy's plan to make New York his base of operations and, by holding the line of the Hudson, to cut off New England from the rest of the Colonies, Washington marched his army to New York, hastily built fortifications and prepared to meet the British assault. But Howe was hard at his heels with vastly superior land forces, and his brother, Admiral Howe, was moving in naval units to control the waters surrounding Manhattan. The city was open to a combined military-naval attack on two sides.

In this "darkest hour of the Revolution," Washington turned to Knowlton for a volunteer among the Rangers who would go behind enemy lines and collect vitally needed information on British strength and plans. Nathan Hale offered to undertake this dangerous espionage mission. When a friend tried to dissuade him, he replied that he wanted to be useful, "and every kind of service, necessary to the public good, becomes honorable by being necessary," even spying.

Assuming the guise of a Dutch schoolmaster—with his degree from Yale for credentials—he left on September 12th, proceeding circumspectly to Long Island where he obtained all for which Washington had asked. He had almost reached the American lines when he was discovered. It was widely believed that his Tory cousin Samuel had betrayed him. Nathan was taken before General Howe. Dispensing with the formality of a trial, Howe ordered that he be executed by hanging the next day. The penalty was in accordance with military law and Hale accepted it calmly.

The 18th century English world found its lofty primer to Stoicism in Addison's tragedy *Cato*. Phrases from *Cato* reverberate through the American Revolution: Patrick Henry was paraphrasing when he cried, "Give me liberty, or give me death."

On his way to the gallows, he must have thought of the moving scene in Addison's *Cato* where the father comes upon his son slain in battle and says:

"How beautiful is death when earned by virtue!
Who would not be that youth? What pity it is
That we can die but once to serve our country."

for his last words, as they have come down to us, were: "I only regret that I have but one life to lose for my country."

Hale died at 21, Washington lived to be 67; one was a promising youth who was not allowed time to prove what he might accomplish, the other accomplished more than anyone might have expected when he was a youth. They had in common a virtue that was perhaps more admired in their time than in ours: fortitude in the face of failure, triumph of the human spirit over fortune's adversities. They had in common a selfless devotion to their country that is perhaps rarer today than in 1776.

And yet perhaps not. To the historic minded, there was an echo of Hale's words in the air when another young man, who was not permitted to live long enough to accomplish what he set out to do, urged his countrymen to "ask not what your country can do for you—ask what you can do for your country."

USS LAFAYETTE (SSBN 616)

Named IN HONOR of the best foreign friend the United States ever had, Marie Joseph Paul Yves Roch Gilbert du Motier, Marquis de Lafayette (1757–1834). Scion of ancient and illustrious French families, he was born in the Château de Chavaniac in Auvergne, France, and educated at the Collège du Plessis in Paris, entering the King's Musketeers at the age of 14. He was 18 and by now a captain when he heard of the revolt of the American Colonies against Britain and read the Declaration of Independence. "At the first news of this quarrel," he later wrote in his memoirs, "my heart was enrolled in it." He instantly decided to make America's cause his own. In part, he was motivated by an ardent desire to hit back at England for the humiliation she had inflicted on France in the Seven Years' War, in which his father had lost his life (at the Battle of Minden, 1759). In part, his generous youthful spirit was stirred at seeing the American Colonies put into effect the ideas of the Enlightenment.

Like most educated Europeans, he was thoroughly familiar with these ideas, especially with the belief of the *philosophes* in a "law of nature" which, if only it could be discovered and applied to human society, would end most human misery, set men free, and enable them to achieve happiness. Newton's discovery of the laws of nature governing the inanimate universe left a deep impression on thinking men, and gave them hope that analogous natural laws might be found for the governance of man in society.

It was a beguiling—though erroneous—notion; a notion which seems to reappear in ever new forms, perhaps because it satisfies a deep human hunger for freedom and justice. On it rested the Roman *jus gentium*, supposedly pure reason incarnate, since it was distilled from principles common to the laws of all the races sojourning at Rome, whose interrelationships it governed. It is still the basis of customary international law, as when Grotius tried to build on the Roman *jus gentium* a law for the governance of the emerging European society of equal and independent states (1625). John Locke used it to evolve a theory of government, entirely secular, in no way depending on divine sanction. And Jefferson, steeped in Locke's philosophy, called upon "the laws of Nature and of Nature's God" to support the political maxims proclaimed by the Declaration of Independence—maxims we hold sacred, and which have now been accepted by all truly democratic countries, not because they are in fact a binding "law of nature," but because men have agreed to accept them as binding law. Unlike the forces of inanimate nature, human beings have free will; therefore, the laws that govern them are not immutable and fixed by nature, but man-made creations of public consensus in free societies, of government fiat in authoritarian countries.

Whatever Europeans came to think of America later on, all those of liberal spirit were immensely impressed with the American experiment which established—by a deliberate constitutive act based on popular consensus—a government such as men had heretofore merely dreamed of and speculated on—a government dedicated to securing liberty and equality for all. This is why aristocrats—Lafayette, Pulaski, Kosciuszko, Du Portail, De Kalb, Von Steuben—wanted to help us win the War for Independence. They were ready to fight, if need be to die (as did Pulaski). None more so than the 19-year-old Lafayette.

He had arranged with Silas Deane, American agent in Paris, for entry into the Continental Army as a major general and made preparations to sail when news of the military disasters of the New York and Long Island campaigns reached France. Though his friends tried to discourage him and his king forbade him to leave, and a *lettre de cachet* was issued should he try to disregard the royal command, Lafayette by a ruse escaped and arrived in Georgetown, N.C., June 13, 1777. Six weeks of arduous travel brought him to Philadelphia where he presented his credentials to a Congress grown somewhat weary of foreign adventurers seeking high-ranking positions in the army. Lafayette, however, offered to serve without pay as a simple volunteer, and Congress resolved (July 31, 1777) "that his services be accepted, and that, in consideration of his zeal, illustrious family and connections, he have the rank and

63

commission of a major-general of the United States." The next day Lafayette met Washington. Between these two men—25 years apart in age—there rapidly developed a close and warm friendship which lasted until Washington's death (Lafayette named his first son Georges Washington).

He fought at Brandywine (receiving a slight wound), at Gloucester, at Monmouth; he shared the hardships of the bitter winter at Valley Forge (1777–78), joined General Greene in the Southern Campaign (1781) where he helped to thwart the attempt of British General Phillips to take Richmond, and played a brilliant part in the victory at Yorktown that same year.

He had come here with only the little English he was able to pick up on the sea voyage and never quite mastered the language of his troops, but he was highly popular with them— "the soldier's friend" they called him. By nature impetuous, he could nevertheless muster great caution and patience— essential qualities during the long waiting period before French military and naval aid arrived—when he had to use his sparse resources of men and material in the most economical way, never allowing the enemy to draw him into a battle he could not hope to win, but harassing them constantly by dodging, parrying and retreating, only to advance and repeat the same maneuvers all over again, thus keeping the British constantly occupied.

Other foreign volunteers fought bravely and competently, but Lafayette, besides being a capable, well-trained officer of great courage, was also extremely rich. He gave half his fortune to the American cause (some $200,000 spent on buying and outfitting a ship, procuring ammunition, etc.). His was the first and last case of a private "aid to America" project, one the American people have never forgotten. At the risk of sounding smug, we may take pride in having proved ourselves more grateful recipients of foreign aid than many others. Not only did we lavish affection and popular acclaim on Lafayette on the three occasions he visited us after the war, but when he lost most of his fortune during the French Revolution, Congress in 1794 voted him $24,425, a sum representing the accumulated pay he had refused while he fought for us, and in 1803 made him a grant of 11,520 acres in Louisiana. Moreover, when he was held prisoner of state (1792–97) in Prussia and Austria, after having been declared a traitor by the revolutionary govern- ment of France (which repudiated his efforts at moderation between factions), the Congress, Washington, and Gouverneur

Morris exerted every effort to obtain his release (without success—it was Napoleon who secured his freedom in 1797).

None of this can, of course, balance our account with Lafayette. The debt we owe him can be neither fully evaluated nor would it have been possible ever to repay it adequately. He was enormously helpful in procuring French financial, military and naval aid, and as a liaison officer between the American and French armies. After his return to France at the end of the war, he continued to serve our interests, helping Jefferson—then our minister to France—to adjust the boundary dispute with Spain, promoting the sale of American tobacco and fishery products, obtaining for us the position of most favored nation in the French market. A constant friend at Paris, he smoothed out innumerable minor problems arising between the two countries and—to use a modern term—was America's best public relations agent abroad.

His last visit here (1824–25), on the invitation of President Monroe was a triumphal tour of which Charles Sumner said that it belonged "to the poetry of history." Americans demonstrated an enthusiasm never before or since accorded a foreigner. Lafayette loved glory and fame and this America gave him in full measure. In 1784, the Maryland General Assembly conferred honorary citizenship in perpetuity upon him and his heirs. Upon adoption of the Constitution this automatically made him an American citizen (honorary citizenship is still possessed by his direct descendants, the Chambrun family, the male line having died out with his grandson in 1881)—the only foreigner so honored in all our history until Congress conferred citizenship on Sir Winston Churchill in 1963.

To his own country, Lafayette left a legacy of American friendship, of good will on the part of America which no temporary misunderstanding has ever extinguished.

USS ETHAN ALLEN (SSBN 608)

Named for Ethan Allen (1738–89), soldier, farmer, political pamphleteer, and frontier philosopher, best known for his exploits as leader of the "Green Mountain Boys" during the American Revolution.

Ethan Allen was born in Litchfield, Connecticut. His family, English in origin, had been farmers in Connecticut for four generations. Ethan was the first Allen to have college aspirations, but his education was cut short by the early death of his father. As the oldest in a large family, it was his responsibility to manage the family farm.

In the 1760's he took up land with two of his brothers in the "New Hampshire Grants," as the area, now Vermont, was called. Vermont was then the "frontier" of New England; still largely a wilderness but beginning to fill up with land-hungry New Englanders who came in search of virgin soil. Even at that early date, farms were being abandoned in some older sections of the country because the primitive agricultural methods of the time—no rotation of crops, little if any use of fertilizer—had exhausted the soil. The settlers in Vermont were the first wave in the continuous succession of migrations from settled regions into the unspoiled wilderness, so characteristic of the American way of conquering a continent.

The settlers were from the start beset by jurisdictional conflicts arising from imprecise colonial charters. Such conflicts were commonplace in the New World which was parceled out in slipshod manner by Europeans ignorant of American geography. From the start, Vermont was in dispute between France and England, since she had been included in grants issued in 1603 by Henry IV of France and in 1606 by James I of England. Some of the fighting in the almost continuous

Anglo-French wars between 1689 and 1763 (when France was finally removed from America) took place there. Vermont was also in dispute between New York and New Hampshire, each seemingly having a valid claim under their respective royal charters. Upon the arrival of settlers with New Hampshire grants, New York brought the dispute before the Privy Council in London which decided in her favor—a decision bitterly resented by the settlers who were New Englanders and did not wish to be ruled by New York. In their fight for independent statehood (which lasted two decades), Ethan Allen became their leader and his Green Mountain Boys their protectors against the hated "Yorkers." More deeply committed to the autonomy of Vermont than to the independence of the confederated Colonies, Ethan Allen yet played a notable—if brief—part in the Revolutionary War.

Every schoolboy knows that he and his Green Mountain Boys—with the help of some men from Connecticut and Massachusetts—took Fort Ticonderoga on May 10, 1775, the very day the Second Continental Congress convened in Philadelphia. As he later told it, Allen ordered the surprised garrison to surrender "in the name of the Great Jehovah and the Continental Congress." In truth, Congress had not ordered the attack. It did, however, accept responsibility for this, the first clearly aggressive military act of the colonists which, in an instant, changed England's trouble with her Massachusetts Colony into a full-scale revolution involving all of her American empire.

John Adams estimated that at the start of the Revolutionary War, one third of the colonists were loyal to England, one third were undecided and one third were committed to independence. The last carried the day because of the fervor of their convictions and the energy with which they took the matter in hand. There can be little doubt that the law-abiding men of the Second Continental Congress had not yet reached agreement on severing all ties with the mother country when they were catapulted into war by such spontaneous popular actions as Ticonderoga, Lexington, and Concord, undertaken on their own initiative by surprisingly small numbers of citizens. Ticonderoga was captured by 83 men. It should be mentioned that the garrison numbered 42. Lafayette was right when he said in reply to a query by Napoleon as to the nature of the American Revolution, that "the greatest interests of the universe were there decided by the skirmishes of picket guards."

Except for a brief period, Ticonderoga remained in American

hands throughout the war, a strategic asset of considerable importance because it controlled the water route into Canada. Of more immediate significance to the American cause was the store of powder and cannon in the fort. John Marshall, in his *Life of George Washington*, reports that 14 mortars, two howitzers, 39 cannon, a ton of lead, and a barrel of flint were captured. This may seem a meager cache by modern standards, but it was of inestimable value to the colonists who at the time had none of the military supplies essential to waging a large-scale war; nor manufacturing facilities where such equipment could be produced; nor enough money to buy it abroad and little chance, if they could have obtained them on credit, of bringing military supplies through the tight blockade maintained by the British Navy. During the first years of the war, before French financial, military, and naval aid arrived, most of our battles were fought with material captured from the enemy.

The Ticonderoga stores were transported across the mountains on ox-drawn sleds during the winter 1775–76, arriving in time to give Washington the equipment that enabled him to mount an offensive strong enough to end the siege of Boston which had been deadlocked for months. On March 17, 1776, General Howe and his British garrison were forced to evacuate the city. It was the first victory of Washington's Continental Army and a great boon for Massachusetts and all of New England, since military operations now moved away from the Northeast where the war had begun.

Ticonderoga, for Ethan Allen, was but a first step toward the grand objective of winning Canada to the American cause, of carrying the Revolution beyond the 13 seaboard Colonies into the vast empire Britain had won from France at the end of the Seven Years' War (or French and Indian Wars as it was known in America). Allen himself had fought in that war (1757) and Congress was in a receptive mood when he suggested that an invasion of Canada would rally the French *habitants* to our standard. Surely, they could feel no attachment to Britain, for had they not been ceded less than a dozen years before? It seemed reasonable to think they might wish to become the 14th "rebellious Colony." But the assumption proved false. By guaranteeing her French subjects their special legal institutions and complete religious liberty (Quebec Act of 1774), England had secured the loyalty of the *habitants*. When a two-pronged attack was mounted on Quebec in the fall of 1775, they remained neutral. The British put up a resolute defense and the Americans retreated in July 1776.

Even so, the hope that Canada might eventually join the revolt against Britain lingered on. Witness the preferred status accorded her in the Articles of Confederation which provided that Canada be admitted at once should she wish to join the Confederation, while all others needed the approval of nine States (Art. XI).

The Canadian expedition proved costly, not least to Ethan Allen who was captured while trying to take Montreal by surprise and held prisoner in England for 3 years until an exchange could be arranged. Upon his return to this country in May 1778, he was cordially received by Washington, voted back pay by Congress, and breveted colonel. He took time out to write the most celebrated book in the prison literature of the American Revolution, the *Narrative of Colonel Ethan Allen's Captivity* (1779), but took no further part in the war. Short-term military service was the custom then; few Americans served for the duration. Many, like Ethan Allen, were motivated exclusively by loyalty to their State.

The objective of the war was political independence, the right to self-government. For most Americans this meant autonomy and self-government for their *State*, despite the existence of a *Continental* Congress and Army. The Articles of Confederation might use such terms as Independence of "America," "Perpetual Union" of the States, and take for its name "the United States of America," but this did not at once create loyalty to the new political entity; certainly not a loyalty taking precedence over loyalty to one's own State. Juridically, the Confederation was not a State but a "league of friendship," a creature of the States composing it, each of which "retained its sovereignty, freedom and independence" (Art. II). Congress under the Articles was not a national legislature but an assembly of plenipotentiaries, appointed and paid for by their home governments. When Washington attempted to administer the oath of allegiance to his New Jersey troops they refused, declaring "New Jersey is our country," and were upheld by their representatives in Congress.

Local patriotism was particularly strong among settlers in frontier regions that were in process of establishing themselves as separate States. If they felt thwarted by the Confederation in matters important to them, negotiation with foreign governments for better terms was apt to seem quite in order. Take the issue of free navigation on the Mississippi and the right of deposit in Spanish New Orleans. This was an economic necessity for settlers in what was to become Kentucky (1792) and

69

Tennessee (1796). When John Jay, Secretary of Foreign Affairs of the Confederation, proposed (1784) to waive the right of deposit in return for commercial advantages chiefly benefiting New England, the settlers were prepared to accede to Spain if this was the only way to obtain this vital outlet for their bulky goods.

Or take Vermont. A constitutional convention declared independence on January 15, 1777, adopted the name Vermont, and approved a constitution modeled closely on that of Pennsylvania, except that it was more democratic (Vermont was the first State to abolish slavery and decree universal manhood). When repeated requests for admission to the Confederation were rejected by Congress, in deference to the objections of New York and New Hampshire, Ethan Allen took steps to obtain a guarantee of independence from Governor Haldimand of Canada. Whether, in return, he promised the Governor neutrality or even union with Canada, or whether he was simply engaged in a maneuver to force the hand of Congress is not known. In any event, his action brought quick results. The difficulties with New Hampshire were composed in 1782, those with New York in 1790, and Vermont was admitted in 1791, the first new State to join the original 13.

Ethan Allen did not live to see this goal achieved, a goal which had absorbed his interest and consumed his energies during most of his adult life. He died 2 years too soon.

USS NATHANAEL GREENE
(SSBN 636)

NAMED FOR one of the ablest American generals of the Revolutionary War. Nathanael Greene (1742–86) was a Rhode Islander by birth, son of a farmer and blacksmith. At the age of 28 he was elected to the colonial legislature and served a total of four 1-year terms. An early and passionate sympathizer with the Revolutionary cause, he joined the militia in 1774, Washington's army in 1775, and was made major general by the Congress in 1776. He fought the war from beginning to end, much of it as right-hand man to George Washington.

There was a certain similarity between these men. "He has an aspect which commands respect," wrote one of Greene's officers, "something of the Washington about it." Both men were disciplinarians, taking great pains to instill in their troops the military virtues of professional soldiers. As early as 1775, in a report describing the first encampment of the Continental Army, it was noted that Greene's Rhode Islanders, unlike most other contingents, set up their tents "like the regular camp of the enemy." But Greene also shared his Commander in Chief's warm concern for the welfare of the men he led, digging so often and so deeply into his own pocket to provide them with clothing, when a careless country failed to do so, that he had trouble discharging his personal debts.

All our native-born troop commanders were self-made soldiers, but Greene was something more. Through intense study of European campaigns—especially those of Louis XIV's Marshal Turenne—he made himself a military theoretician. His understanding of the art of war was second only to Washington's. This was all the more surprising in that Greene was of the Quaker faith. Indeed his passionate interest in military strategy led to his expulsion from the Society of Friends. Strangely too, this interest came late – at the age of 32. He seems to have been stimulated solely by deep devotion to the cause of American liberty. Once victory was won, he returned to farming and twice refused the office of Secretary of War.

Though he learned his military science from Europeans, Nathanael Greene's approach to warfare was distinctly American. He was devoid of vainglory and ever ready to adopt unorthodox tactics. War was not a game to him but a grim business. His object was not to win battles but to clear the British from American soil. Until the last months of the war their forces were superior to ours in numbers, training and equipment. Moreover, geography favored the enemy. The configuration of our coastline, with its many deep indentations, allowed the British, who had ample shipping, to move troops rapidly inland, as well as from any point on one of these waterways to any point on another. In contrast, our own forces had to move on foot over difficult terrain with few good roads. The niggardly provisioning of our troops made this particularly slow and painful. We have the poignant remark of an officer that the road to Trenton could be "easily traced, as there was a little snow on the ground, which was tinged here and there with blood from the feet of the men who wore broken shoes."

Greene's talent as a strategist is best seen in his successful campaign to regain the South which had fallen to the enemy and was occupied by British regulars and Tory militia holding strong positions in a chain of small forts. In the face of stronger enemy forces, Greene divided his own and attacked, thus violating all the established rules of warfare. But as historian Lynn Montross wrote: "Some of the greatest victories of history have been won by generals who refused to be bound by the rules. Greene joined this select list . . . when his right wing, led by Morgan, destroyed a small British army in the tactical masterpiece of the Revolution – a battle so brilliantly conceived that it served as model for future American operations." He was referring to the Battle of Cowpens.

Though subsequent encounters resulted in technical victory for the enemy, each engagement furthered Greene's over-all purpose. Each cost the British greater losses in men killed and wounded; each made their occupation of fortified strong points less profitable; each forced them to move back toward the coast. Thus Greene regained the South in but 9 months. He was particularly skillful in coordinating the operations of his regular troops with those of patriot partisan bands. One might well call him the first strategist making joint use of guerrillas and organized army contingents—a new concept at the time.

Thomas Jefferson wrote of Greene that he was "second to no one in enterprise, in resource, in sound judgment, promptitude of decision, and every other military talent." These are talents as important today as in the past, as necessary in naval as in army operations.

USS CASIMIR PULASKI (SSBN 633)

NAMED FOR a man whose all too brief life was dedicated to the fight for freedom, Casimir Pulaski. First for the freedom of his native country, Poland, and when this fight was lost, for the freedom of our own country. Born a Polish nobleman, he died an American Revolutionary War hero.

Pulaski was an active participant in the last desperate efforts of Polish patriots to preserve their country's freedom from Russian encroachment. When the Polish cause was lost he fled, his life and property forfeit. With Benjamin Franklin's help he reached our shores and joined Washington's army. He was one of a small band of foreign officers who, though of aristocratic birth, made the cause of the American Revolution their own and fought valiantly for it.

Pulaski's signal military exploits at the Battle of Brandywine won him the commission of brigadier general from the Continental Congress. A brilliant cavalryman, he awakened American generals to the need of a better cavalry. He became a favorite of General Washington and with his approval formed "Pulaski's Legion," an independent force composed primarily of European trained cavalry and infantrymen.

Pulaski was mortally wounded leading his legion in a cavalry charge at the Battle of Savannah, Oct. 11, 1779, a day which has been proclaimed "Pulaski Day" by Congress.

General Washington wrote to him:

"I assure you Sir, I have a high sense of your merit and services and the principles that influenced the part you have taken in the affairs of this country. The disinterested and unremitted zeal you have manifested in the service gives you a title to the esteem of the citizens of America, and have assured you mine."

USS VON STEUBEN (SSBN 632)

NAMED FOR a Prussian-born soldier who served with distinction in the American Revolutionary Army. Frederick William Augustus von Steuben arrived in this country in 1777 and offered his services to Congress as a volunteer without military rank. He was accepted as such, but Congress soon recognized the value of his services and made him inspector general or drillmaster with the rank of major general. Von Steuben served until the end of the war, retiring to Steuben-ville in the State of New York where he died in 1794, much honored by the Congress and the American people.

He was one of the small band of foreign officers whose memory we honor because they made our cause their own, and this at a time when the odds ran heavily against us. It is difficult to remember today how unequal were the protagonists in that 7-year struggle: 13 loosely allied, often contentious little States pitted against the greatest empire in the world; a pitifully small, ill-equipped and badly supported force of citizen soldiers serving brief terms of duty, facing a substantial body of regular soldiers and professional officers backed by a navy that ruled the seas. Though many Americans were superb guerrilla fighters, neither officers nor men had knowledge and experience in the art of war. As Charles A. Beard wrote, "there was not available a single army officer experienced in the stratagems of combat on a large scale, as distinguished from local fighting."

It was by supplying the missing professional knowledge and experience that von Steuben made his great contribution to the war effort. He himself had been trained in the best military school of the time: Frederick the Great's army, which he entered at age 14, ultimately becoming the king's aide-de-camp. This veteran of many wars was astonishingly successful in applying European military principles and practices to the special needs of Washington's army. Discarding everything not strictly essential to winning battles, he was able to transform highly individualistic part-time volunteers into a disciplined army, and to do this in as many months as it normally took years abroad. Despite his insistence on strict discipline, he was well-liked by the soldiers. The secret of his success was that he understood the American psyche and temperament, even though he did not know their language. As he wrote to a fellow Prussian, "the genius of this nation is not in the least to be compared with that of the Prussians, Austrians or French. You say to *your* soldier, 'Do this,' and he doeth it; but I am obliged to say, 'This is the reason why you ought to do that,' and he does it." No higher tribute could have been paid the American Revolutionary soldier.

Von Steuben's view of the proper relationship between officers and men was surprisingly modern and "democratic." In his instructions to company officers, he warned that "a captain cannot be too careful of the company the state has committed to his charge. He must pay the greatest attention to the health of his men, their discipline, arms, accoutrements, ammunition, clothes and necessaries. His first object should be to gain the love of his men by treating them with every possible kindness and humanity, inquiring into their complaints and, when well-founded, seeing them redressed. He should know every man of his company by name and character."

Just before resigning his commission to Congress, Washington made it his last official act as Commander in Chief of the American armies to write a warm and highly appreciative letter to von Steuben. As the historian George Bancroft wrote, von Steuben "served under our flag with implicit fidelity, with indefatigable industry, and a courage that shrank from no danger. His presence was important both in the camp and in the field of battle, from the butts of Valley Forge to Yorktown, and he remained with us til his death."

USS DANIEL BOONE (SSBN 629)

NAMED FOR Daniel Boone (1734–1820), most famous of frontiersmen and Indian fighters, skillful guide of the first pioneers who crossed the Appalachian Mountains and settled permanently in Kentucky, a man of infinite resourcefulness, courage, and perseverance. One of his adventures is said to have been used by James Fenimore Cooper in *The Last of the Mohicans*. In fact, Cooper's hero Leatherstocking was probably modeled after Boone. Lord Byron devoted seven stanzas of *Don Juan* (1823) to him which made Boone posthumously world famous.*

The Boones were English Quakers who came to this country in 1717, settling first in Pennsylvania where Daniel was born (in Oley, near Reading). His grandfather was a weaver and surveyor, his father a blacksmith and stock raiser. The family moved to the Yadkin Valley in North Carolina, near the frontier, when he was 16. Daniel had the kind of childhood boys dream about, yet no other could have prepared him so well for the tough life he had chosen.

There was time to roam the woods, hunt and fish, observe animals, enjoy the solitude of the wilderness. And these things, which he liked best to do, made him an expert woodsman and crack shot. The chores expected of him taught him much else.

---

*Canto 8, Stanzas LXI–LXVII. These sing an ode to the American pioneers. "The free-born forest found and kept them free, and fresh as is a torrent or a tree. And tall, and strong, and swift of foot were they . . . Simple they were, not savage; and their rifles, though very true, were not yet used for trifles . . . Serene, not sullen were the solitudes of this unsighing people of the woods." Of Boone, Byron wrote that he "was happiest amongst mortals," and "left behind a name for which men vainly decimate the throng, not only famous, but of that *good* fame, without which glory's but a tavern song."

From his grandfather, he picked up the rudiments of surveying; as a helper in his father's blacksmith shop he learned enough metalwork to repair rifles. These were useful skills for a frontiersman, as was his ability to "think Indian" which he acquired through intimate acquaintance with friendly Indians who were always about, visiting the settlement. The Quakers had established amicable relations with them before Daniel was born. He became a first-rate Indian fighter because he understood Indian ways, Indian psychology, as few white men did. Many a time in later life, he managed to extricate himself and others from desperate situations only because he knew exactly how the Indian would react to a given stimulus.

Between Daniel and the Indians there was a curious mutual attraction. He was by profession a hunter, by preference a wanderer in the wilderness, leading a life not unlike their own. They respected him and liked him, and tried several times to adopt him into their tribe. Yet he was their enemy because he led settlers into land they rightly claimed as their own. And so they stole his goods, twice bankrupting him, and when they captured him, they threatened torture and death, but he always got away. In mutual trickery, he invariably had the best of them. He could not have managed them so skillfully, had he not felt a measure of sympathy for this doomed race.

There had been no schools when he grew up, so he was taught the three R's at home, and obviously in not too strenuous a fashion for his book learning was sketchy, his spelling erratic, his handwriting a scrawl, his arithmetic shaky. It is unlikely that he ever read a book. These educational deficiencies were no drawback on the frontier, but they may explain in part why he could not cope with civilization. Legal technicalities, in particular, were beyond him. Though he opened up vast territories, losing two sons and a brother in the effort, every one of his own land claims proved defective and was voided. He might have died without "as much land as would make a grave," had not Congress in 1814—when he was a very old man—reinstated him in a grant of 1,000 arpents (850 acres).

Boone first heard about Kentucky in 1769 when an itinerant peddler stopped at his cabin. He was John Finley, a man Boone had known when both served as wagoners accompanying a North Carolina regiment in the ill-starred Braddock campaign (1755). As he sat by the fireplace, Finley spun such marvelous tales of Kentucky where he had traded and hunted with the Indians that Boone readily consented to go along on a hunting and exploration trip. Finley only knew the water route down the Ohio; Boone was to find a trail into Kentucky across the mountains. Four others went along on what was to be a 2-year trip full of adventures and miscellaneous mishaps. But they found the famous "Warrior's Path" (so called because it was used by Indian war parties), and followed it to a hill from which they could look down upon Kentucky, spread before them lush and green—a land of fertile soil and vast sycamore, oak, and chestnut forests, and game abundant beyond man's imagination. Boone was determined to settle in this paradise and many were ready to follow if he would but lead them. That the royal edict of 1763 barred white settlement west of the Appalachians—at the so called "Proclamation Line"—seems to have worried no one. Designed to protect the Indians, the edict was considered unjust by the colonists and was generally disregarded by them.

A first colonizing expedition (1773) failed when Boone and his group of some 30 men were driven back by the Indians. A second attempt, 2 years later, succeeded. This was a large-scale settlement project underwritten by Judge Richard Henderson's Transylvania Company. It envisaged establishment of a 14th Colony, to be named Transylvania, patterned after earlier proprietary Colonies. The plan was for the company to buy 20 million acres from the Cherokees and parcel out the land to settlers on payment of a perpetual quit rent, reserving large tracts to Henderson and others who had supplied the necessary capital. Boone was engaged as agent, charged with negotiating the land purchase, guiding the settlers and their livestock and other property across the mountains, and helping establish the new Colony.

Traveling among the Cherokees, Boone soon found them prepared to sell if the price was right. After much haggling, the company offered to pay 10,000 pounds in trade goods chosen by the chiefs. More than 1,000 Indians came to witness the final arguments pro and con. No pressure was exerted on them, except possibly the psychological one of heaping the merchandise in a vast mound for all to see. Upon conclusion of the treaty of sale (March 1775), a great feast was laid on by the company. But many of the Indians were angry when they found that, distributed among them all, the great mound yielded but a pittance to any one of them. Boone's biographer, John Bakeless, tells of one disgusted brave who "complained that his share was only a shirt that he could easily have earned in a day's hunting on the land they had given away." Chief Oconostota spoke movingly of what the white man's penetration beyond the Alleghenies would mean to the Indians. "This is only the beginning," he warned. "The invader has crossed the great sea in ships; . . . and now he has penetrated the wilderness and overcome the ruggedness of the mountains. Neither will he stop here. He will force the Indian steadily before him across the Mississippi ever towards the west . . . till the red man be no longer a roamer of the forests and a pursuer of wild game." At one time the Indians broke off negotiations but in the end they agreed to sell.

Boone's men had been standing by. They began at once to hack out the famed "Wilderness Road," and in April the first group of settlers were brought in. A month later elections had been held, a government was functioning, the building and fortification of Boonesboro was under way. Services were held on May 28, under a large elm tree and, for the first and last time, so Bakeless records, a prayer for the royal family was offered. "Next day came a letter describing 'the battle of Boston,' and within three years His Majesty's officers were leading Indian forces against Boonesboro."

The fort was saved by Boone's cunning and the fortitude of its small garrison of men, women, and children. There followed more than a decade of incessant Indian raids, the British encouraging their allies to do as they pleased with the settlers. The lovely land was turned into "a dark and bloody ground" filled with widows and orphans. Throughout our Western frontier regions, the Indians were on the warpath.

Reading of ambush, kidnaping, torture, and murder among the settlers, one cannot help but feel that much of their suffering could have been avoided, had they only planned more carefully, moved more slowly, and taken elementary defensive measures. With hindsight, it is evident that they ought to have proceeded more circumspectly when on the march, stopping to make camp before they were too exhausted to post sentinels; that they should have moved and settled in larger groups so that cabins could have been tight and fortifications could have been built by some, while the others hunted and planted crops. One might even wonder whether it might not have been more sensible for them to have learned better farming methods which would have kept the farms they left behind fruitful for generations, instead of gambling all on finding better land to the west. (It was said "that Kentucky soil, planted and cultivated produced 20 bushels of corn an acre, merely planted, 10 bushels; not even planted, 7.")

But carelessness, impatience, lack of discipline are as much part of the character of pioneers, as incredible hardihood and courage. Who ever heard of a cautious man conquering a continent? These were ordinary people not given to weighing all the circumstances before taking action. They had the good sense to recognize that this country was a Utopia into which anyone might enter if he was strong and brave enough, and nothing could have kept them out.

As for Judge Henderson's dream of founding Transylvania, it was short-lived. Virginia would allow no part of her domain to detach itself and establish an independent government. In 1776, she organized the area as a county (named Kentucky), and 2 years later she voided the land claims of the Transylvania Company. But in the long and bitter war years that followed, she could neither protect the settlers nor send them arms. When enough of them had arrived—and they kept coming steadily, undeterred by marauding Indians—they organized themselves as a State and, in 1792, were admitted to the Union. Having had to fight for survival on their own, they owed no loyalty to Virginia.

As the population grew and the Indian menace receded, Boone began to feel "crowded" and to sense he was no longer the indispensable man he once had been. So he left for Missouri which was wild and empty enough to suit him and where the hunting was still good. His life had a curious symmetry. It fell into three parts, each roughly 30 years in duration. In the first and last he was the hunter, free and footloose in the wilderness, a romantic figure out of our past. In the middle period, he helped found a State where there had been only a blank spot on the map of Virginia. This part of his life, when he was main-stay, guide, and protector of settlers moving into unknown and dangerous regions, when he served a pioneer community as leader of the militia, sheriff, surveyor, and legislator has the greater interest for us today.

Here we see, through the events of one man's life, compressed into three decades, the evolution from Indian territory to American State through which in turn every section of our Nation has passed, leaving as a sediment in the popular mind a proprietary view of government that is the very rock on which our democratic institutions rest: a firm conviction that government is no more than a mechanism created by people to serve their common needs, legitimate only as long as it has the consent of the governed.

Jefferson expressed this concept of government most suc-cinctly in his *A Summary View of the Rights of British America* (1774). He reminded King George III that his colonial subjects owed England no debt for "America was conquered, and her settlements made and firmly established, at the expense of individuals and not of the British public. Their own blood was spilt in acquiring lands for their settlement, their own fortunes expended in making that settlement effectual. For themselves they fought, for themselves they conquered, and for themselves alone they have right to hold."

USS LEWIS AND CLARK (SSBN 644)

NAMED FOR Meriwether Lewis (1774–1809) and William Clark (1770–1838), the Virginia-born captains under whose joint command a small American Army unit (three sergeants, 24 men, one Indian and two French Canadian interpreters) crossed from St. Louis to the mouth of the Columbia River and back, thus completing one of the great transcontinental voyages of exploration, ranking in importance with those of Balboa (1513) and Mackenzie (1793).

Planned and personally supervised by President Jefferson, the expedition had as its objective the exploration of "the Mississippi River, and such principal streams of it, as, by its course and communication with the waters of the Pacific Ocean . . . may offer the most direct and practicable water communication across this continent." If such a water route could be found, much of the lucrative fur trade, then largely in Canadian hands, might be diverted to American seaports. The President had long been interested in exploring this possibility; had, in fact, given aid to three previous attempts that came to nothing. He obtained from the Congress authorization and an initial grant of $2,500 in January 1803, a few months before the uncharted territory to be traversed by Lewis and Clark passed into our possession through the Louisiana Purchase. The expedition got underway, May 1804, in a bateau and two pirogues and did not return until nearly 2½ years later.

It is difficult for us to realize the importance of water transportation in those days. Men were inclined to believe certain navigable routes must exist simply because they so ardently wished for them. Thus, the hope of reaching the Orient by sailing westward was not relinquished even after it became known that the American land mass stood as a barrier between the Atlantic and Pacific Oceans; this hope was merely transferred northward to the inland waterways of North America where for 300 years Spaniards, Frenchmen, and Englishmen diligently searched for the mythical Northwest Passage first postulated by Verrazano in 1524. To discover this passage was one of the avowed objects of the Hudson Bay Company.

Some envisaged it as a strait across Canada at the latitude of Hudson Bay, others as a "commingling of the headwaters" of major eastward and westward flowing rivers. Both versions of the myth were inscribed, as late as 1767, in Jonathan Carver's map of America. Explorers kept the myth alive by asserting as fact what was pure fantasy. Thus, in 1765, Robert Rogers stated categorically that between the sources of the Missouri and the "Great River of the West" the portage was not above 30 miles. His River of the West was pure figment of the imagination but, oddly enough, speculation placed it near the actual location of the Columbia. No one then knew of the Rocky Mountains or imagined that such a barrier might divide America's eastern and western rivers.

It must be counted a major gain of the Lewis and Clark Expedition that it laid to rest forever the myth of a navigable passage across the continent. It established, by actual observation that the sources of the Missouri and Columbia lay too far apart for an easy portage and that neither river was truly navigable in its upper reaches. A feasible route from St. Louis to the Pacific was, indeed, mapped out, but 430 miles of it ran overland through rugged terrain, and the 3,555 miles by river were part way navigable by canoe only. Not until a century later did Amundsen find the only true Northwest Passage which does not, of course, bisect the continent but runs along Baffin Island through the Arctic Ocean. In 1960, the nuclear submarine *Seadragon* traversed the passage under water.

If then the Lewis and Clark Expedition could find no natural and easy cross-continental water route, it accomplished what in the end proved more important: It greatly strengthened our claim to the Oregon Territory, originally based on the discovery of the Columbia River in 1793 by Captain Robert Gray of the American ship *Columbia Rediviva*. Over the route mapped by Lewis and Clark soon came American trappers, and in 1811 Fort Astoria was built at the mouth of the Columbia, the first permanent settlement in the Oregon country.

America won the race to the Pacific by a hair's breadth, for Canadian traders were fast approaching the coast. Mackenzie had traversed Canada from Lake Athabaska to the mouth of the Bella Coola as early as 1793, Simon Fraser came down the river named for him in 1808, and David Thompson followed part of the Lewis and Clark route in 1811. When he reached the mouth of the Columbia, he saw the American flag flying over Fort Astoria — it had been raised but a few months earlier! As the historian John Bakeless writes: "Because of the Corps of Discovery, Oregon is American today. And ten white stars in the blue field of Old Glory stand for States of the Union that one by one grew up in the farms and mills, cities and homesteads, along the trail where weary men in tattered elk-skin cursed the rocks that tore their feet, sweated at the tow rope, poled against the savage current of the muddy Missouri, stumbled in the chilly streams of the Rockies, and staggered down the western end of the Lolo Trail." It had been a hard journey and a long one. When Clark wrote in his diary, November 7, 1805, "Ocean in view! Oh Joy!" the weary explorers doubtless felt much the same triumph and relief as the men on the three small Spanish caravels when they heard the lookout on the *Pinta* cry "Tierra! Tierra!"

Charting a course — 4,000 miles each way — through unknown territory inhabited by numerous, often hostile Indians, was surely difficult enough, but many other tasks were imposed on Lewis and Clark by Jefferson. He instructed them to keep a daily record of the weather and an accurate description of the route traversed; to ascertain "by celestial observation, the geography of the country;" describe in detail its fauna, flora, and mineral wealth; report on the character, customs, and languages of the Indians they encountered and try to win their friendship for the United States. It has been truly said that these tasks would seem superhuman had not the diligent and intrepid commanders fulfilled them all very nearly to the letter. Except for one sergeant who died of what seems to have been appendicitis, no life was lost. The total cost of the enterprise was a modest $40,000.

Wherever one dips into the early history of our country, one is amazed at the number and variety of men of outstanding ability and courage produced by a Nation with fewer people than Denmark has today!

Luck played some part, but the success of the expedition was due to the care with which its personnel and equipment were selected, the skill with which it was led, and the disciplined manner in which it proceeded. The captains spent the winter of 1803 in St. Louis, then the westernmost outpost of civilization, collecting all available information from woodsmen and trappers; when they set out on their journey, they had learned everything any white man then knew about the country they were to penetrate.

Lewis and Clark were ideally suited to their task. Close friends of similar background, sons of planters, they had much experience of command and of wilderness life. They fought as regular army officers, Lewis for a time under Clark. Both were highly intelligent; Lewis more analytical, Clark more practical. Lewis had received a better education; moreover, Jefferson had sent him to Philadelphia to study intensively such matters as astronomy, botany, map making, manipulation of instruments for meteorological observations – all essential to the conduct of a scientific expedition. Clark, however, had geographical genius and a gift for winning the friendship of the Indians. They trusted him because they sensed that he respected them as fellow human beings. When critical situations developed, both captains handled the Indians with consummate skill. "In personal dealings with them," wrote Bernard De Voto, "they made no mistakes at all."

At Jefferson's request, Lewis and Clark kept daily journals (as did some of the men). The journals were first published in 1814 and have been reissued several times. Straightforward, factual, often written under trying circumstances, after days of physical exertion and danger, these journals tell of a fabulous voyage of discovery that can still be read for their sheer fascination as an adventure story.

But they are more than that. They are a sort of American Domesday Book, an inventory of the vast and rich lands we bought from France at the bargain price of 4 cents an acre. Many of the beautiful sights the captains described – the cascades of the Columbia River, the vast and somber forests of giant pines in the Northwest – have long since disappeared, bulldozed out of existence in the name of progress. As Bernard De Voto comments sadly in the preface of his edition, *The Journals of Lewis and Clark,* no American will ever again see the beauty or feel the majesty that overwhelmed Lewis when he first came across the Great Falls of the Missouri. Were it not for these journals we might forget how beautiful the country was when it was first seen by these intrepid explorers.

USS JOHN MARSHALL (SSBN 611)

NAMED FOR John Marshall (1755–1835), fourth Chief Justice of the Supreme Court and, in the estimation of many, the greatest. Wrote Judge Story, his colleague on the bench for many years: "Providence grants such men to the human family only on great occasions to accomplish its own great end." By the sheer power of his intellect and personality, Marshall raised the Federal Judiciary, least important of the three branches of government when he took office, to the prestigious and authoritative position it holds to this day. Through his long tenure (1801–35), the independence of the Supreme Court was intermittently in jeopardy, yet at no other period in its history did it render such signal service to the Nation as judicial interpreter and guardian of the Federal charter. Marshall himself has no equal as expounder of the Constitution, nor has anyone surpassed him in judicial statesmanship.

His head, said Rufus King, was "the best organized" he had ever known. His capacity for swiftly absorbing masses of material and extracting what the occasion demanded was nothing short of phenomenal. He could "develop a subject by a single glance of the mind," according to Attorney General Wirt, and do so seemingly without effort: isolating at once the crucial point at issue, discovering and applying the appropriate constitutional provision, examining and disposing of every possible opposition, building his argument step by step to its inevitable conclusion, and persuading his colleagues on the bench, the American bar in general, and ultimately the public at large of the correctness of his constitutional judgments. It has been said that "the Constitution in its most important aspects is the Constitution as he interpreted it."

Marshall's title to fame rests on his achievements as Chief Justice but this was not his first public office. He served 11 years in the Virginia Legislature (1782–91, 1795–97). He was a member of the State ratifying convention and fought vigorously for adoption of the Constitution. Washington and John Adams offered him important positions (Cabinet, judiciary, diplomatic mission). But, with heavy family responsibilities and no private fortune, he felt impelled to decline; a leading member of the Virginia bar, his income from private practice far exceeded any Federal salary. He finally consented to serve on the XYZ mission to France (1797–98), where he acquitted himself so well that upon his return he was elected to the House of Representatives, even though he was a Federalist and the tide was running strongly against his party. Adams appointed him Secretary of State and, while Marshall still held this post (1800–01), Chief Justice — a far from popular choice. But history proved Adams right. Twenty-five years later, he remarked: "My gift of John Marshall to the people of the United States was the proudest act of my life."

Born in a log cabin on the Virginia frontier in what 4 years later became Fauquier County, Va., Marshall came, on the paternal side, of an obscure and humble family. The first of the name in America, a poor Welshman, probably arrived in the latter part of the 17th century. John's father Thomas was a self-made, self-educated man for whose unusual abilities and strength of character his famous son had boundless admiration. "It was a theme," wrote Judge Story, "on which he broke out with a spontaneous eloquence," attributing to his father "the solid foundation" of all his own success in life. Through his mother, who was of gentle birth, John was kin to most of the notable Randolphs and Lees whose names dot our early history. Thomas Jefferson was his cousin; Army Chief of Staff George C. Marshall was a collateral descendant. The Marshalls were one of those "rising" families in which so many of the Nation's great have been nurtured.

Though never rich, Thomas Marshall improved his fortunes as his family grew. When John, eldest of his 15 children, was 18 he moved them into a large and, for the times, almost elegant house which still stands as a wing of "Oak Hill," the mansion later built by John Marshall's eldest son. Besides managing his farm, Thomas was George Washington's surveying assistant; later he opened his own office in Kentucky (1783). A leader in the community, he served as sheriff, vestryman, county clerk, and member of the House of Burgesses. John remembered him as "a watchful parent and an affectionate instructive friend," who taught him the outdoor skills frontiersmen needed and the love of literature which was to give him his chief satisfaction in life (Pope was their favorite author).

Until 20, John Marshall knew only the simple life of a self-contained wilderness farm where nearly all the necessities of life were homemade and the education of children was a family enterprise. Even as his father was John's principal tutor, so John took a hand in teaching his younger brothers and sisters. Of formal schooling there was almost none. John got his start in Latin and the classics from briefly attending Parson Campbell's academy (Monroe was a classmate), and being tutored a year or so at home by a young Scottish clergyman. He continued on his own, reading Horace and Livy, "with no other aide than my Dictionary." At 17, his father gave him Blackstone's *Commentaries*, the first American edition of this readable and lucid survey of the common law having just appeared. Written with the educated layman rather than the professional in mind, it proved uncommonly useful in 18th century America (where it was more widely read than in England). The *Commentaries* and a 6-week course given by George Wythe at William and Mary, were all the preparation Marshall had when he offered for the bar and was accepted. Yet he was to rise to such eminence that Oliver Wendell Holmes said of him: "If American law were to be represented by a single figure, sceptic and worshipper alike would agree without dispute that the figure could be one alone, and that one John Marshall." Americans, in those days, acquired an astonishing amount of "learning," and an amazing command of the English language, simply by reading and rereading, learning by heart and endlessly discussing a few good books. The Marshalls lived frugally and wore homespun, but books and conversation about public events and political and literary ideas were an essential part of their lives; this is what made them a "rising" family.

They were early adherents to the cause of liberty, Patrick Henry having struck a responsive chord with his stirring call to resist Britain's encroachments on colonial liberties. At the first rumblings of the Revolution, father and son (one 45, the other not yet 20) joined the Culpeper Minute Men (whose hunting shirts had as their emblem Henry's "Liberty or Death." They participated in the fighting at Great Bridge and Norfolk which forced Governor Dunmore to take refuge on a British warship and soon after to depart for England, leaving Virginia in the hands of the rebels and in relative peace for 5 years. In July 1776, both Marshalls received commissions in the Continental Army; they served with distinction through most of the war. John fought at Brandywine, Germantown, Monmouth, Stony Point; he shared with his father and two brothers the hardships of the winter at Valley Forge.

The war deeply influenced Marshall's political thinking. It got him into the habit, as he later wrote, of "considering America as my country and Congress as my government"—though a weak and ineffective one. The conditions under which the war was fought made him a Federalist for life. It is safe to say that in expounding the Constitution Marshall never forgot that, had this powerful instrument of union bound them together, the colonists would have been spared much suffering and the war might perhaps have been won sooner. As it was, they were not only inferior to the enemy in trained men, war material, and essential supplies; they also lacked the means to make full use of the resources at hand. They knew of no associations of sovereign states with self-operating organs which might have served them as models, nor were they used to cooperating with each other. Under Britain, their external relations had been exclusively with the mother country and these were coercive, not cooperative. Without precedent, tradition, experience, or time to plan how they might best organize for this, their first joint enterprise, they found themselves at war. In the time-honored manner of Englishmen facing a crisis unprepared, they improvised. Out of an ad hoc meeting of colonial delegates called together to consult on ways of resisting Britain's Coercive Acts (in colonial parlance, The Intolerable Acts), there evolved the first agency for joint action—The Congress. Much as they differ, today's Congress stands in direct line of descent to this first imperfect Federal organ and can thus claim to antedate independence (Treaty of Peace, 1783) by 8 years.

At this meeting—called the First Continental Congress—all the Colonies except Georgia were represented. Thirteen Parliamentary acts were declared to violate colonial rights, the delegates pledging economic sanctions until the acts were repealed; should their grievances remain unredressed, they resolved to reconvene the following year. Hostilities having broken out at Lexington and Concord (Apr. 19, 1775), the Second Continental Congress constituted itself a standing consultative body for the coordination of all the activities shared by the Colonies (May 15, 1775). *Inter alia*, the Congress directed the war, conducted foreign affairs, issued paper money, negotiated loans to which it pledged the credit of the Colonies, and proclaimed their independence—all this without legal warrant. Its position was not regularized until the Articles of Confederation came into effect (1781) a few months before the surrender of Cornwallis at Yorktown which brought hostilities to a virtual end.

The Articles were drafted by a congressional committee (one member for each State), debated for over a year in Congress, and finally submitted to the States (1777) as representing the only proposal offering "any tolerable prospect of a general ratification." Most States accepted within a year or so but Maryland held out until disposal of the former crown lands had been arranged to her satisfaction. A treaty rather than a Constitution, the Articles altered in no way the loose association born of the necessities of the war. Congress retained the character of a diplomatic conference, its members appointed, dismissed, and paid by their respective sovereigns, wholly dependent on the States for execution of its decrees. It was called a Government and expected to perform governmental functions, but the powers indispensable to, and normally possessed by governments were withheld by the States.

The Confederation—now for the first time "officially" named The United States of America—rested on faith alone; there were no sanctions for infraction of the Articles. During the war, common danger had to some extent served as a bond; when peace came there was nothing to hold the States to their Federal obligations. Though pledged "to abide by the determinations of the united states in congress assembled," in all matters properly before that body (Art. XIII), even so small a State as Rhode Island, with but one sixtieth of the combined population of all 13 States, could with impunity veto action agreed upon by the other 12. No sooner was peace concluded than some States engaged in mutual discriminations and commercial wars; treaty obligations, jointly assumed, were violated by many; almost all defaulted on their debts or paid them with worthless paper money which creditors were forced by State law to accept as legal tender. The Confederation could not function as a sovereign State; nor, for that matter, could the individual States. Five years after the long hard fight for freedom had been won, the country was close to chaos. Pressed to act, Congress called a meeting to consider revision of the Articles; every State except Rhode Island sent delegates. To grasp the magnitude of the crisis, one needs but to read the proceedings of the Philadelphia Convention (1787). What is there of disorder, poverty, humiliation, asked Hamilton, "which does not form a part of the dark catalogue of our public misfortunes?"

The delegates took to heart Washington's admonition "to probe the defects" of the Confederation "to the bottom" and to "provide a radical cure." Few had a good word to say for Congress or for the States whose "refractory and inattentive conduct" had brought the country to the verge of dissolution; most of them, said Charles Pinckney, "have neglected altogether the performance of their Federal Duties, and whenever their State-policy, or interests prompted, used their retained Sovereignty, to the injury and disgrace of the Federal Head." Governor Randolph of Virginia, whose own plan of government was a radical cure indeed, seems to have been the only one with a kind word for the framers of the Articles of Confederation. They did the best that could be done, he said, "in the then infancy of the science of constitutions & of confederacies," when the problems that caused the Confederation to fail could have been foreseen by no one, "and perhaps nothing better could be obtained from the jealousy of the states with regard to their sovereignty." Nothing better could in fact be *legally* obtained a decade later, the jealousy of the States remaining as formidable a block to action in 1787 as it had been in 1777.

The Philadelphia Convention had been called "for the sole and express purpose of revising" the Articles, but amendment required the consent of all the States and this would have been unobtainable for any effective reform. Certain that the inadequacy of the existing Union endangered its very existence, the delegates disregarded their instructions and proceeded to draft a new plan of government submitting it not, as required, to the States but to the people acting through special conventions. Van Buren called it "an heroic and lawless act," and so it was, though retroactively legitimized by the American people when they adopted the Constitution. The overall majority was slim, however, and the Federal charter might well have been rejected had not the ratification campaign been conducted with great skill and persistence.

In sharp contrast to their near-unanimous acceptance of popular government (once the Loyalists had left or been silenced), Americans were deeply divided on the kind of Union they wanted—a division going back to the start of the war. Britain's decision to put down the rebellion by force confronted the revolutionaries with *two* urgent tasks: winning the war, and securing the fruits of the Revolution (by establishing in the former Colonies new governments based on the consent of the governed). The first required united effort, the second did not. Most Americans concentrated on one or the other, seldom on both tasks. The choice then made determined in large part their eventual stand for or against a strong Union.

Those involved in the war from start to finish—whether fighting in the field or directing the war effort in a civilian capacity—learned at firsthand how prejudicial to its conduct was the weakness of the Confederation. Dealing with matters transcending State boundaries, they began to think in continental terms. In the postwar chaos they saw a portent of the eventual breakup of the country into several independent confederacies; no great, prosperous or even merely peaceable future seemed possible to them, except under a properly functioning Federal Government. The strengthening of the Federal machinery was therefore a simple matter of practical necessity. Nonparticipants in the war, lacking an intimate acquaintance with the day-to-day problems of Federal action, seldom shared this view. Those involved in the revision of State constitutions and laws tended, moreover, to mistrust federalism as in some way alien to revolutionary America. In *their* political creed, the States were the principal seat of the democratic tendencies of the Revolution; they were the strongest bulwarks of individual liberty; their emergence as sovereign entities a revolutionary gain that ought not to be sacrificed for the sake of more efficient Federal action. The division at bottom was between those who believed popular government could be preserved in a large union of States and those who feared it would be lost and therefore wanted none of it. "Whether we remain in one confederacy," wrote Jefferson in 1803, "or form into Atlantic and Mississippi confederations, I believe not very important to the happiness of either part."

In time, of course, even adherents of State power came to realize the futility of the Confederation. Some worked hard for the Constitution and, once adopted, there was a closing of ranks, a desire to give the new experiment a chance. But the truce lasted only 4 years. The old division reappeared, now crystallized in official party programs: The Federalists wanted the National Government to exercise its constitutional powers to the fullest; the Jeffersonian Republicans demanded strict construction of the Constitution, so as to limit national and enlarge State power. The Federalists came in with Washington, established the Government, and cleared up the financial chaos bequeathed by irresponsible State action. In 1800, resurgent States' rightism swept them out of office in a campaign fought with unusual rancor. The Federalists found themselves targets of such favorite 18th century epithets as "aristo-cratic" and "monarchist"—words as imprecise and emotion laden as "undemocratic" sometimes is today. Odd as they sound, flung by rich slave owning planters at such self-made men as Hamilton or John Adams or Marshall, they stuck; the motives of the Federalists have been suspect ever since. Yet it was they and their successors, the Whigs, who tried to hold the Union together when States' rightism threatened to destroy it—none with more courage and quiet determination than John Marshall.

He took office 1 month before Jefferson was inaugurated (it was Marshall who administered the oath to the new Presi-dent). The cousins, so similar in background, were bitter politi-cal opponents. For a number of years Marshall was under threat of impeachment at the hands of his kinsman—not for malfeasance but for decisions contravening the political be-liefs of the party in power; removal by impeachment was the only legal way to get around the constitutional guarantee of tenure "during good behavior." It seemed to many Republi-cans that continuance in office of Federalist judges after the decisive defeat of their party was a brazen flouting of the people's will. A constitutional amendment was proposed pro-viding that "the Judges of the Supreme Court and all other Courts of the United States shall be removed from office by the President on joint address of both Houses of Congress request-ing the same." Nothing came of these and numerous other attempts to impose political restraints on the judiciary, though criticism never let up, not even when natural attrition altered the composition of the Federal courts; by 1811, all but one of Marshall's colleagues were Republican appointees. Such was the force of his personality that his influence continued unim-paired. In most instances, and in *all* the important cases, Mar-shall spoke for a unanimous or near-unanimous court. Of 1,215 decisions handed down between 1801 and 1835, he deliv-ered the opinion in 519 (and filed a dissent in nine); only 5 per-cent involved constitutional questions but these touched upon nearly every important part of the Constitution as it existed before the Civil War. Marshall found himself in the minority only once (and then barely so) on a matter of constitutional construction (*Ogden* v. *Saunders*, 1827).

To a modern reader, his decisions seem so "right" that it is difficult to understand the grounds on which he could have been accused of unduly enlarging national or restricting State power. Far from "stretching" the Constitution, as both his critics and his admirers aver, Marshall adhered closely to its text, following the recognized canons of interpretation "applicable to formal and solemn instruments of constitutional law," to wit: if a word has more than one meaning, that which most effectually accomplishes the end in view applies. Said Marshall, ". . . We must never forget that it is a constitution we are expounding" — an instrument laying down broad general principles which cannot in the nature of the thing possess the precision and detail of a statute or a code of laws. The court is not bound to construe words "more restrictively than they naturally import."

How closely his judgments accord with the "sense" of the Constitutional Convention we can judge better than Americans of Marshall's day, for we have available — as they had not — the full record of its proceedings. The journal Madison kept was then still resting among his private papers (published 1840). Held in strict secrecy, with armed guards at the doors (all Revolutionary assemblies were secret), little was known of the deliberations that produced the Constitution. Without this knowledge, the somewhat imprecise textual basis of the judicial power lent itself to conflicting interpretations. Gouverneur Morris, member of the Committee of Style which cast the document into its final form, admitted as much. He wrote in 1814 that he believed the text of the Constitution to have been made as clear as the English language permits, *excepting* the part relating to the judiciary. "On that subject, conflicting opinions had been maintained with so much professional astuteness, that it became necessary to select phrases, which expressing my own notions would not alarm others, nor shock their selflove." This may be why the Constitution does not mention judicial review, even though it was the intent of the framers to make the courts responsible for carrying out the mandates of the Federal charter, in particular, for holding the States to their constitutional obligations. The transcript shows clearly that Article III, Section 2 (the "judicial" clause) and Article VI (the "supremacy" clause) of the Constitution vest in the courts — with the Supreme Court as final authority — the right and duty to declare invalid any State law contravening the Federal charter. This right and duty of judicial review is confirmed in the Judiciary Act of 1789 (now in 28 U.S.C. 1257), written by a congressional committee, half of whose members came fresh from the Convention of Philadelphia.

The metamorphosis of the two clauses makes fascinating reading. When the Convention began its proceedings, it had before it the "Randolph Plan" which contained a proposal (Resolve #8) for a "council of revision," to consist of the Executive and an unspecified number of members of the judiciary. All Federal and State laws (before they "shall operate") were to be submitted to this council and if rejected were to be void *unless* reenacted (Randolph left open whether by a simple or qualified majority). The proposal, according to Madison, was "extensively favored at the outset." The delegates were agreed that Congress should be held in check lest, becoming all-powerful, it overshadow the other branches of government. One delegate went so far as to warn that "the public liberty is in greater danger from legislative usurpation than from any other source." And on no other matter was the Convention so at one as in its determination to incorporate a "coercive" principle in their plan of government that would impel the States to obey Federal laws and treaties. Madison put the matter in a nutshell when he said: "The necessity of a general Govt. proceeds from the propensity of the States to pursue their particular interests in opposition to the general interest. This propensity will continue to disturb the system, unless effectually controuled." In the end, it was decided to work the Randolph proposal into two separate measures: one providing for a check on Congress by the President, the other on the States by the judiciary. The first was accomplished within a week; the second took all summer.

A move to withdraw congressional acts from the council of revision and substitute a qualified presidential veto (that could be overruled by a two thirds vote) was carried eight to two; there was little debate. It was more difficult to find effective ways to control the States. Nothing short of a "negative on their laws" will control them, said Madison. Whose "negative" was the problem. The council of revision was dropped because of "insuperable objections, arising from the extent of the Country, and the multiplicity of State laws." A suggestion that the veto be given to the President in consultation with his Cabinet was at once abandoned; that it be lodged in Congress was rejected as too "terrible to the States." On July 17, Luther Martin moved adoption of a clause taken from the "New Jersey Plan," viz. "that the Legislative acts of the United States made by virtue and in pursuance of the articles of Union and all treaties made and ratified under the authority of the United States shall be the supreme law of the respective States . . . and that the judiciaries of the several States shall be bound thereby in their decisions, anything in the respective laws of the individual States to the contrary notwithstanding." With a few changes, this became the "supremacy" clause of the

Constitution. Rutledge proposed late in August that the words "This Constitution" be added, and the Committee of Style introduced the famous phrase from the Magna Carta "the supreme law of the land." The original intent remains clearly evident. It was to impose the law of the Union on its constituent members, the States. The clause, said Madison, became the one and only "safeguard to the Constitution and laws of the Union, agst. the encroachment of its members and anarchy among themselves."

Meanwhile, the original wording of the judiciary clause in both the Randolph and New Jersey Plans was being broadened by giving the Federal courts jurisdiction over "all cases . . . arising under this constitution, the laws of the United States and treaties made . . . under their authority" (Art. III, Sec. 2). This was necessary, said Madison, because "confidence can [not] be put in the State Tribunals as guardians of the National authority and interests. In all the States these are more or less dependt. on the Legislature." Citing instances of legislative interference with State judges, he concluded that "a power of negativing the improper laws of the States is at once the most mild & certain means of preserving the harmony of the system."

Perhaps it was mild, but it encompassed the *legal* subjugation of the States to Federal authority. When they "converted their league into a government," said Marshall, "the whole character in which the States appear, underwent a change." They became "members of one great empire," stripped of much of their former sovereignty—a transformation not accepted by a substantial segment of the American people until forced upon them by the sword.

During his 35 years as Chief Justice, Marshall declared a total of 18 State laws invalid (compare this with 360 declared void between 1927 and 1962). He did so with great circumspection and "in no doubtful case." Half the 18 were acts clearly proscribed by the Constitution; eight "for impairing the obligations of contracts" (notably *Dartmouth College* v. *Woodward*, 1819); one for emitting "bills of credit" (*Craig* v. *Missouri*, 1830). The relevant constitutional prohibition in both cases was Article I, Sec. 10, included in the Constitution, said Marshall, to put an end to widespread "abuse" and "mischief" committed by the States under the Confederation. Nearly all the others involved State acts intruding into the sphere reserved to the National Government. The most famous of these is *Gibbons* v. *Ogden* (1824) in which Marshall sustained the plenary power of Congress over interstate commerce (Art. I, Sec. 8). This decision, said his biographer, "did more to knit the American people into an indivisible Nation than any other one force in our history, excepting only war." One of Marshall's most "controversial" decisions was *McCulloch* v. *Maryland* (1819) in which he held invalid a State act contravening the *implied* powers of Congress. His interpretation of the so-called "sweeping" clause (Art. I, Sec. 8) which permits Congress "to make all laws which shall be necessary and proper for carrying into execution" its delegated powers, accords with the intent of the Constitution-makers that Congress be unhampered in its choice of means for carrying out the tasks assigned to it. This principle first enunciated by Hamilton, made definitive by Marshall, has since been affirmed in scores of decisions.

Marshall's best-known case is *Marbury* v. *Madison* (1803) in which he asserted the right of the Supreme Court to declare a congressional act unconstitutional, thereby gaining for the judiciary a position of equality with the two other branches of Government—important at the time if the court was to carry out the work assigned it by the Constitution. It was the only case of this kind during his long tenure and for 20 years following his death (compared to 42 Federal acts voided between 1899 and 1964). Whether the framers of the Constitution intended the "supremacy" clause to authorize judicial review of *Federal* acts has been endlessly debated. Since the Union is no longer in danger of being torn apart either by an allegedly "all-powerful" Congress or by intransigent States, it has been suggested that a change might be desirable. As the time of the writing of the Constitution recedes further and further into the past, the effort to find in its words definitive rules overriding the will of the people as expressed by their representatives in Congress becomes increasingly untenable. Half a century ago, Oliver Wendell Holmes said, "the United States would not come to an end if we lost our power to declare an Act of Congress void."

A possible solution might be to ease the amending process (perhaps allowing a majority in Congress to propose amendments and two thirds of the State legislatures or State conventions to ratify them). We have a precedent in the Constitution itself which simplified the amending process of the Articles of Confederation (curiously enough, *adoption* of the Constitution itself was made easier than subsequent *amendment*). Jefferson's remarks might be given some thought. Those who wish the Constitution "to be immortal" he said, should "be attentive by amendments to make it keep pace with the advance of the age in science and experience." He was troubled that men not elected by the people nor accountable to them should have final authority over laws reflecting the *contemporary* will of the people. He found the assertion untenable that the Constitution stands above acts of Congress because it represents the will of the people while legislation represents only the will of the people's agents in Congress. For what difference is there between delegates to a constitutional convention or State ratification convention and members of Congress? Elected by the people, all are agents of the people. Other countries with *written* constitutions (the main basis of Marshall's decision), even those with Federal systems, do not place this restraint on the national legislature. "A judiciary independent of a king or executive alone is a good thing," said Jefferson, "but independence of the will of the nation is a solecism, at least in a republican government."

No less important than Marshall's judgments were the statements in which he analyzed the constitutional principles upon which they rested—a sort of continuing "gloss" on the Constitution in the manner used so successfully by Hamilton in *The Federalist*. James Bryce said of them "that the luminous exactness of their reasoning and the fine political sense which pervades them, have never been surpassed and rarely equalled by the most famous jurists of modern Europe or ancient Rome." As clause after clause came before him, Marshall fleshed in the bare skeleton of the Federal charter, building a corpus of constitutional law binding the Union together at a time when it was often in danger of falling apart. Had it not been for him, said Jeremiah Mason, one of the great jurists of the day, "the Union would have fallen to pieces before the General Government had got well under way . . . John Marshall has saved the Union, if it is saved" (1833).

USS FRANCIS SCOTT KEY (SSBN 657)

NAMED FOR the author of our national anthem. An only son, Francis Scott Key (1779–1843) was born at Terra Rubra in what was then Frederick County, Md. This plantation had been owned since 1750 by the Keys, a wealthy family of cavalier ancestry. Great-grandfather Philip Key, who had been a well-to-do lawyer in England, came to this country in 1726, having obtained from Lord Baltimore the grant of a large tract of land (about 3,000 acres), beautifully situated along the Wicomico. Succeeding generations followed his example of successfully combining management of a large plantation with public service and the practice of law.

His grandson, John Ross Key, father of Francis, served as justice of the peace and associate district judge. Twenty-one when the Revolutionary War began, he enlisted at once. In answer to a call for expert riflemen to join the Army at Boston, he led a detachment of frontier fighters from Frederick to Boston in record time—520 miles in 22 days. These were the first soldiers from the South to reach New England, the first of the famous "Maryland line." With their mountain rifles, tomahawks, leather hunting shirts and moccasins, Boston found them a strange but reassuring sight.

Taking occasional leave to look after his plantation, John Ross stayed in the Army until victory was won. He fought with Lafayette at the siege of Yorktown and was a friend of George Washington who visited Terra Rubra when Francis Scott was a boy of 12. Years later, when he was a successful lawyer, Francis never accepted a fee from the old soldiers who had fought with his father. They were his childhood heroes.

In the family tradition which he himself continued with his own 11 children, Francis Scott Key was tutored by his parents.

He entered St. John's College at 14. After graduation, he read law in the office of Judge Chase of the General Court in Annapolis, and at 22 was established in practice with Roger B. Taney, a fellow law clerk, lifelong friend and future brother-in-law who became Chief Justice of the Supreme Court in 1836. Key settled in Georgetown in 1802 and became one of the leaders of the Maryland bar.

Men of his background and competence in the law customarily entered politics, but Francis had no taste for the rough-and-tumble of political life. Within his own circle of family and friends he constantly experienced the disruptive power of political controversy. His father and favorite uncle took opposite sides in the Revolutionary War; his two best friends — Randolph of Roanoke and Roger Taney — were his political opponents. He had witnessed the attack in Baltimore on the headquarters of a Federalist paper and the murder by an angry mob of one of his law clients who had contributed to the paper. Francis shared with the Founding Fathers and many of the leading men of his own generation a fear of political parties. People then took their party allegiance as seriously as in an earlier age they had taken their religion, reacting violently against those who differed with them. As yet, the unity of the Nation was so fragile that factional disputes often brought threats of secession.

Key did, however, get somewhat involved in politics in the Jacksonian era. He campaigned for Jackson, whom he admired greatly, and accepted under him the post of District Attorney of the District of Columbia. In 1833, he undertook for the President an important peacemaking mission. Alabama was threatening to secede over a controversy with the Federal Government involving the Creek Indians. This mission he completed with skill and dispatch.

Though he shunned political office, Francis had a strong sense of civic responsibility. He devoted much time, effort and money to a variety of causes that engaged his sympathy and interest. One was free education for poor children. Largely on his initiative, the first Lancaster elementary school in America was established in Georgetown. He gave it generous financial support and participated actively in its management. Another cause in which he became deeply involved was the problem of the manumitted slaves who had difficulty competing in the free labor market. Key grew up on a plantation worked by slaves but he came to reject slavery and freed them all. He shared the belief, widespread at the time among antislavery elements, that the most humane way to liquidate this inhumane institution was to provide free transportation to their African homeland for all freedmen who desired to return. He was a member of the American Colonization Society and a founder of Liberia.

It was on one of his humanitarian missions that Key penned the stirring words of *The Star-Spangled Banner*. The occasion was an episode in the War of 1812. All through the year 1814, British Admiral Cockburn had waged "inglorious warfare on the hen-houses, cow-barns, and movable property along the shores of Chesapeake Bay"—as Samuel Eliot Morison pithily wrote. The admiral and his colleague, General Ross, quartered themselves in the home of Dr. Beanes, an elderly and highly respected physician who lived in Upper Marlborough. For weeks Beanes was a gracious though involuntary host to numerous British officers, treating their wounded and furnishing them with whatever they demanded. The British forces finally withdrew. He was celebrating with friends the departure of his unwelcome guests when he was disturbed by straggling sailors and soldiers who had left the ranks to plunder and were making a nuisance of themselves in the local tavern. Advancing at the head of a group of angry citizens, Dr. Beanes had the troublemakers thrown into jail. He did so believing that Upper Marlborough had a right to put down the disturbance of these individuals who no longer were part of an organized military body.

Admiral Cockburn took a different view. He had the doctor arrested and thrown into the forecastle of his flagship, the *Tonnant*. Seized in the middle of the night, Dr. Beanes was barely given time to dress before he was placed upon a hard-gaited horse and compelled to ride 30 miles. Throughout, he was treated most harshly. Friends who sought to effect his release were brusquely turned away and not even allowed to give him the necessaries he had not been able to take along.

Key was acquainted with the elderly physician who in his youth had been attached to Washington's army, and who had tended the wounded of Valley Forge and Brandywine. He went at once to the President and obtained his permission to plead Dr. Beanes' case before the admiral. With Colonel Skinner, the American agent in charge of exchange of prisoners, Key set out in a small boat for the *Tonnant*. For a long while Cockburn adamantly refused to treat the doctor as a prisoner of war, to consider exchange, or to permit Key to talk with him. Beanes, said he, deserved hanging. In the end Key's tact and persuasive skill and the testimony—cannily brought along—of many letters from wounded British officers who had been treated by the doctor finally secured his release.

The three Americans were not, however, permitted to leave at once. Cockburn was about to attack Fort McHenry and take the city of Baltimore where, he boasted, he would make his winter quarters "even if it rained militia." All that stood in the way of his occupying the city was Fort McHenry which the citizens of Baltimore had hastily strengthened with earth-works. Key, Skinner and Beanes, detained in their small boat for a day and a night of heavy bombardment, paced the deck anxiously. When, in the early morning light of September 14, 1814, they saw the flag still flying atop the fort, Key felt moved to write on an old envelope the poem that became our national anthem.

It seems paradoxical that this rousing war song was written by a man who had long opposed the war which produced it. Key was not alone in his misgivings as to the justice or wisdom of declaring war on Britain (voted by Congress 79 to 49 in the House, 19 to 13 in the Senate). Indeed, the country has seldom if ever been so divided during a war. But Key's patriotism was aroused when we suffered reverses. On land, the war in general went badly for us; nowhere worse than in the Chesapeake region. Our hastily summoned, ill-trained and badly led militia were no match for Cockburn's sailors and marines.

Washington was taken in August 1814, its public buildings burned. In the House of Representatives all the furniture was piled into a heap and set to the torch. As Key's biographer Victor Weybright wrote, "in smoke, ashes, and flames the great library which Jefferson had begun and fostered, the historic archives, the priceless furnishings of a noble public building, perished forever." Key wrote his poem at a historic moment. Cockburn's failure to take Fort McHenry signalled a turn in the fortunes of war; the worst was over.

To write verse was second nature to Key, but previously this had been merely a pleasant social gift. He thought of himself as an "album poet," not a writer of publishable verse. Interestingly enough, one of his direct ancestors had been a real poet, John Key, who lived in the 15th century and called himself "humble poet laureate to His Majesty Edward IV." *The Star-Spangled Banner* was Key's one serious poetic effort besides a hymn or two; indeed, it is the only achievement by which he is known. It was an instant success. Long before Congress officially designated it the national anthem (in 1931), it had become the nation's favorite patriotic song. And this, despite the fact that the melody (written by an English composer for the London Anacreontic Society), is difficult for untrained voices.

The song's popularity, I think, is due entirely to Key's words. He wrote a hymn to the American flag. He caught the mystique the flag has for us, who are a Nation not by consanguinity, not by a long common history but by devotion to an abstract concept, the concept of what the ideal society should be, the concept of liberty under law. Denis W. Brogan, an Englishman who understands us uncommonly well, once tried to explain to his countrymen what the flag means to Americans. It is more, he said, "than a mere symbol among many others. It is the regimental color of a regiment in which all Americans are enrolled." The 13 stripes remind us of our small beginnings, the 50 stars of how large we have grown. It was the sight of the flag still flying after an anxious night watch that inspired Key to surpass himself and, in a sense, to become the poet laureate of the American people.

USS TECUMSEH (SSBN 628)

NAMED FOR Tecumseh (1768–1813), the great Shawnee chief of whom historian Henry Trumbull said "was the most extraordinary Indian that has appeared in history"; more unusual than Pontiac (1720–69), the Ottawa chief on whom Tecumseh modeled himself and whose life paralleled his own in many respects.

Tecumseh's cause was the oldest in history – liberty, freedom for his people to live in their own way on land possessed by them since time immemorial. A man of unusual intelligence and perception, Tecumseh clearly foresaw the inevitable destruction of his race unless the Indians could hold back the relentless tide of western migration and avoid all contact with the whites. He saw nothing of value in their civilization for his people. To build a strong Indian confederacy became his consuming passion. He worked tirelessly, traveling the length and breadth of the Northwest and Southwest, urging every Indian tribe to join his league so that it might become strong enough to resist further white encroachment. Many have testified to his eloquence. Wrote General Dale, a frontiersman who in 1811 attended one the last great councils held by Tecumseh: "I have heard many great orators; never one with the oral powers of Tecumseh or the same command of the muscles of his face. Had I been deaf, the play of his countenance would have told me what he said."

Born in the Shawnee village of Old Piqua, near what is now Springfield, Ohio, Tecumseh was the son of a minor Shawnee chief and a Creek or Cherokee mother. Orphaned at 6, he was adopted by Chief Blackfish who taught him the arts of hunting and war, and treated him – as customary among Indians – with great kindness. His childhood was therefore a happy one. At an impressionable age, he met the great Shawnee war chief Cornstalk who told him of the glorious deeds of Pontiac under whom Cornstalk had fought, thus awakening in Tecumseh at an early age the ardent wish to try once again for the goal the Ottawa chief had failed to achieve — creation of an Indian state, a sanctuary for the Indian way of life.

Though he grew up amicably enough with white foster brothers adopted by Blackfish who had lost his own son (for a brief while in 1778, Daniel Boone was such a foster "brother"), Tecumseh's personal experiences and his observations of white behavior were such that, as he said, he " could not look upon the face of a white man without feeling the flesh crawl on his bones." All but one of his brothers died in battle as did his father who was killed in Lord Dunmore's war (1774). Old Piqua was burned to the ground by George Rogers Clark during the Revolution (1780). The man he most admired as a youth, Cornstalk, was treacherously murdered (with his son) when he came to warn the garrison at Fort Randolph of new Indian dangers (1777).

Used to the stern but fair Indian code of justice, the double standard of the whites infuriated him. While the Indians turned over to the American authorities every murderer of a white man (to be forthwith hanged without ceremony), no white jury ever convicted a white man who had murdered an Indian or relinquished a white murderer to the tribe of his victim. But worst of all was the ruthless appropriation of Indian lands, especially the practice of inducing whiskey-sodden minor chiefs to put their X mark on treaties of cession.

By Indian custom, no individual chief had the right to cede land, for, as Tecumseh was to reiterate over and over again, "the land never was divided but belongs to all, for the use of every one. No groups among us have a right to sell, even to one another, much less to strangers who want all and will not do with less." Once he exclaimed, "Sell a country! Why not sell the air, the clouds and the great sea, as well as the earth? Did not the Great Spirit make them all for the use of his children?" Protesting the Treaty of Fort Wayne (1809) which had been wrested by the Governor of the Indiana Territory, William H. Harrison, from what the Governor himself called "the most depraved wretches on earth," Tecumseh remarked sadly: "Once, and until lately, there were no white men on all this island . . . it then belonged to the red men, children of the same parents, placed on it by the Great Spirit that made them, to keep it, to traverse it, to enjoy its productions and to fill it

106

with the same race. Once they were a happy race. Now they are made miserable by the white people who are never contented but are always encroaching." In one of his most eloquent passages, Tecumseh cried out: "I am the maker of my own fortune. And oh, that I might make the fortune of my red people, and of my country, as great as the conceptions of my mind, when I think of the Great Spirit that rules this universe! I would not then come to Governor Harrison and ask him to tear up the treaty [of Fort Wayne] and obliterate the landmarks; but I would say to him, 'Sir, you have permission to return to your own country.'"

The Treaty of Fort Wayne aroused such ire among the Indians that it proved a mighty stimulus to Tecumseh's confederacy. Alarmed, Harrison sent for Tecumseh intending to chastise him but found himself instead on the defensive. As Henry Adams tells it, Tecumseh said: "Brother, since 1795 you have killed some of the Shawnee, Winnebagoes, Delawares, and Miamis, and you have taken our land from us; and I do not see how we can remain at peace with you if you continue to do so." Earnestly protesting that he did not wish to make war, Tecumseh nevertheless stated bluntly that he would resist any attempt by Harrison to possess himself of the ceded land. He begged the Governor to prevail upon the President to give up these lands and promise to make no treaties in the future without the consent of all the tribes. In return, he pledged himself to become a faithful ally of the United States. Told that such a proposal had no chance of finding favor, Tecumseh replied: "Well, as the great chief is to decide the matter, I hope the Great Spirit will put sense enough into his head to induce him to direct you to give up this land. It is true, he is so far off he will not be injured by the war; he may sit still in his town and drink his wine, while you and I will have to fight it out." With which shrewd observation of the different ways a war affects those who rule and those who fight, Tecumseh departed.

Of all the colonizers, the Dutch alone both recognized the Indians' right to their land *and also acted on this admission.* In Dutch law, title to land required first a voluntary act of cession by the Indians, then a government grant. When Peter Minuit paid 60 gulden for the 20,000 acres of woodland called Manhattan, this was in purchasing power a considerable sum, many times more than $24 today. Often cited as an illustration of how the Indians were robbed of their land, historian Boorstin points out that "the remarkable fact was not the price they paid the Indians, but rather that the Dutch felt it necessary to pay any price at all."

In their contacts with the whites, none proved as ruinous to Indian property rights (and to Indian self-respect) as that with the Americans. Although the Federal Government—at least some individuals in the Government—recognized Indian title to the land on which they had lived for thousands of years, the settlers and their State governments denied this, on grounds that were perhaps best stated by Governor Lumpkin of Georgia, in justification of his attempt to drive the Cherokees out of his State: "I believe the earth was formed especially for the cultivation of the ground, and none but civilized men will cultivate the earth to any great extent . . . therefore I do not believe a savage race of heathens found in the occupancy of a large and fertile domain of country have any exclusive right to the same." John M. Oskison, Tecumseh's biographer, remarks acidly that at that time the Cherokees "had attained under progressive leadership a state of civilization even more advanced than that of their white neighbors."

In contrast, Washington's instructions to the first Governor of the Northwest Territory bade him respect the boundaries of Indian lands, and stipulated that anyone crossing them without license from the American Government "may be treated in such manner as the Indians may see fit." In *Worcester* v. *Georgia* (1832), John Marshall said that "the Indian nations had always been considered . . . the undisputed possessors of the soil . . ." In *Cherokee Nation* v. *Georgia* (1831), he held that "the Indians are acknowledged to have unquestionable, and heretofore, unquestioned right to the lands they occupy." But when President Jackson disregarded the Court, allegedly declaring "John Marshall has made his decision, now let him enforce it," he doubtless reflected the majority sentiment of Western settlers who felt, with Daniel Boone, that they had been "ordained by God to settle the wilderness."

Jefferson, as President (1801–09), took a more equivocal stand than Washington. His passionate wish was for America to remain a republic of independent yeomen and this required much land for the ever growing numbers of would-be settlers. Professing his love of the Indians on numerous occasions, he yet did not understand them at all. When he asked that they "assemble their scattered warriors and form towns and villages, abandoning their nomadic life and becoming farmers," not even his offer to supply them with "horses, cattle, hogs and implements of husbandry" made an impress on the Indians who were hunters and despised farming as not much better than slavery. He kept assuring them that "farming was easy to learn," hinting at the same time that there was, in fact, no other alternative. "Instead then, my children," he once said, "of the gloomy prospect you have drawn of your total disappearance from the face of the earth, *which is true if you continue to hunt the deer and buffalo and go to war* (my italics), you see what a brilliant aspect is offered to your future history if you give up war and hunting and adopt the culture of the earth, and raise domestic animals."

Tecumseh discerned behind these benevolent words the same lust for land that animated the settlers. Indeed it revealed itself inadvertently in Jefferson's artless remark that if the Indians are induced to "withdraw themselves to the culture of a small piece of land, they will perceive how useless to them are extensive forests and will be willing to pare them off from time to time." He ordered the opening of trading posts where Indian chiefs would be granted easy credit for "we observe that when these debts get beyond what the individual can pay," the chiefs become willing to cede land.

On more than one occasion, Tecumseh tactlessly pointed out that the Federal Government was paying off the Revolutionary War debt with its huge profits from the sale of Indian lands. The Government paid $2.5 million to the Indians (in annuities) for 190 million acres and sold them for $213 million. Private speculators, buying at the Government price of about $2 an acre, sold to settlers at $5-25 on credit, the first failure to pay an installment resulting in repossession of the land and subsequent resale, often many times over. Where profits were so great, so easily made, it may, perhaps, have been too much to expect that the rights of an alien race of inferior power would be respected.

Certainly, the treaties guaranteeing such rights were but scraps of paper. General Benjamin Cowen, a student of Indian affairs, records that "through all the colonial times since the first treaty when the Plymouth governor made old Massasoit drunk and stole his land, Indian treaties were made to be broken, and from the first treaty made by our government, that with the Delawares at Fort Pitt in 1778 . . . down to the last treaty with the tribes huddled together in the arid lands of the Far West—in all over 900 treaties—every one of the number was broken in one or more important particulars by the whites." In truth, the Indians had no "unalienable" rights, not even the right to regenerate themselves by heeding the sermon preached by Tecumseh's brother, the Prophet, who urged them to return to the old Indian ways.

Many came to the community which the two brothers established on the Tippecanoe River, pledging themselves to abstain from alcohol, to isolate themselves from the whites and buy none of their products, to become self-sufficient by growing corn to supplement their game and fish. When Tecumseh told Harrison that they also "endeavored to level all distinctions, to destroy the village chiefs by whom all mischief is done . . . who sell our land to the Americans," the Governor thought this a dangerous precedent. At the first opportune moment, Tecumseh being absent, he fell on the settlement and razed it to the ground (1811). Thirty years later, he won the Presidency with the slogan "Tippecanoe and Tyler too." The immediate result, however, was to drive Tecumseh into the arms of the British, thus proving to Harrison's satisfaction that he had been right all along to suspect a British conspiracy behind Tecumseh's confederacy.

That the Indians saw in Britain a potential ally was natural. Before 1763 they had looked on France as an ally against Britain and for the same reason — having few settlers, neither of these countries was then pressing upon Indian land (as did the Americans). Tecumseh ridiculed the idea that Indian resentment was being fostered by Britain; it needed no artificial stimulus. True, in the Revolutionary War Britain used her Indian allies to ravage our Western settlements but the situation had changed. Now she was fully occupied fighting Napoleon on the Continent and weakly garrisoned in Canada. She had no wish to see the border inflamed. There is evidence the British held Tecumseh back. But when Tippecanoe was attacked and destroyed, he abandoned the "path of peace" he had followed so long despite constant provocation. He became Britain's ally in the war that was declared by Congress on June 18, 1812.

Ironically enough, the war carried Tecumseh to the pinnacle of his career; so close to his goal that he could almost seize it with his hands. With 5,000 warriors under his command and nearly all the Indians living between the Great Lakes and the Gulf and as far west as the Mississippi as his allies, he wielded power such as no Indian had ever known before. Alone and with his British allies he won victories that destroyed American power in parts of the West. Settlers were fleeing eastward in large numbers. But the moment passed. Perry won a victory on Lake Erie and things went a little better for the Americans. Detroit, which had surrendered in 1812 was recovered in 1813. Harrison won the Battle of the Thames (October 1813) and 5 months later Jackson decisively defeated the Creeks, Tecumseh's southern allies, at the Battle of Horseshoe Bend. Tecumseh himself lost his life at the Thames. Exhorting his warriors to "be brave, stand firm, shoot straight,"

110

he had plunged into the fighting never to be seen again. His body was spirited away by the Indians.

Had he lived, Britain might have pushed through her proposal at Ghent for creating an Indian state north of the Ohio to serve as a buffer between Canada and the United States — she made a try but gave up in the face of the determined opposition of the American commissioners. Had he lived, Tecumseh might have become the head of such a state, nominally free but under British protection. Who can tell? His cause died with him. There was no one to take his place. The last great effort of the Indians to regain a portion of their land and their freedom, indeed their very soul, was lost forever. Thereafter theirs was a tragic tale of steady deterioration, of reduction to the status of wards of a Government showing little sympathy and less understanding for their needs and interests.

It was Tecumseh's fate to have been born too late to reestablish Indian power. The tide had turned irrevocably against his race in the 1760's. At about that time they lost their numerical superiority which had up to then mitigated to some extent the disadvantages a Stone Age race faces in trying to hold back an enemy with a technically superior civilization. There were probably as many as two million Indians when the whites first appeared. By 1765, the latter had gained numerical parity and thereafter the ratio grew rapidly worse for the Indians who seldom had more than one or two children against the prolific settlers' seven or eight. By 1790, the whites outnumbered the red men four to one. In 1763 the Indians also lost their strategic advantage as a balance wheel between two major powers contesting the Continent. England and France both had sought them as allies when they were at war. But France was so completely defeated in the Seven Years' War that she had to relinquish all her American possessions.

Tall, straight, and lean, a stirring orator, a superbly skilled hunter and warrior, Tecumseh rose to his towering position among the Indians on merit, not by reason of birth as son of a chief. It was Indian practice to let men prove by their actions that they were fit to lead. There were no elections. Men were chosen by tacit acceptance as each individual warrior submitted to the leadership of a man he honored as his chief. Tecumseh's hold on the Indians was extraordinary; he was a very great chief. How great comes out best, perhaps, in a report written to the War Department in 1811 by his implacable opponent, Governor Harrison. It may stand as a final summing up:

"The implicit obedience and respect which the followers of Tecumseh pay him is really astonishing and more than any other circumstance bespeaks him one of those uncommon geniuses, which spring up occasionally to produce revolutions and overturn the established order of things. If it were not for the vicinity of the U.S., he would perhaps be the founder of an Empire that would rival in glory that of Mexico or Peru."

USS KAMEHAMEHA (SSBN 642)

NAMED FOR a man who was neither by birth nor choice American, who knew little about America, had few close contacts with Americans and never set foot on American soil. Scion of a royal family, he belonged to an alien race and religion. His political preference was for Britain, not for the United States. He was Kamehameha, king of Hawaii from 1810 to 1819.

If it seems strange that the name of a Hawaiian king should be borne by an American warship, the paradox resolves itself when we remember that he was the most striking figure in Hawaiian history and Hawaii is now our 50th State. We honor his memory because in our philosophy the heritage of every State of the Union is part of our common heritage. There is room in the pantheon of America's great for the heroes of every sector of this vast Nation.

Kamehameha was a great warrior. Having fallen heir in 1782 to a small chieftaincy, he set out to conquer all the islands. Others had tried before but he was the first to succeed. It took 28 years before all resistance was quelled, but the bitter fratricidal fight brought an end to the continuous inter-island wars that mar so much of Hawaiian history.

Kamehameha proved himself an extraordinarily able and wise ruler. His power was absolute but he used it benevolently. Under him the people were assured of justice and domestic peace. It was said of Hawaii under Kamehameha—as of Saxon England under King Alfred—that along any highway a child, woman or old man could lie down to sleep in perfect safety.

At whatever time he had lived, Kamehameha would have deserved to be called "the Great," but his achievements were enhanced by the fact that they occurred at a time when Hawaii needed as never before to be united and well governed. His adult life coincided with the dangerous and difficult period that followed Captain Cook's discovery of the islands in 1778 when trading ships from Europe and America in ever-growing numbers made the islands their way station for rest and revictualing.

The visiting seamen brought weapons and tools that aroused the admiration of the Hawaiians, but also new vices and diseases that decimated their number. The rowdy behavior of the visitors was a constant threat to the independence of the islands, for any incident brought with it the danger of foreign intervention. By maintaining public order and treating foreigners with scrupulous honesty and cordial hospitality, Kamehameha gained his people almost a century of political freedom.

After a thousand years of self-contained remoteness, the Hawaiians were ill-prepared to cope with the sudden influx of strange new ideas and ways of life. An indigenous Stone Age culture, no matter how highly developed, rarely survives contact with modernity. Kamehameha, who had grown up in old Hawaii, cherished its ancient religion and customs but realized his people must master modern techniques. He had an eye for what was good and what was bad in foreign ways. Against the latter he sought to protect his people, while enlisting the help and friendship of several foreigners in order to acquire such technology as would be useful for Hawaii. He deserves much of the credit for easing the transition from an old to a new culture, and for whatever remains today of the spirit of old Hawaii and its attractive way of life.

It is fitting that one of our swift new nuclear submarines should bear the name of this illustrious son of a race of intrepid seafarers whose swift canoes made landfall with amazing accuracy across the wide spaces of the Pacific, whose superb seamanship and knowledge of stars, winds and currents still arouse wonder and admiration.

USS JAMES MONROE (SSBN 622)

NAMED FOR James Monroe (1758–1831), fifth President of the United States, best known as the author of the Doctrine that bears his name. The immediate purpose of the Doctrine— which it brilliantly achieved—was to prevent the sending of a Franco-Spanish expedition to reconquer the South American colonies, then about to win their independence from Spain, and to prevent Russia from seizing California. The impetus came from Britain which proposed a joint Anglo-American note of protest which was to include a self-denying pledge by both nations to seek no further territory in the Hemisphere. Monroe decided to act on his own.

He consulted Jefferson, the party's greatest elder statesman, who was agreeable to accepting the proposal, but added, "Do we wish to acquire to our own confederacy any one or more of the Spanish provinces? I candidly confess that I have ever looked on Cuba as the most interesting addition which could be made to our system of States." Calhoun, too, was ready: . . . "even if it should pledge the US not to take Cuba or Texas." The view embodied in the Doctrine only barred the transfer of any territory in the Western Hemisphere to a *European* power.

In his annual message to Congress, December 2, 1823, he made two policy statements. The *first* reiterated Washington's principle of noninvolvement in European affairs: "In matters relating to themselves we have never taken any part, nor does it comport with our policy so to do." The *second* declared the Americas forever closed to colonization or interference by European states: "We should consider any attempt on their part to extend their system to any portion of this hemisphere as dangerous to our peace and safety." As to the former Spanish-American colonies, "we could not view any interposition for the purpose of oppressing them, or controlling in any other manner their destiny, by any European power, in any other light than as the manifestation of an unfriendly disposition toward the United States."

Monroe's message, wrote Webster, "met with the entire concurrence and the hearty approbation of the country." It was enthusiastically received in England, one member of Parliament declaring that no recent event had "dispersed greater joy, exultation, and gratitude over all the free men of Europe." The President's assertion that the principles of his message were American "doctrine" was an impressive act of statesmanship, made all the more remarkable by the fact that Europe's power vastly exceeded our own. Now that these principles have become "American" in the wider sense of a multilateral hemispheric doctrine (Act of Havana, 1940), they serve a somewhat different but no less important purpose.

Domestic circumstances and national interest had their effect on the timing and text of the Doctrine. Until the negotiations for acquiring Florida were concluded, the United States was careful to take no steps that might offend the Spanish Government. As soon as Florida was safely in our hands, there followed in quick succession American recognition of the independence of the former Spanish colonies, the establishment of diplomatic relations, and finally the Monroe Doctrine. Similar factors made Cuba a special case. Instructions to our minister at Madrid in 1829 noted "the interest of the southern section of the Union that no attempt should be made in that island to throw off the yoke of Spanish dependence, the first effect of which would be the sudden emancipation of a numerous slave population, the result of which could not but be very sensibly felt upon the adjacent shores of the United States."

Monroe was notably successful, also, in enlarging the area of the United States and delineating its boundaries to the north and west. His part in negotiating the Louisiana Purchase deserves greater recognition than is usually accorded. Jefferson sent him to Paris in 1803 to assist Robert R. Livingston, our regular envoy, in obtaining from Napoleon an irrevocable guarantee of the right of navigation on the Mississippi and, if possible, to purchase a narrow strip of land to the east of the mouth of the river for $2 million. Free navigation and trading rights on the river had long been objectives sought by Western farmers for whom the Mississippi offered the only feasible transport for their bulky goods. Monroe himself had fought hard for these rights since his early days in the Continental Congress.

When Napoleon unexpectedly offered to sell all of the territory he had wrested from Spain in 1800, the American envoys accepted at once (after whittling down the asking price by one third to a mere $15 million). They had no authority to buy this vast territory (900,000 square miles), nor funds to pay for it. There was no certainty that their action would be approved by the American Government. They seized the opportunity and took the risk; in consequence an area as large as that of the original 13 Colonies, and eventually to contain 13 new States or parts thereof, was added to the Union.

Monroe had a hand in the acquisition of Florida as well. It was bought during his administration (1819), which also saw the settlement of longstanding boundary disputes with Spain, Russia, and Britain. As part of the Florida settlement (1819), Spain relinquished her claims to California north of the 42nd parallel. In 1824, Russia (then seeking to assert authority over Oregon) was induced to abandon all claims south of 54 degrees 40. Finally, by agreement with Britain (1818), the 49th parallel was made the boundary line as far west as the Rocky Mountains (Polk extended it to the Pacific in 1846). Part of the credit for Monroe's diplomatic successes must be ascribed to John Quincy Adams, his able Secretary of State.

Part Scottish, part Welsh by descent, Monroe was born in Westmoreland County, Va., where his family had been settled since 1647. He attended Parson Campbell's academy, entered William and Mary at 16, and left 2 years later to join the Revolutionary War. Commissioned a lieutenant in a Virginia regiment of the Continental Army, he fought in the battles of Harlem, White Plains, and Trenton (where he was wounded), Brandywine, Germantown and Monmouth, resigning after 4 years' service with the rank of major. At 22, he entered the office of Thomas Jefferson, then Governor of Virginia, to study law (1780–83). A warm personal and political friendship soon developed between the two which lasted until Jefferson's death in 1826. Their close association decisively influenced the future course of Monroe's life. Elected at 24 to the Virginia House of Delegates and the Governor's Council, he embarked on a public career (alternately serving his State and the Nation) which continued with but a few brief intervals of private life until, at 67, he stepped down from the Presidency.

As a young man, Monroe was a provincial Virginian. His interests did not extend beyond his native State. He vigorously opposed the Constitution. But as his years of public service accumulated, he learned to think in continental terms and, in the end, became one of our strong Presidents. Lacking the brilliance of the Founding Fathers, his success has been attributed to "untiring application and indomitable perseverance." Perhaps it should also be attributed to a practice we followed in the first 40 years of our life under the Constitution. This was to choose for the Presidency men who had, so to speak, served an 8-year apprenticeship by holding top administrative posts, as Vice President or Secretary of State to their predecessor (Jefferson had been both); Washington, during his 8 years as Commander in Chief of the Continental Army, was in effect Secretary of War as well. In the crucial years when the American experiment got under way, this practice insured us guidance by men who, if not always brilliant, inevitably had much experience in the difficult art of managing a Federal Republic.

An easy way to call to mind our first six Presidents is to visualize them as a procession with Washington at the head (1789–97), and the famous Virginia Dynasty (Jefferson, Madison, Monroe) in the middle, preceded by one Massachusetts President (John Adams, 1797–1801) and followed by the other (his son John Quincy, 1825–29). The party changeover in 1800 did not break the continuity at the top level of government. As the defeated Federalist President (John Adams) moved out of the White House, his Vice President (Thomas Jefferson) moved in.

Jefferson, like all reformers, tended to think in abstractions and absolutes. It was a measure of his greatness that once in control of the National Government, the practical side of his nature took over as it did to an even greater extent with his Republican successors in the Presidency. The election of 1800 had been so bitterly fought, some of the Republicans regarded it as a second Revolution. But once in office and faced with the task of governing, the victorious Republicans found that many of the Federalist measures they had fiercely attacked on ideological grounds were practical necessities. Constrained to adopt these or similar measures, they discovered that their fear of them had been unwarranted. The longer the Republicans held office, the readier they were to reverse doctrinaire positions when the actual running of the country showed these to be unworkable. They had the good sense to learn by experience but they did so on an ad hoc basis, without abandoning their political philosophy. This has tended to obscure the extent to which Federalist policies survived after the party lost all political control; survived, it would seem, on merit.

During the bitter party strife preceding their defeat by the Republicans, the Federalists had been most vehemently attacked on two points: their broad construction of the Constitution and their preference for Britain as against Revolutionary France. On these very points, the Republicans reversed themselves almost at once. The Lousiana Purchase could be justified only by carrying the Federalist dogma of "implied powers" to its ultimate limit. And as for Jefferson's Embargo Act (1807), it aroused the same feeling of outrage as being contrary to the spirit of the Constitution that Adams' Alien and Sedition Acts (1798) had aroused in Jefferson himself; more people were injured by the former than by the latter. Nothing illustrates more dramatically the evanescence of seemingly unalterable dogma when confronted with reality than Jefferson's *volte-face* vis-a-vis France and Britain. In 1802, he was ready to conclude an alliance with Britain (as he wrote our envoy in Paris) should Napoleon refuse us free navigation on the Mississippi and the port of New Orleans. He had reason to fear Napoleon might establish an empire on our western flank, but then Adams had reason to fear Revolutionary France might undermine our political institutions – the country was full of her agents. When Monroe asked advice on how to respond to the British proposal for a joint protest against European encroachment on Latin America, Jefferson and Madison recommended joint action with Britain while Adams' son, John Quincy, pressed energetically for unilateral American action (the Monroe Doctrine).

During Madison's administration, almost the whole of Henry Clay's so-called "American System" was enacted into law – a protective tariff, the Second Bank of the United States, and the first large naval appropriations measure which allocated $1 million per annum for 3 years to build warships. This was Hamilton's program, the very program that had caused the break between Madison and Hamilton and led to foundation of Jefferson's Republican Party. It was the War of 1812 and its aftermath that demonstrated the wisdom of these measures. Hamilton's *Report on Manufactures* was rediscovered and found eminently relevant to the situation in 1815 when belligerent interference with trade came to an end and America's war-born "infant industries" clamored for Government protection against wholesale dumping of European goods. Jefferson admitted having erred in opposing industry. He had not foreseen that dependence on foreign products would diminish our economic freedom (Hamilton saw this clearly). "We must now place the manufacturer by the side of the agriculturalist," said Jefferson in 1815, "experience has taught me that manufactures are now as necessary to our independence as to our comfort." During his second term, a small step was even taken toward the Federalist concept of aid to the economy in general: Congress appropriated money for constructing the Cumberland Road (1806).

In his First Inaugural Address, Jefferson sought to heal the wounds of party strife by saying, "we are all Republicans, we are all Federalists." They were prophetic words—for a time at least. As Federalist measures were enacted, those who had remained faithful to the defeated party were reconciled with the Republicans and joined their ranks. During Monroe's visit to New England in 1817, the Boston *Columbian Sentinel* coined the expression "Era of Good Feeling" which has ever since been applied to his administration (1817–25).

Though it did not seem so at the time, it may have been fortuitous that the American political experiment was launched at the very moment Europe plunged into a 25-year period of incessant war, revolution and turmoil. Preoccupied with their own problems, the European powers were not in a position to exert as much influence on the American Continent as they might have wished. At the same time, their belligerent activities made enough trouble to pull us together. When peace returned to Europe in 1815, we no longer needed to fear foreign military aggression. As our industry developed, we were able to escape European economic dominance. And so we began to concentrate more and more on domestic issues. These turned out to be far more divisive than our earlier political controversies; perhaps because they took the form of sectional conflicts involving important economic interests rather than disputes of an essentially philosophical nature.

USS SIMON BOLIVAR (SSBN 641)

N AMED FOR a great American soldier, patriot and states-man. Simon Bolivar (1783–1830) was *American* in the broad sense of the word prevailing south of the border, where it is applied to citizens of the entire Western Hemisphere, north, central and south.

Not only for us, but for all who share this vast continent with us, the word has a magic of its own. It stands for what we have in common, what gives us a sense of belonging to the same family of nations, despite the fact that we differ in many important respects. Not the least of the bonds uniting us is a revolutionary heritage that is peculiarly American.

What sets America's wars of independence apart from other struggles for colonial emancipation is that they were fought for political liberty, pure and simple. They were wars led in the north by Englishmen and in the south by Spaniards against men of their own race, language and culture who would deny them the right to self-government. The leaders of the revolt laid down their "lives, their fortunes and their sacred honor" from motives of pure patriotism unadulterated by desire for personal advantage. They were already successful and impor-tant men in their communities; they did not expect independ-ence to enrich them or to enhance their status. They fought for the ideal of liberty at great personal risk. None risked more and gained less personally than Simon Bolivar.

Born in Caracas, Venezuela in 1783—the year England recognized the independence of the United States—the son of a wealthy and aristocratic Spanish family long settled in the colony, Bolivar was educated abroad and, until the age of 27, lived the pleasant life of a rich planter. But from the moment of the first revolt in Caracas against Spain in 1810 to the end of his brief life of but 47 years, Bolivar served almost continuously as leader of the revolt. He richly deserved the title *Liberator* bestowed on him by his countrymen, for he succeeded in driving the Spaniards from the vast area now occupied by the Republics of Panama, Colombia, Venezuela, Ecuador and Peru. At one time or another he was not only the military leader but civilian chief as well of one or more of these Republics; for a brief time all were united under him.

The Hispanic-American wars of independence lasted twice as long as did our own, and were fought over a vastly larger area and more intractable terrain. In population, the adversaries were more evenly matched, there being 11 million Spaniards to 15 million colonials, while we had but a third as large a population as England. Spain at the time was weakened by the Napoleonic Wars while England was the premier maritime empire of the world. On the other hand, the Spanish colonials had to fight with no outside help except for individual volunteers who flocked to Bolivar's army as they did to Washington's. No major country gave aid as we received from France. Only little Haiti, under President Pétion, supported the cause of freedom by giving men and materiel to Bolivar at a time when he sorely needed them.

Of his military feats, Thomas Carlyle said that Bolivar rode "fighting all the way, through torrid deserts, hot mud swamps, through ice-chasms beyond the curve of perpetual frost — more miles than Ulysses ever sailed." He "marched over the Andes more than once, a feat analogous to Hannibal's and seemed to think little of it. Often beaten, banished from the firm land, he always returned again, truculently fought again."

Henry Clay called Bolivar the Washington of South America. Indeed, there are striking similarities, but the differences in temperament and in the turn of their lives are equally great. Both were self-taught soldiers. Bartolomé Mitre, famed Argentinean statesman, journalist, author and historian said that though Bolivar "had no military education, he possessed the talents of a great revolutionary leader and the inspiration of genius . . . He formed his plans quickly and executed them with daring resolution, while he lost no time in securing the fruits of his victory." And, speaking of his reconquest of western Venezuela, he remarked that "never, with such small means, was so much accomplished over so vast an extent of country, in so short a time."

Like Washington, Bolivar had that quality without which no man becomes a great military leader — a capacity to bear adversity with fortitude and to rise from defeat to win victory. His Spanish adversary General Morillo said that Bolivar was "more fearful vanquished than victorious"—just as of Washington one might well say that his finest hour was Valley Forge. Both cared for the welfare of their troops and were generous toward them. Both in their lifetime received much public adoration, both have a secure place in history as liberators of their nations. A South American Republic was named for Bolivar, an American State for Washington.

But, while Washington remained popular and died venerated by his countrymen on the estate he loved so well, Bolivar lost the support of his people and died penniless of a lung ailment which might not have proved fatal had he spared himself. Toward the end he was discouraged and said that "those of us who have toiled for liberty in South America have but plowed the sea." Hendrik Willem Van Loon, in his biography writes an epitaph that is more just. "If those words, spoken in the bitterness of his final defeat and loneliness, had truly been the summing up of his restless labors, the life of Simon Bolivar might well have been considered a hopeless failure. Whereas a single glance at the map of the southern half of our continent proclaims the glory of his achievements. Half a dozen free and independent nations, arisen from among the ruins of Spain's imperial ambitions, are surely a monument of which any human being might well feel proud."

USS ANDREW JACKSON (SSBN 619)

NAMED FOR Andrew Jackson (1767–1845), seventh President of the United States, focal point and standard bearer of a popular movement that has with some justice been called revolutionary though it triumphed through the "democratic process," that is, by winning the endorsement of a majority of the electorate. Jackson's election was not, however, the normal or routine kind that rotates parties in and out of office in response to minor changes in public opinion, usually temporary and reversible; it was unusual in that it registered a major political shift, manifesting itself in the eclipse of an old and the emergence of a new party.

Such electoral "revolutions" occur rarely. There were only three (1800, 1828, 1861) during the first century of American independence. In the first of these elections, political control of the National Government passed from the Federalists to Jefferson's Republican Party; in the second from the Republicans to Jackson's Democratic Party; in the third, from the Democrats to Lincoln's new Republican Party. Of the Presidents elected on these occasions, none was more closely identified by background, temperament and achievement, with the movement that carried him into the White House, than Jackson.

His birthplace was a backwoods settlement at Waxhaw, Lancaster County, S.C. The Jacksons, poor immigrants from northern Ireland, had come to America in 1765 with their two eldest sons. Misfortune pursued them from the start. The father died shortly before Andrew Jackson was born, leaving the little family destitute and forced to seek shelter with distant relations. All except the future President perished in the Revolutionary War. The eldest son was killed in 1779; the second died 2 years later of wounds neglected while a prisoner of the British; the mother died of prison fever while nursing the sick in Charleston (1781).

Jackson was only 13 when he witnessed the massacre at Waxhaw of 380 Virginia militia who were trying to surrender to Tarleton and his horsemen of evil repute — Northern Loyalist volunteers who were responsible for some of the worst ravages perpetrated in the war. "Tarleton's Quarters" became the rallying cry of embattled farmers striking back at the British (as a reminder that it was that officer's practice to butcher American soldiers who had surrendered to him). Though a mere boy, Jackson joined the untrained, unpaid guerillas who had found a natural leader in Colonel Sumter, a farmer who took up soldiering — and proved uncommonly good at it — after the enemy had burnt his home and driven his family into the woods. Taken prisoner in the Battle of Hanging Rock (1781), Jackson received a vicious saber cut marking him for life because he refused to black a British officer's boots. He almost died of the smallpox and never lost his intense dislike of the British.

When peace returned to the South, he was 14 and all alone in the world. He tried his hand at various trades without notable success. At 17 he decided to study law, a formidable undertaking for one who had no money and almost no education. He got the money by selling his horse, read law for 2 years at Salisbury, N.C., passed his bar examination, and with a fellow law clerk set out (1787) on the trail leading westward into what is now Tennessee. In 1788, the two friends opened their own law office in Nashville. They prospered, even though they were fonder of horse-racing, cock-fighting and similar amusements than of Blackstone. The litigious West needed young lawyers hardy enough for the rigors of frontier practice. It offered splendid opportunities to speculate in land and make a fortune. Before he was 30, Jackson owned a large cotton plantation with numerous slaves, on which he later built himself an elegant mansion, the Hermitage. He took an interest in politics, though only intermittently, won election as delegate to the convention that drew up the constitution for the new State of Tennessee (1796), served briefly in both Houses of Congress (1796-97 and 1823-25) and sat as a judge on the Tennessee Supreme Court (1798-1804) — all in all, not an outstanding public career.

He made his mark elsewhere. In the 5 years from 1813 to 1818, "Old Hickory" (as he was called by his troops for his toughness and endurance) won important victories in three military campaigns. At the head of the Tennessee militia, he crushingly defeated the Creek Indians (Battle of Horseshoe Bend, 1814), which led to his being commissioned a major general in the U.S. Army, charged with the defense of New Orleans. His victory over Wellington's veterans under Pakenham (1815), won him national attention. American predilection for successful citizen-soldiers put him in line for the highest office should he seek it. Not even the difficulties he caused the Government by over-zealous conduct of the Seminole War could dim his prospects. Sent to chastise some Indians who were raiding along the Alabama-Georgia border, he exceeded his instructions, pursued them across the border into their sanctuary in Spanish Florida, captured Pensacola and hanged two British subjects for allegedly having stirred up the Seminoles.

From the consequences of this rash act (which brought the country face to face with the possibility of war with both Britain and Spain), he was saved by Monroe's Secretary of State, John Quincy Adams, the only Cabinet member to advise the President against disavowing Jackson's actions. Adams, who was one of our most astute diplomatists, cleverly used the incident to pressure Spain into ceding Florida. Paradoxically, he thus vindicated the man who a decade later would defeat him in an election fought with extraordinary rancor. Jackson emerged more popular than ever. He appealed particularly to the rapidly growing segment of the population that was gaining political influence as the electoral base was being broadened *geographically*, with the movement of masses of people into the western wilderness, and *socially*, after widespread adoption of manhood suffrage.

At the end of the Revolutionary War, the line of settlement along the Atlantic coast extended at most to a depth of 250 miles, often much less. A few thousand had penetrated through four gaps in the Appalachian mountain chain, establishing themselves precariously in Kentucky and Tennessee. Once peace was concluded (1783), the trickle became a mass movement, 2½ million going West between 1790 and 1820. When Washington was inaugurated, the Mississippi valley had perhaps 100,000 inhabitants; when Jackson ran for President it had four million, a fortyfold increase. Total population had only trebled (nearly all through natural increase, for Americans then averaged 7.5 children per family and immigration did not yet exceed 6,000 per annum, prorated over a 50 year period).

With nine western frontier States in the Union (out of a total of 24), the political views of the men who were hewing farms and communities out of the virgin forest were bound to gain influence in the affairs of the Nation. But while population growth automatically enhanced the political power of the West, it brought no corresponding growth in economic power. Angry at being perennially in debt to Eastern creditors, Western farmers to a man voted for Jackson who shared their hatred of the "money power" that had arisen in a country but recently possessed of neither millionaires nor paupers. His followers presented Jackson to the public as the "modern Cincinnatus," retired to his farm there to cultivate "with his own hand the soil that he defended from the grasp of a foreign foe." In vain did his opponents point out that Jackson was the owner not of a farm but a large plantation worked by slaves and superintended by overseers. They could make no dent in his image as the "farmer of Tennessee."

From the West, which regarded the right to vote as implicit in Democracy, manhood suffrage spread eastward. One by one, the original 13 States abandoned the notion that a man ought to prove he had a stake in the community before being permitted to vote (as by possession of some property, service in the militia, or payment of taxes). Several enfranchised their small farmers, farm hands, mechanics and laborers just in time for them to vote for Jackson whose rapid rise to wealth and a respected position in society, despite his humble birth and lack of education, seemed to them the very embodiment of their own dreams and aspirations. He was, indeed, the average man writ large.

Jefferson might "feel much alarmed at the prospect of seeing General Jackson President," declaring he is "one of the most unfit men I know for such a place," though admittedly "an able military chief;" indeed, warning that Jackson was a "dangerous man," given to wild outbursts of passion, willful and inclined to ride roughshod over the law. But Jackson had in high degree the qualities most admired by the man in the street—vigor, energy, straightforwardness, courage, an iron will to succeed. That he was deficient in the qualities heretofore demanded of presidential candidates increased, if anything, his immense popularity. Bancroft reflected public opinion in his eulogy of Jackson (1845) when he spoke with admiration of this "unlettered man of the West . . . little versed in books, unconnected by science with the traditions of the past," but possessing a mind "nursed in freedom" by the "ancient forests" in which he had grown to manhood.

That little was known of his views on the major issues of the day did not matter. He ran neither on a record nor on a

82-336 O - 72 - 10

specific political program, but on his charisma as the avowed champion of the people who, as his friend Van Buren tells it, was convinced that "to labour for the good of the masses was a special mission assigned him by his creator." In the election of 1824, he received more votes than any of the other three candidates (John Q. Adams, Clay, Crawford), though not the required majority, and the House made Adams President. But he won handsomely in 1828, and again in 1832.

Jackson was the first popular leader, the first Westerner, the first "man of the people" to enter the White House. His election marked a break with tradition, a departure from long-held ideas about the nature of popular government. The new democratic creed of which Jackson was the symbol rejected certain theories and practices going back to the Founding Fathers and hitherto accepted by the American people; in particular the postulate that "right and obligation are correlative," in the sense in which it was understood to mean that those wishing to exercise a political right must be competent to discharge the public responsibilities involved.

This had not been a matter of being less democratic—Jefferson subscribed to it no less than Washington or Hamilton—but rather of being more concerned with trying to make certain that elected and appointed public officials be properly "qualified" for their particular tasks. The Founders were acutely aware of the risk they were taking with their new experiment in popular government. They knew that, like any other government, it would not endure unless it was competently managed. Our first six Presidents were natural *aristoi*, as Jefferson understood the term—men of learning, intelligence, experience; trained, in a sense, for the Presidency by long and distinguished public service. In making their own appointments to national offices, they followed Washington's lead, establishing equally high standards of fitness and probity.

But high standards inevitably exclude those who cannot meet them. This, to Jackson and his followers, was unacceptable. They were not prepared, for the sake of competence, to relinquish equality. It seemed to them all the more reasonable that the rewards of political life be distributed as equally as possible and not reserved to the specially qualified since they believed no special qualifications were needed for any public office. Even in Jackson's day, when government functioned in a limited sphere and the duties of public servants were relatively uncomplicated, this was an erroneous supposition. For modern governments it is, of course, untenable. Unfortunately, the

Jacksonian notion of "rights" divorced from competence and merit persists in nonpolitical areas (education, for example) where it works great mischief.

Jackson himself had a fine, if untutored, mind. As President, he acted decisively on every issue confronting him. He was successful where common sense and vigor could resolve the problem, less so where understanding and knowledge, such as only education and experience can provide, were required. The two actions that won him the greatest popularity had disastrous consequences for the country.

Among his successes must be counted the satisfactory settlement of longstanding disputes with Britain (access to West Indian trade) and France (payment of American spoilation claims), and his masterful handling of the nullification crisis of 1832 when the tariff legislation had so infuriated South Carolina that she went to the brink of secession. He brought her back by a judicious mixture of force and conciliation. At a time when sectional interest all too often took precedence in men's minds, it was one of Jackson's great merits that he never wavered in his devotion to the Union.

His war on the Bank of the United States, on the other hand, proved costly to the country. Simple ignorance of economics, reinforced by personal hatred (he suspected the Bank of working for his political opponents) blinded him to its value as fiscal agent of the Government and guardian of the Nation's currency and credit. When Congress renewed the Bank's charter in 1832, he proceeded to slay the "hydra-headed monster," symbol (to him) of the "money power," with a veto message that must have taken an hour and a half to deliver. It was a masterpiece of propaganda (prepared by his Attorney General, Roger Taney), as effective as it was unfair. The Bank did not perform its task, he said; it was a Government-supported monopoly making rich men richer at the expense of the taxpayer; it was unconstitutional. Four years before its charter expired, he began to withdraw Government funds and deposit them in his "pet" banks. He tried to stem the ensuing orgy of speculation by ordering that all payments to the Government be made in gold and silver. His arbitrary actions, for which the Senate censored him (though his friends managed to have the censure expurgated from the record), are generally believed to have helped precipitate the panic of 1837, the worst the country had so far experienced, and the longest (6 years). Wildcat banking and a fluctuating currency continued for decades to come, ruining many whose interests he had wanted to protect, while doing little harm to the "money power" he so disliked.

For his policy of "rotation in office" — at the time even more popular than his war on the Bank—Jackson has since been severely criticized, not least by succeeding Presidents who found themselves beseiged by importunate office seekers. His conviction that the "duties of all public officers are, or at least admit of being made, so plain and simple that men of intelligence may readily qualify themselves for their performance," fastened on the Federal Government the corrupt and inefficient spoils system already existing in some States, New York in particular. That State's representative in the Senate, William L. Marcy, replied to Clay's condemnation of patronage with these words: "The politicians of the United States . . . boldly preach what they practice . . . they see nothing wrong in the rule that to the victor belong the spoils of the enemy." Only after a long and bitter fight was the damage undone and America provided with a civil service based on merit and the "open career for talent" — years after every other advanced country had done so.

On the Presidency, Jackson left a deep impress. Where men like Washington, the Adamses, Monroe, had sought to place it above partisanship, Jackson acted as the policy-making head of his party and succeeding Presidents have followed his example. He raised the office to heights of power neither envisaged by the Constitution nor desired by his predecessors. Defying the Supreme Court when he felt it exceeded its jurisdiction, he once declared that the Court "ought not to control the coordinate authorities of this Government," for each of them must "be guided by its own opinion of the Constitution." There was more than political bias in Clay's warning (1833) that the powers of Congress were being paralyzed by excessive use of the executive veto; that the "concentration of all power in the hands of one man" was "tending towards a total change of the pure republican character of the government." But the majority of the people could find no fault in Jackson. He was one of the few Presidents to leave the White House with his popularity not only unimpaired but greater than when first elected.

Jackson gave his name to a party, a period, a point of view of great significance in shaping America. His party remained dominant for three decades and in the party his influence remained preeminent until he died. Jackson's era, rather than our own, marks the apogee of the average man, the moment in history when his faculties found their greatest scope, when he most fully came into his own. Manhood suffrage translated for the first time his numerical preponderance into political power. Public issues were uncomplicated; he could understand them and therefore participate actively in political life, with all this means to a man's dignity and importance. A land full of riches and empty of people put success within his grasp. In the 1830's, four out of five Americans (outside the South) were independent property owners, mainly small farmers, and the fifth had a good chance of eventually joining the rest. Permanent dependence on public or private charity of fellow countrymen was almost unheard of. The Nation's most important task—conquest of the continent—average men could and did do superlatively well. Pioneer life was hard but it made for real equality.

Few have summed up so well what gave Jacksonian America its distinctive, its unique pattern of life and thought than de Tocqueville, who wrote: "It is not impossible to conceive the surpassing liberty which the Americans enjoy; some idea may likewise be formed of the extreme equality which subsists among them, but the political activity which pervades the United States must be seen in order to be understood." After pondering the spectacle, he concluded, "I am not sure that upon the whole this is not the greatest advantage of democracy."

USS JAMES K. POLK (SSBN 645)

N AMED FOR James K. Polk (1795–1849), ablest President between Jackson and Lincoln, and one of the few who rose from log cabin to White House. Born in North Carolina, the eldest of 10 children of a plain farmer, Polk grew to manhood in Duck River, Tenn., a rude frontier settlement on the edge of the wilderness. His ancestors were Scottish Covenanters who migrated to Ireland early in the 17th century and to America a hundred years later, settling first in Maryland and later moving westward in search of a freer and better life. The future President's family found in Tennessee the hoped-for Land of Promise where unremitting toil was all that was needed to attain prosperity and an honored place in the community. Young Polk worked long hours on the farm and, since there were no schools, was taught the three R's by his parents. He was good at mathematics and liked to read. When he reached 17, his father was able to grant him his wish for an education leading to a professional career.

Though never in robust health, Polk was all his life a prodigious worker. He accomplished much because he had enormous drive and great talent for systematic and sustained mental labor. It took him but 3 years of formal instruction to make up his educational deficiencies. At 20, he was admitted to the University of North Carolina with sophomore standing, graduating with first honors in mathematics and classics. He read law and, before he was 26, had become one of the leading practitioners in Columbia, Tenn., as well as a promising candidate for public office.

After one term in the State legislature, he entered the U.S. House of Representatives where he served from 1825 to 1839, the last 4 years as Speaker and leader of the Jacksonian forces.

Polk would have preferred to remain in Congress but was drafted by his party to run for Governor of Tennessee, to save the State for the party. Elected in 1839, he lost in 1841 and 1843 – the only setbacks in an otherwise uniformly successful career. In those days, rival candidates used to travel the country together, putting up at the same inns, often sleeping in the same bed, taking turns addressing the same meetings to which voters flocked from distant parts, as much for entertainment as for political discussion. Polk ran on his record as Governor. He had given his State an excellent administration, rescued it from near bankruptcy, and initiated significant reforms. His rival, semiliterate but shrewd, never discussed issues but took pains to amuse the audience. He won, it seems, chiefly because he was the better storyteller!

Polk was being considered for Vice President when the Texas and Oregon issues burst upon the country causing a deadlock that could be broken only by nominating Polk as a compromise candidate for President. The 1844 election was one of the most hotly contested the Nation had ever experienced. The issues between Democrats and Whigs were sharply drawn, feelings ran high, the country was almost evenly divided. Odd as it seems today, the candidates for the Presidency did not campaign actively since it was then considered unseemly to give the appearance of seeking this high office. Polk won with 170 electoral votes to 105 for Clay. Though at 49 he was the youngest President, he was committed to a more ambitious, more precisely stated administration program than any of his predecessors. All of it was carried out in the single term to which he had limited himself voluntarily when accepting the nomination of his party.

In the *domestic* field, Polk's achievements proved ephemeral, but his views, consistently Jacksonian, still have historic interest. He was a strict constitutionalist because he was certain this alone could preserve the Union. He opposed the protective tariff because he deemed it "unjust to tax the labor of one class of society to support and fatten another." He feared that Federal funds for internal improvements would destroy State sovereignty. It was better "to live as free men in a trackless wilderness than ride as vassals down a broad highway." He wanted Federal funds kept separate from the private banking system to prevent their being used for credit expansion and cheap money. The Federal Government, he thought, should be brought back to "what it was intended to be, a plain economical government." In the *foreign* field, Polk's success was both spectacular and of enduring importance to the Nation.

An ardent expansionist, as was natural given his pioneer background, Polk added more territory to the United States than any previous President except Jefferson.

He settled the 40-year-old Northwest Boundary Dispute by skillful diplomacy and admirable nerve in face of a possible two-front war, inducing Britain to relinquish her long-standing demand for a boundary along the Columbia River, which would have cost us the State of Washington, in exchange for abandonment of our claim to what is now British Columbia. On the basis of discovery and settlement, this was the most we could justifiably ask or, for that matter, realistically hope to obtain without resorting to war. Our southwest boundary was moved to its present location as a result of Polk's able management of the Mexican War and the ensuing peace negotiations. Mexico was generously compensated for the loss of California and New Mexico though not of Texas which had been lost 10 years earlier in exactly the same way as Mexico herself had been lost to Spain—by a successful indigenous revolt. We paid Mexico considerably more per acre than Napoleon had charged us for the Louisiana Purchase in 1803. When Polk left office, the United States stretched from "sea to shining sea."

Polk stood out among leading figures of his day in his unfaltering devotion to the national interest, uninfluenced by personal or parochial considerations, yet most 19th century historians accused him of precipitating the Mexican-American War in the interest of slavery expansion. This verdict has since been reversed in consequence of the publication early in this century of relevant official documents from the archives of Texas, Mexico, and Great Britain, which made it possible to see the issue more accurately. When Polk took office, the annexation of Texas was already an accomplished fact. Having warned us she would consider this "equivalent to a declaration of war," Mexico promptly severed diplomatic relations. Both sides moved troops to the Mexican-Texas border. Unfortunately, the two countries disagreed as to whether the Rio Grande or the Nueces constituted the boundary. It was in the disputed territory between these rivers that hostilities broke out spontaneously and a war began that neither country really wanted.

That Polk was able to execute his entire domestic and foreign program is the more remarkable in that he was neither a charismatic leader identified with some great popular movement, nor a politican adept at manipulating people and events. How he was able to resolve the great issues pressing upon him can best be understood by reading the diary he kept while in office.

The President emerges from its pages an able and astute administrator who approached every problem with a logical mind and a keen sense of political realities, who gained his objectives by stating them with precision and justifying them with well-reasoned argument. One cannot but feel that he understood the issues he dealt with better than most of his experts, whether they involved war strategy, military supply, diplomatic negotiations or how to get congressional approval for his measures. The nominally dominant Democrats were so rent by faction that every executive request was attacked by at least one element in his party, with the enthusiastic support of the Whigs.

Written for personal use, as a reminder of the official happenings crowding his overfull days, the diary gives an intimate glimpse into the Executive Office during a transitional period in our history. It was a time when, as a result of war, technological change, and the physical growth of the country, certain aspects of the democratic process and certain political habits had become outmoded, although the American people were not yet prepared to relinquish them. Take the fine old tradition that every citizen had access to the President. It had become an intolerable burden, for the business of the Nation was now so large it demanded all a President's time and energy. Polk found that "no President who performs his duty faithfully and conscientiously can have any leisure." He rarely took even a brief vacation and often had to toil far into the night to complete official tasks for which he found no time during the day, so besieged was he with people wanting to shake his hand or pay their respects, and with office seekers and patronage-soliciting politicians who, as he wryly put it, seemed to feel that providing jobs was "the chief end of Government."

Or take the persistence of divisive geographic and ideological interests which, in Polk's time, tended to take precedence over the national interest. So much so that politicians in all sections of the country indulged in the mischief of threatening to break up the Union whenever national action went against their parochial interests. The well-publicized quarrels in the Senate, which were caused by intrusion of these divisive factors into every foreign policy issue, were a serious handicap to Polk when he was engaged in difficult negotiations with Britain over Oregon, or sought by diplomatic means to end the war with Mexico. The American people and their leaders had not yet accepted the maxim we now take for granted that "politics end at the water's edge."

One cannot read Polk's diary without warming to this thoughtful man of uncompromising integrity whose political philosophy, as he once said, "was not of yesterday," but "formed upon mature consideration," and adhered to whether expedient at the moment or not. Having achieved the objectives of his administration, he refused renomination in order to retire to private life. He died 3 months after leaving the White House.

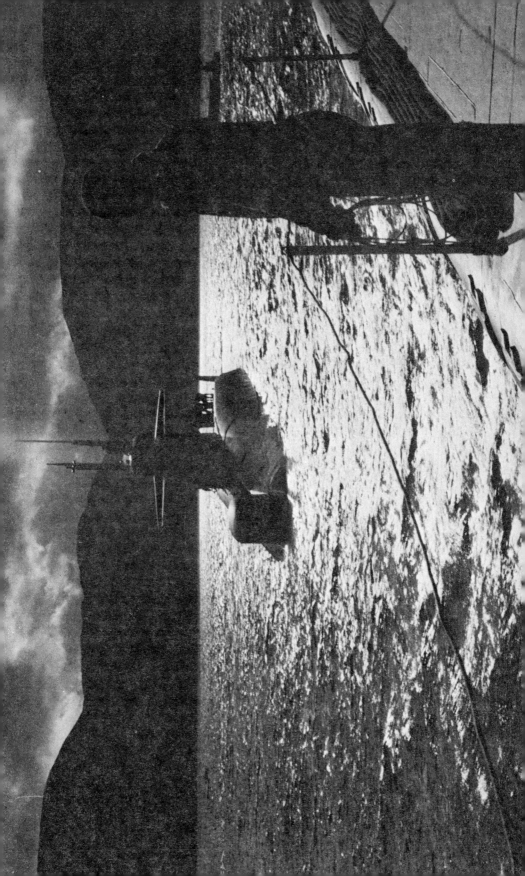

USS SAM HOUSTON (SSBN 609)

Named for Samuel Houston (1793–1863) one of the most colorful of American frontier-statesmen and a commanding presence in the early history of Texas. Famed as the victor of the Battle of San Jacinto, which won Texas her independence and made him first President of the new Republic, he deserves the greater acclaim for his courageous and farsighted efforts to preserve the Union in the face of determined opposition by his State and his region and at the cost of jeopardizing his political career in a vain attempt to stem the tide of secession.

Houston was born at Timber Ridge Plantation in Rockbridge County, Va. His family had been settled there since 1730 when great-grandfather John arrived from Ulster, accompanied by his mother, wife and six children. One of the most prominent citizens among Virginia's Presbyterian settlers beyond the Blue Ridge, he fought in the French and Indian Wars, served as magistrate, and built a stone church and several roads that were still in use two centuries later. The family continued to prosper until Sam Houston's father, a veteran of the Revolutionary War, decided to make the militia his career—a gentlemanly profession but one which dissipated most of his very considerable patrimony. Upon his death in 1807, his widow took her nine children and moved to East Tennessee (then a frontier region of North Carolina), where she was able to

USS Sam Houston (SSBN 609) *as she returns in 1963, to Holy Loch, Scotland from the first Polaris patrol in the Mediterranean Sea.*

purchase 400 acres of land and build a home for her fatherless family, all of them taking a hand at clearing and cultivating the new farm.

Sam Houston had no taste for frontier farming which demanded hard and monotonous labor and yielded meager rewards. It seemed to him that the neighboring Cherokee Indians lived more sensibly by hunting and fishing than the white settlers by toiling in their fields. Certainly theirs was a more carefree life and one whose every need could be satisfied with little effort. When his elder brothers found Sam a position as clerk in the local trader's store, this work proved no more to his liking. One day he disappeared without trace.

An intensive search for the 15-year-old truant was instituted by the settlement, but it was months before word trickled back that he was living with the Cherokees and had been adopted by their chief. The story goes that when his two older brothers went there to bring him back, they found Sam reading a translation of the *Iliad* under a tree. Begging them not to disturb him, to let him "read on in peace," he stated categorically that he much preferred "measuring deer tracks to tape," and liked "the wild liberty of the Red men better than the tyranny of his brothers." Not until he was 18 did he return home, greatly scandalizing his mother with his wild appearance and Indian ways.

Houston never forgot the years he spent among the Indians and what he learned of their lore. The closest friends of his youth were Cherokee boys and girls. To them he was known as "The Raven," the Indian name given him when he was adopted by Chief Oo-loo-te-ka. Near the end of his life, he once remarked that though he had seen "all there is to live for," he yet found "nothing half so sweet to remember as (his) sojourn among the untutored children of the forest." He was that rarity among frontiersmen — a true friend of the Indians, a man who respected them and tried to obtain justice for them. But he was no more successful in winning recognition for Indian rights than in preventing the breakup of the Union. In 1838, President Van Buren ordered the forcible removal of the Cherokees to the Indian Territory in Oklahoma where they were put down among hostile tribes. The long "trail of tears" had (temporarily) come to an end.

Houston distinguished himself in the War of 1812 serving in the Tennessee militia under Andrew Jackson, whose friend and loyal follower he became. Though severely wounded in the Battle of Horseshoe Bend (1814), he remained in the army until 1818 at which time he resigned his commission and took up the study of law. His formal schooling had been of the scantiest—a couple of years in public school, one or two terms at the Maryville academy—but in only 6 months he completed an 18-month study program laid out for him by Judge Trimble of Nashville, an old friend of the family. After being admitted to the bar, he practiced law in nearby Lebanon and was almost at once appointed prosecuting attorney (attorney-general) of the Nashville District.

Possessing all the qualities that appealed to a frontier community—a commanding presence, a fine military record, astounding vigor and extraordinary eloquence as a stump speaker—it was inevitable that he would succeed in politics. In 1823 he ran for Congress and was elected to the House without opposition; he easily won a second term in 1825, and the governorship of Tennessee in 1827. So far his life had followed a pattern that repeated itself time and time again in the lives of public figures of that day. Houston himself described it accurately in a remark he made in 1824: "Five years since I came to this place without education more than ordinary—without friends—without cash—and almost without acquaintances—consequently without much credit—and here among talents and distinctions I have made my stand! or rather the people have made it for me." Still true to the pattern, he married the daughter of one of the richest and most influential families of his State. But 3 short months later, the pattern was broken, his career at an end. His bride left him for home; Houston resigned from the governorship, turned his back on civilization and went to live with his Cherokee friends. No one knows why a man well on the road to the Presidency should have taken the breakup of his marriage so hard or, for that matter, why the marriage broke up at all.

Houston was welcomed with open arms by the Cherokees. Runners carried news of his return to every wigwam and there was a week of celebration. Soon he was established in a trading post and had married one of the companions of his youth, a collateral ancestress of Will Rogers. For half a dozen years he worked on behalf of his Indian friends: as adviser, arbitrator of their disputes with other tribes, and defender of their treaty rights. Almost yearly he made the long trip to Washington to plead their cause before the Government, usually dressed in Indian garb, for the Cherokees had formally made him a member of their tribe and Houston had resumed his Indian name, The Raven.

Only gradually, as if reluctantly, did he find the way back from his self-imposed exile. At first he went abroad only on

141

Indian business, as in 1832 when President Jackson commissioned him to negotiate a treaty with the Comanches (enemies of his own Cherokee tribe) in Texas, which was then a department of the Mexican State of Coahuila. After several visits during which he found himself drawn into the quarrels between the American settlers and the Mexican authorities, he decided to stay (spring 1835). Henceforth his life is identified with Texas.

With the preliminaries leading to the War of Independence he had little if anything to do, but it was he who brought it to a victorious end. The last chance for a peaceful settlement of the dispute between the American settlers (numbering 20–30,000) and Mexico (population six million) was lost when their petition for detachment from the State of Coahuila and establishment as a separate Mexican state was rejected and Austin, sent to present the resolves of the Convention of San Felipe, was thrown in prison by Santa Anna. On March 2, 1836, Texas declared herself independent; on the 4th, Sam Houston was chosen Commander of the Texas Army (some 743 raw recruits); on the 6th, the Alamo, which had been held by 188 Texans against an assaulting force of 3,000 Mexicans under Santa Anna, was taken and the entire garrison massacred (as were 300 defenders of Goliad 3 weeks later). By mid-April, the Mexicans had reached Galveston Bay and the war seemed almost lost.

Houston, who had been steadily retreating while building up his small force, drawing Santa Anna after himself towards the San Jacinto, suddenly launched a surprise attack (April 21, 1836) and completely defeated the enemy who outnumbered him two to one. The battle lasted but 15 minutes. Shouting "Remember the Alamo," the Texans charged with irresistible force, shooting 630 and capturing all but 50 of the original 1,200, including Santa Anna who promptly signed a treaty ordering the retreat of all his remaining forces and pledging his support of Texan independence. Houston's little army had lost six killed and 25 wounded, including its commander. Urging that Santa Anna be used as a hostage to secure peace, Houston left for New Orleans to have his wounds attended. Six months later he took the oath of office as President of the new Republic (1836–38).

He was reelected for a second term (1841–44) and, after admission of Texas to the Union, became one of its first two Senators, serving from 1846 to 1859, a staunch Union-Democrat in the tradition of Andrew Jackson, for whom the preservation of the Union always took precedence over State or regional interests. He refused to sign the "Southern Address" of 1849 for "it would excite the Southern people and drive them further from their Northern friends." Accused by Southerners of being a "traitor," he replied that he had been "actuated by as patriotic motives as any gentleman, North or South." In a moving speech, the most telling point he made was that he knew "neither North nor South" but "only the Union"; that on the floor of Congress he was a "representative of the whole American people."

He voted for the Compromise of 1850 and against the Kansas-Nebraska Bill of 1854, the only Southerner to do so. Clay and Webster had but recently died and the eagle above the chair of the Presiding Officer of the Senate was draped in black, "as if" said Houston, "it deplored the misfortune which had fallen upon us, or as a fearful omen of the future calamities which await our nation in the event this bill should become law . . . By these associations, I adjure you to regard the contract once made to harmonize and preserve this Union. *Maintain the Missouri Compromise!* Stir not up agitation! Give us peace!" He was denounced at mass meetings in the South and censored by the Texas legislature and the State Democratic Convention. His political career seemed to have come to an end. But how right he proved to be!

So popular was he among his people that they elected him Governor in 1859. In this position he labored hard to prevent the secession of Texas and, after he had been overwhelmingly overruled (34,794 to 11,255) by the Secession Convention, to keep Texas out of the Confederacy. For refusing to swear allegiance to the latter, he was deposed (1861). He died 2 years later—too early to see his premonitions vindicated.

82-336 O - 72 - 11

USS HENRY CLAY (SSBN 625)

NAMED FOR Henry Clay (1777–1852), one of the ablest parliamentarians of his time, a gifted orator whose mind, voice, and manner gave his arguments compelling force; a statesman whose personal charm and magnetism helped persuade embattled opponents to make the mutual concessions that dissolved deadlock into compromise.

Henry Clay was born in a part of Hanover County, Va., called The Slashes, at a time when the region was the scene of bitter fighting in the Revolutionary War. His ancestors, who came from England shortly after the founding of Jamestown (1607), were never able to rise above respectable poverty. Clay's father, a Baptist minister, died when the boy was 4. His widow was left with nine children and little else. After her remarriage, 10 years later, the family moved to Richmond. The stepfather, who took a kindly interest in Henry, procured him a position as clerk, first in a store, then in the High Court of Chancery. Apart from 3 years in a country school, this was all the help Clay's family was able to give him. Everything Henry Clay accomplished in life, he achieved entirely on his own.

He took the first step up the ladder when his clear and legible penmanship won him a position as secretary to the Chancellor of the High Court, who saw promise in the bright and industrious boy, lent him books, and finally advised him to study law. Thus it happened that the backwoods boy began to read for the bar under Virginia's greatest legal luminary, for the

USS HENRY CLAY (SSBN 625) *on initial sea trials in 1964.*

Chancellor was none other than George Wythe who had been Jefferson's teacher and friend. Clay finished his studies in the office of Robert Brooke, a former Governor and future Attorney General of Virginia. His association with these men taught him more than the law, for they introduced him into their social circle where he acquired the ease and charming manners that would stand him in good stead in his future career.

At 20, he passed his bar examinations and set out for Lexington, Ky., across the mountains, on the Wilderness Road hacked out by Daniel Boone and his men 20 years earlier. People still traveled in groups at that time for there remained a danger from marauding Indians. Clay arrived safely, opened a law office, and was soon reputed the best criminal lawyer in Kentucky; it was said that he never lost a client. Once, late in life, when his mind spun back to those early years, he remarked, "I remember how comfortable I thought I should be if I could make one hundred pounds, Virginia money, per year, and with what delight I received the first fifteen shillings fee. My hopes were more than realized. I immediately rushed into a successful and lucrative practice." The rapidity of his success can be measured by the growth of his taxable property which consisted of one horse in 1799; two horses and three slaves in 1800; 125 acres of first-class land and 6,400 of second-rate, a town house, 15 livestock, and eight slaves in 1805. By 1811 he had bought the land that was to become his beautiful country estate of Ashland where he grew corn, hemp, and other crops, and raised thoroughbred cattle and some of the finest race horses in the State.

Even while the law was building him a private fortune, it was losing to politics in Clay's life. Here, too, success came speedily. He served his apprenticeship in the Kentucky Legislature (1803–10), which made him Speaker in 1808 and twice sent him to Washington to fill unexpired Senate terms (1806–07, 1810–11). After his departure for the second of these terms, he never again served his State officially except in a national capacity, but to the end of his life he could count on the large and loyal following he had left behind. He would hold their minds and emotions in his hand and be sustained by them in every crisis of his political life.

From his first public appearance at 21, when he denounced the Sedition Act (1798) before a large crowd in Lexington, to the day when for the last time he feebly answered the roll call from the Senate floor, Clay gave 40 years to public service, retaining a bare dozen for private life. He served six terms in the House and some 15 years in the Senate; he represented the

United States in the peace negotiations with Britain at Ghent, and was John Q. Adams' Secretary of State.

Elected to the U.S. House of Representatives in 1811, he was at once chosen Speaker by the young "war hawks" of the West and South who organized the Twelfth Congress and pushed Madison into our second armed conflict with Britain over the vehement protest of the maritime States of the Northeast. Although the ostensible aim of the "war hawks" was for "free trade and seamen's rights," their real goal was conquest. The Westerners wanted Canada, believing Britain's removal from the continent would end Indian resistance to the demands made by land hungry American settlers; the Southerners had their eyes on Florida and Texas. The Congress they controlled paid no heed to the fact that Britain had atoned for the Chesapeake outrage and was about to suspend her offensive Orders in Council (she did so 2 days before we declared war), or that France interfered quite as much with our trade as England.

Woodrow Wilson called the war "clumsy, foolhardy, haphazard"; one might add, futile. Totally unprepared, we did not win. The peace treaty merely confirmed the *status quo ante.* Her commerce and shipping ruined by the war, New England came close to secession. Historically, the doctrine of constitutional secession, as distinct from the Lockean right of revolution, was first elaborated by the New England Federalists. Delegates from the States of that region met in secret at Hartford (1814–15) and adopted a number of antiwar resolutions based squarely on Jefferson's States' right doctrine. *Inter alia,* constitutional amendments were proposed requiring a two-thirds vote of Congress before embargoes could be imposed or war declared (except in case of actual invasion); nullification was threatened if a conscription bill then before Congress were passed. Nothing came of this. As a delegation was on its way to Washington to lay the resolutions before Congress, the war came to an end. But not before Daniel Webster, Congressman from New Hampshire, delivered an angry attack in the House, so extreme that his remarks were not published for nearly a hundred years. The majority, he said, seemed to act on the supposition "that the government possesses over us a power more tyrannical, more arbitrary, more dangerous, more allied to blood and murder, more full of every form of mischief . . . than has been exercised by any civilized government in modern times."

The War of 1812 was the most extreme instance in its time of two regions capturing the Federal Government and pursuing a national policy so obnoxious to the third that the bond of Union was loosened thereby. Clay's influence, more than any other man's precipitated that war. Perhaps he learned a lesson. In any event, it was in the immediate postwar years that he came to recognize the disruptive effects of regional conflicts and to make their abatement his primary concern.

In a country as large as ours, as various in climate and soil, as deficient (until well into the 19th century) in means of overland transport, such conflicts were inevitable. They go back to the beginning of our life as a Nation and beyond; they shaped the Constitution, gave impetus to our first political parties, precipitated a number of constitutional crises, and very nearly wrote finis to the whole American experiment in federated self-government.

Most Americans (down to the Civil War) were independent farmers producing little beyond what was consumed by their families and sold in the local market. But the country's dominant economic pursuits were concentrated geographically, centering in the South on staple crops (chiefly for export), in the Northeast on commerce and shipping, in the Northwest on diversified agriculture (later supplemented throughout the North by large-scale manufacturing). Clay saw clearly that these interests *naturally* drew the American people together within their particular regions, while placing the regions themselves in opposition to each other.

Unlike most statesmen of his time, Clay was not content with mere verbal expressions of devotion to the Union, but sought to strengthen the Federal bond by positive action pursued on two levels: on the one, he attempted by legislation to promote the growth of a balanced national economy, hoping thus to tie the great regions together in mutually profitable economic interdependence; on the other, he resolved by ingeniously balanced compromises three major conflicts (1820, 1833, 1850), any one of which might have torn the Union asunder.

His legislative program—later called the "American System"—encompassed a protective tariff to develop the industrial base of the economy and create a domestic market for farm surplus, Federal subsidies for internal improvements (roads, canals) to facilitate the overland transport of bulky goods, a National Bank to insure the monetary stability commerce needs, and an adequate navy to keep America safe from foreign attack.

In essence, these measures were an updated version of the program first proposed 25 years earlier by Hamilton, leader of the Federalists. That it should have been Clay, a Jeffersonian Republican, who fathered the "American System" was paradoxical, opposition to that program having been the primary reason for the founding of his own party in 1792 and for its electoral victory 8 years later.

The Jeffersonians objected to Hamilton's broad interpretation of the Constitution. They demanded that the constitutional grant of powers to the Federal Government be strictly construed lest the reserved rights of the States be usurped. Every action of the Federalists seemed to them to lead to a "dangerous consolidation" of the Government in Washington. The very name chosen for the new opposition party was indicative of its antithesis to the Federalists whom Jefferson was wont to call "monarchists" or "monocrats", and whom he charged with planning "a change from the present republican form of government to that of a monarchy, of which the English Constitution is to be the model." But in the intervening years circumstances, hence opinions, changed. When Clay put forth his program, it appealed to many previously opposed.

The Jeffersonians won so decisively in 1800 that for the next quarter of a century they remained in virtually undisputed control of the Government. As often happens, the shift from opposition to ruling party wrought changes in their political outlook. Within a few years, they lost the fear of Federal power which played so important a part in their campaign oratory. "Buffeted by gales from abroad and by passions at home," wrote Charles A. Beard, they were soon "exercising powers greater than any ever claimed by Hamilton and defending the constitutionality of laws which they had once rebuffed." Confronted with the practical problems involved in governing the country, they were bound to see (though they never admitted it) that much of their criticism of the Federalists had been unwarranted.

Notably so their denunciation of the Federalist buildup of a small but respectable army and navy as "unrepublican" militarism. Upon coming to power, the Jeffersonian Republicans lost no time dismantling the country's military defenses. They cut the army almost in two, and they sold all but 13 ships of the navy, replacing them with 200 small sailing vessels (each mounting but a single gun) which were to be kept in storage sheds during peacetime and manned by volunteers in case of actual invasion — "somewhat after the manner of a village fire department," as historian Wilfred E. Binkley put it. This, Jefferson said, "was the only *water* defense which can be of use to us, and protect us from the ruinous folly of a navy." But, of course, the little boats could not protect our shipping against belligerent depredations during the titanic struggle between France and Britain for control of Europe which erupted shortly after Jefferson took office, and lasted nearly a decade (1805–15). (In fact, American naval weakness invited violation of our neutral rights by both belligerents as well as British impressment of our sailors.) Nor could they prevent the British from laying waste to the Chesapeake shoreline and burning the Capitol in Washington during the War of 1812. Had Britain not been busy fighting elsewhere, the dismantling of our military forces might have had disastrous consequences for America.

If the war years thus vindicated Federalist foresight in seeking to provide the country with adequate defenses, our humiliating dependence on smuggled foreign manufactures proved the fallacy of Republican denigration of Hamilton's economic measures. Even Jefferson, that arch-agrarian, came to see that industry was as important to the welfare of the country as agriculture. And Monroe, in his First Inaugural Address (1817), promised "systematic and fostering care of the government for our manufactures."

So, too, with Hamilton's Bank of the United States, that pet aversion of the Jeffersonians. Having allowed its charter to lapse in 1811, they found it extremely difficult to finance the war and were left with a disorganized currency and a general suspension of specie payments when peace was restored.

The war gained us none of our objectives, yet in its aftermath a wave of patriotic sentiment swept the country which favored Clay's legislative program. The desire to enhance the power of the Nation took precedence (for the moment) over regional concerns. Perhaps because of Jackson's splendid victory at New Orleans (though it came too late to affect the outcome) most Americans were soon convinced we had won the war and once again humbled proud Britain. The Republican Party—the former "war hawks"—assumed a nationalism rivaling that of the Federalists (they were later called National Republicans). Led by Clay and Calhoun, they pushed much of the "American System" through Congress within a single year.

Even the agricultural sections (with no selfish interest in the promotion of manufacturing) were now prepared to accept a protective tariff. By cutting off normal English imports for over a decade, war and revolution in Europe created a sanctuary in which domestic industries were able to develop. These "infant industries" could not have survived if foreign goods stored abroad in anticipation of peace had been allowed unhindered entry into the American market. With little opposition, a moderate tariff was enacted in 1816. To aid the Government in its fiscal policies and guarantee a sound paper currency, the Second Bank of the United States was chartered. Nothing perhaps illustrates the change in party sentiment better than the fact that Republican papers reprinted Hamilton's bank report of December 13, 1790. Once bitterly attacked as advocating unconstitutional class legislation, the report was now cited to support the 1816 bill chartering the Second Bank. That same year the largest naval appropriations to date were voted. The army was placed on a respectable footing and West Point was remodeled on Washington's original plan.

Despite its promising start, Clay's program failed in the end. The first serious setback came in 1817 when a bill authorizing Federal subsidies for internal improvements (counterpart of tariff protection in Clay's formula) was vetoed by Madison on the ground that such subsidies required authorization by a constitutional amendment. (Subsequent bills were vetoed by Monroe in 1822 and Jackson in 1830.) Nor was Clay able to put through his alternative – a Distribution Scheme which would have enabled the States to support such improvements by transferring to them the Federal surplus from the sale of western lands.

Postwar nationalism proved a transient, in a sense a premature phenomenon. Public interest soon shifted from concern with building a strong national economy to the simpler objective of taking possession of our continental patrimony. (Soon "Manifest Destiny" was to become the battle cry of the agrarian imperialists.) In the 1828 election, Clay's "national" faction lost out to the "democratic" wing which took control of the party and carried its leader, Andrew Jackson, into the Presidency (in the process dropping the name "Republican" and becoming the Jacksonian "Democracy").

Clay rallied the elements opposed to Jackson (and his "executive usurpations") in a new party (1834), called Whigs after the English party which fought royal tyranny in the 17th and 18th centuries. The Whigs elected two Presidents and won a number of congressional elections but never held office long enough to put Clay's program into operation. They could not match the appeal of the exuberant expansionism and heady egalitarianism of the Jacksonians, nor effectively counteract their accusation that Clay's program favored the rich and the Eastern "money power." Jackson found it easy to arouse popular suspicion of features of the "American System" imperfectly understood by the people, notably the Bank. Destroyed by him, it could never be revived. But, in final analysis, what doomed Clay's legislative program was a growing divergence between the economies of the North and the South which precluded

151

consensus on a common economic policy. Its main features, in particular the protective tariff, cornerstone of the "American System," became fiercely divisive regional issues.

The South turned against the tariff while Northern majorities in Congress pushed for ever higher duties. In the early postwar period, protection of American manufactures had been favored by the South. Indeed, the tariff of 1816 was largely the work of two South Carolinians, Calhoun and Lowndes. She was herself then engaged in an attempt to diversify her economy by establishing industries, and had hopes that—with cotton and abundant water power (besides iron and coal deposits) at her disposal—she might rival New England, then the foremost industrial region of the country. But she could not mobilize the necessary capital and skilled labor, and the attempt failed. By the end of the 1820's, it was plain to see that the march of industry across the Continent had come to a halt—a permanent halt, so it was then believed—at the line dividing the free States of the North and the slave States of the South. The dichotomy of their respective economies was further sharpened by the coincident emergence of the South as the world's largest cotton producer and the country's premier exporting region. The interests of the North and the South, wrote Lord Acton, were now "perfectly distinct." The South, because of her large export business, needed "the utmost freedom of imports, in order not to barter at a disadvantage in the world market," while the North, "unable to compete with European manufacturers," needed restrictions on imports by protective tariffs, in order to "secure the monopoly of the home market."

It was the invention of a New England schoolteacher (Eli Whitney) which inadvertently froze the South into an economic pattern that set her apart from the rest of the Nation. His saw gin—by mechanizing separation of the tenacious lint from the green seeds of the short-staple cotton fiber—transformed a hitherto almost worthless weed into an extremely valuable commercial crop, the most profitable crop ever raised by the South. To make room for more cotton acreage, the handicraft industries and foodgrowing farms which previously supplied the South with consumer necessities (if not luxuries) were swept away, leaving the region thereafter dependent on the outside for all the manufactures and most of the food she consumed. Preoccupation with cotton growing precluded economic diversification, and the South came to believe herself destined to remain forever wedded to a staple economy, exporting most of what it produced and importing most of what it consumed.

152

As a staple grower, the South was enormously successful. She had no serious competitors either at home or abroad. During the first half of the 19th century, she produced seven-eighths of the world's total cotton crop, besides large quantities of sugar, rice, and hemp. Through improved seeds and curing processes, she regained her position as premier tobacco grower which had been temporarily lost after independence. In Lord Acton's words she "was teeming with agricultural produce for which there was a great European demand." The bulk of her products had perforce to be exported since it far exceeded domestic needs. Less than a quarter of her cotton, for example, could be utilized by American industry. And this despite the fact that the United States was the second largest consumer of the raw fiber (England ranking first by a wide margin).

To the South, it made economic sense that the ships carrying her products abroad should be loaded on the return journey with English manufactures, then still the best and cheapest in the world. Just so had she traded in colonial times, the mother country placing no burdens on the exchange. In fact, England's mercantilist policies actively nurtured this trade by granting the colonists bounties on agricultural products, guaranteeing them a protected market in England and the West Indies, and making imported manufactures available on easy terms (to the extent even of rescinding duties on certain European goods if they were transshipped to the Colonies— so-called "drawbacks").

Once aware she could not herself profit from industry, the South looked on the duties that Federal tariff laws obliged her to pay as but so many millions of dollars taken out of the pockets of her people handed over to Northern manufacturers— a form of unequal taxation she considered all the more unjust in view of the great economic value of what she produced.

Her exports benefited the country's balance of trade. By 1830 (and through the next three decades) her share of total U.S. exports never fell below 60 percent—an amount all out of proportion to her relative size and population. The fees collected for handling her commercial transactions profited the very regions most insistent on raising duties. (Diverted into the so-called "cotton triangle," the toll levied on Southern exports and imports by New York City, for example, was estimated at 40 cents on the dollar.)

Southern resentment reached the explosive point in 1828 with passage of the so-called "tariff of abominations" (which tripled the rates of the 1816 act). Coming at a time of depressed world cotton prices, the new Federal exactions were doubly

153

obnoxious, especially to the older States of the South whose land was declining in productivity because of the wasteful methods of cotton culture. Already hard pressed to compete with the new States of the Deep South with their still unravaged virgin soils, they saw in the tariff the instrument of their ultimate ruin. Led by South Carolina, half the Southern State legislatures adopted protest resolutions. But Congress paid no heed. The new tariff enacted in 1832 gave no real relief to the South.

It was then the South became convinced that in a Union in which she was in the minority, her economic needs were not going to be satisfied unless she could by constitutional means prevent the majority from passing laws detrimental to her. So greatly did her needs now differ from those of the country at large that *any* intrusion of the Government into the economy was against her interest. To hold such intrusions to a minimum, she now turned to strict constructionism and the States' rights and nullification doctrines first enunciated by Jefferson and incorporated in the Kentucky and Virginia Resolves in 1798–99. As an alternative, should these constitutional means fail, she was already considering secession. Henceforth the South opposed all demands of the free areas of the country for such economic assistance from the Federal Government as protective tariffs, internal improvements, subsidies for transatlantic shipping and the like.

When (after 1763) the government in London taxed the American Colonies without their consent to help defray the costs of Empire, they counted for nothing the economic advantages they enjoyed as members of that Empire and severed the tie with the mother country. Just so, the South now began to question whether the advantages she enjoyed as a member of the Union were worth the price of being taxed against her will by the Government in Washington to help build up domestic industries.

The 1828 resolutions of the South Carolina Legislature pronounced the "tariff of abominations" oppressive, unjust, and unconstitutional. They are accompanied by a lengthy essay written by Calhoun — the *South Carolina Exposition* — presenting what was to become the acknowledged Southern version of the States' rights and nullification doctrines (public addresses and letters written in 1831 and 1832 gave them their final embodiment). For Calhoun, this meant a total reversal of the political position he had heretofore taken. A close colleague of Clay's in the nationalist faction of the Republican Party, he now became the most influential spokesman for Southern regionalism.

Protective tariffs were unconstitutional, he said. The commerce clause empowered the Government to levy duties for revenue purposes, but not to protect the manufacturing regions against foreign competition. The Constitution did not authorize the Government "to descend from its high appointed duty and become the agent of a portion of the community to extort under the guise of protection, tribute from the rest of the community." If one of the States of the minority considered any particular Federal act to be *ultra vires*, it clearly had the right to suspend the operation of the act within its own domain. Protective tariffs, being of this nature, were therefore "void and of no effect," the Constitution itself nullifying acts not authorized under its terms.

A spirited rejoinder came from Madison who, though in his eighties, was still actively concerned with the proper interpretation of the Constitution. The States, he pointed out, had yielded control of foreign commerce to the Federal Government. "In all nations this regulating power embraced the protection of domestic manufactures by duties and restrictions on imports." Had an exception been made by the Constitution, the American people would "present the solitary and strange spectacle of a nation disarming itself of a power exercised by every nation" in the world. This, Madison maintained, was clearly understood at the time the Constitution was framed—in proof of which he pointed to the tariff of 1789, the first piece of legislation passed by the First Congress sitting under the Constitution, many of whose members (including Madison) had been delegates of the Convention which drew up the Constitution or of the State conventions which ratified it.

While the primary purpose of the 1789 tariff was to provide urgently needed revenue for the Federal Government, its intent (as stated in the preamble) also was "encouragement and protection of manufactures" (a term which in that pre-industrial age applied to handicraft industries, small in scale and—in America—usually owner-operated). Responding to a flood of petitions from mechanics and artisans in the Northern States, Congress had levied moderate duties (at the average rate of 8½ percent *ad valorem*) on such articles as iron, nails, glass, cordage, which the ex-colonials were as yet unable to produce as cheaply as the mother country. The authority of Congress to protect home industries was taken for granted, not only by those who had favored adoption of the Constitution, but by those who had opposed it as well. What then could justify denying this power to Congress 40 years later?

Dismissing out of hand all attempts to deduce from the official records of the Constitution "that it was intended to withhold from Congress a power to protect manufactures by commercial regulations," Madison declared bluntly that "no such inference can be sustained." In searching for the meaning of any particular phrase, "it should never be forgotten, that the great object of the Convention was to provide by a new Constitution, a remedy for the defects of the existing one." One of these defects was that the Confederation Congress had not been given authority to regulate commerce, each State remaining free to pursue its own trade policies. The result was that all suffered from commercial anarchy at home and none were able to deal effectively with commercial aggression from without. Indeed, it was the need for joint action in handling the country's commercial problems which gave the final impetus to reform the whole Federal system.

These were telling arguments. Especially so, coming from Madison who spoke with greater authority than any other contemporary American. He had been a prime mover in the events that led to adoption of the Constitution and he was (in 1828) the sole surviving member of the Constitutional Convention, as well as the guardian of the most accurate and detailed account of its proceedings—to wit, his own diary which was not released for publication until after his death in 1836.

The Constitutional Convention of 1787 had its genesis in the commercial convention at Annapolis the preceding year, to which (at Madison's urging) Virginia had invited her sister States to discuss "how far a uniform system in their commercial relations will be necessary to their common interest and their permanent harmony." The Annapolis meeting issued a report recommending that all 13 States convene the following year at Philadelphia "to render the constitution of the Federal Government adequate to the exigencies of the Union," and in particular to give consideration to "the trade and commerce of the United States." Clear-cut as to purpose, definite as to time and place, this call from Annapolis spurred Congress and the States to action.

It was evident to everyone in the Constitutional Convention that the power to regulate commerce and navigation would have to be transferred from "the states individually to the states collectively"—to use a phrase beloved by Madison. But *how* this power was to be exercised was in dispute from the start.

156

Having lost the imperial trading privileges that nourished their trade and shipping, the Northern States demanded complete and unfettered Federal control through the normal legislative process (i.e. by majority decision in the Congress). The postwar years showed conclusively that individually they could prevent neither the flooding of the American market by English goods nor the preemption of the American carrying trade by English ships. In 1787, nine out of 10 ships in American ports were flying the British ensign, and 90 percent of American exports (chiefly Southern staples) were being shipped in British bottoms. The situation was ruinous for the North where commerce and shipping were of great importance. But for the South — having neither — it was advantageous since foreign competition kept down the commodity prices and freight rates she had to pay.

Being numerically inferior, the South was reluctant to yield powers to the Federal Government that might be used to her detriment by Northern majorities. To secure their region a veto over legislation imposing undue economic burdens, the Southern delegates demanded a two-thirds vote for commercial and navigation laws. The Northern delegates were adamantly opposed, fearing the South might use this veto power to block passage of laws vitally needed by their own region. For 3 months the impasse seemed unbreakable. Not until the last 2 weeks of deliberations was a compromise solution found.

In return for substantial Northern concessions, the Southern delegates dropped their demand for a two-thirds vote and agreed to the commerce clause as it now stands. The South won the "Federal ratio" (which allowed her to count three-fifths of her slaves for purposes of apportioning seats in the House of Representatives — as well as direct taxes). The North agreed to prohibition of export taxes (to protect the interests of Southern staple exporters) and to the inclusion of the fugitive slave clause (which precluded the free States from granting asylum to runaway slaves). To reach agreement, both sides had to make sacrifices that did not come easily. But without such compromises, the Constitution could not have been written.

The delegates represented sovereign States which could neither legally nor forcibly be coerced into acceding to changes in the existing Federal system. "The Union," said the Articles of Confederation, "shall be perpetual," and the Articles "shall be inviolably observed by every state." According to Article XIII, alterations could be made only if unanimously agreed to in Congress and "confirmed by the legislatures of every state."

No single State or combination of States would at that time have been either willing or able to compel another's assent to abrogation of the Articles by the Constitution. (Necessity, of course, might force the hand of a reluctant State, as happened with the two stragglers whose ratifications came in after the Constitution had been declared in force.) Every clause in this charter representing mutual accommodations of divergent views and interests was a treaty in miniature, negotiated by the delegates as agents of principals who acknowledged no sovereign above them, and validated by the people of the several States through specially elected ratification conventions.

Of necessity, the end result was not a document ideally conceived in the abstract but the best plan of government attainable at the time. "That it will meet the full and entire approbation of every State is not perhaps to be expected," wrote Washington in his letter transmitting the Constitution to the Congress for submission to the States. "But each will doubtless consider, that had her interests been alone consulted, the consequences might have been particularly disagreeable or injurious to others." Summarizing with admirable brevity and clarity the difficulties encountered by the delegates at Philadelphia, he called the Constitution "the result of a spirit of amity, and of that mutual deference and concession which the peculiarity of our political situation rendered indispensable."

The political situation at the end of the Revolutionary War was one of confusion and distress, internal dissension and external weakness, "filling every well informed patriot with the most acute anxieties," as Madison said. The bonds of union were fragile, the danger of a breakup ever present, with powerful neighbors ready to pick up the pieces, the British to the north, the Spanish to the west and south. The American States had been able (with the help of France) to win the war loosely allied, each State retaining "its sovereignty, freedom and independence" (Articles of Confederation, II), but to survive and prosper they needed a stronger union, a more effective common government. This could be had only at the cost of sacrificing the independence the States had just won in 8 years of hard fighting. It was obviously impracticable, Washington wrote in his letter of transmittal, "to secure all rights of independent sovereignty to each state and yet provide for the interest and safety of all." We perhaps can understand better than past generations of Americans how hard it must have been for the States to surrender their newly won freedom. We, after all, have been witness to the agonizingly slow and reluctant move of the European states towards political union.

There were no precedents to guide the American States and their delegates in the Convention. Never before had a Confederation of sovereign States by voluntary agreement transformed itself into a Federal Republic in which sovereignty was divided between the central government and the constituent States. To "draw a precise line between those rights which must be surrendered, and those which may be retained" by the States was a difficult enough task by itself, wrote Washington, but it was rendered even more difficult "on the present occasion" because of the "difference of the several States as to their situation, extent, habits, and particular interests." The existence of divergent and conflicting *regional* interests was still another complicating factor. But the delegates kept steadily in view what appeared to them "the greatest interest of every true American, the consolidation of our Union, in which is involved our prosperity, felicity, safety and perhaps our national existence." And this important consideration led each State to be less right "than might otherwise have been expected." As it finally emerged after 4 months of debates, disputes, and deadlocks (each eventually resolved by mutual concessions), the Constitution was truly a miracle of compromise and balanced power.

But of itself, it could not prevent sectional strife. The delegates at Philadelphia had hoped regionalism would abate. In a generation, they told each other, we shall all be simply *Americans.* No one then foresaw the divergent paths North and South would take. After 40 years under the Constitution, the parties to the carefully balanced North-South compromises of the Constitution were faced with consequences of their mutual concessions they had not anticipated and were no longer willing to accept. Little was left of the "spirit of amity" of which Washington spoke, while the danger from without which motivated these compromises had disappeared entirely. And so they tried to renege on them by reinterpreting the Constitution which, being a basic charter, was of necessity couched in general terms lending themselves to conflicting interpretations. During the Missouri crisis (1819–20), the North tried to deny the "Federal ratio" to slave States carved out of the Louisiana Territory by claiming that the word "states" in Article I, sec. 2 of the Constitution referred to the 13 original States only. During the tariff crisis (1828–33), the South denied the validity of protective tariffs on the ground that the word "commerce" did not include manufactures. Neither claim is borne out by the language of the Constitution or the records we have of the intent of its framers.

159

This constitutional issue remained alive and unresolved throughout the "middle" period, the nationalist and States' rights arguments being reiterated again and again. Historians record a score or more instances where now one State, one part of the country, now another claimed the right to disregard the majority will on the ground that Federal action exceeded constitutional authority; and almost as many where erstwhile nullifiers denounced nullification by others when the tables were turned. Within Jefferson's own party, nationalist policies based on a broad construction of the Constitution had appeared almost as soon as it ceased having an effective opposition; to counteract them, so did a States' rights opposition of which Calhoun was to become the most influential theoretician.

When Congress disregarded the protests of the South and enacted the tariff of 1832, South Carolina called a special State convention which (on November 24, 1832) passed an Ordinance of Nullification declaring both tariffs "unauthorized by the Constitution," and therefore "null, void, and no law, nor binding upon this State, its officers and citizens." Forbidding Federal officials to collect duties within the State, the Ordinance threatened immediate secession if an attempt were made to do so by force. An army of 12,000 men was raised, public officials (except members of the legislature) were required to take an oath of allegiance to the State, and appeals to the U.S. Supreme Court of any case arising under the Ordinance were forbidden. President Jackson declared that "disunion by armed force is treason" and took prompt measures to put down the revolt.

No other State heeded South Carolina's appeal to join her in defiance of the Federal Government (though the South was virtually unanimous in condemning the tariffs as unjust and unconstitutional). It was widely feared, however, that should fighting begin, the South would rally to her support and the insurrection become general. The drift towards civil war was stopped when Clay offered a settlement saving face all around. He proposed enactment of a compromise tariff, retaining the protective principle but providing for gradual reduction of existing rates over a 10-year period until they reached the level of the tariff of 1816. In return, the supremacy of national law was to be upheld by passing a pending bill authorizing armed enforcement of the law, if necessary. Clay's Compromise Tariff and the Force Bill were duly passed, and signed by Jackson on March 2, 1833.

As a means of forcing the majority to abide by the minority's strict construction of the constitutional limits of Federal power, nullification thus proved highly successful, even though its legality was by implication denied in the Force Bill. The South gained her objective. Except during brief intervals when the Whigs controlled Congress, tariffs went steadily downward, even though the growth of industrialization outside the South won the support of ever larger numbers for protective duties. Thus, more than twice as many Western votes went against than for the tariff of 1857 which reduced rates to a point that placed the United States virtually among the free trade nations. So, too, with Federal subsidies for internal improvements. There was increasing demand for such aid, principally from the West which the South managed to thwart. But the frustrations and discontents she thus engendered sparked the first truly effective opposition to the long reign of the Southern dominated Democratic Party.

In the light of subsequent events, the soundness of Clay's program is evident. Though his party was as short-lived as the Federalists (it dissolved in 1854), a remnant formed the nucleus of the new opposition party which took the name "Republican" which Jackson had discarded in 1828 (thus causing confusion ever after to American school boys and foreign visitors trying to make sense of our party nomenclature). Abraham Lincoln, a life-long Whig, joined the Republicans in 1856 and 4 years later ran successfully for the Presidency on a platform which included Clay's program *in toto* (initiating a half century of eclipse of the Democrats). The defection of the Southern delegations from Congress in 1861 finally enabled the Northern majority to obtain the tariffs they had sought for over three decades.

The nullification crisis of 1828–33 was the second major regional conflict resolved by Clay; the first (which turned on the issue of slavery in the territory bought from France in 1803) occurred in the midst of the Era of Good Feeling when Missouri asked (1819) to be admitted as a slave State. The Northern-controlled House amended the bill of admission by prohibiting introduction of slaves into the new State, and providing for gradual emancipation of those already in the territory (about 10,000); the Senate, where the South held the balance of power, rejected the bill. Congress adjourned, the issue went to the people, and intense sectional antagonisms were let loose. North and South, uttering threats of secession, stood lined up against each other in the positions on which 40 years hence they would go to war. In the end, Clay's "reconciling formula" was accepted, though not without difficulty (the debate in the House was acrimonious and caused a 29-hour continuous session—the longest to date), but the Missouri Compromise laid the issue to rest for a generation.

Missouri was admitted with slavery, Maine without, thus making a total of 12 free and 12 slave States. North of a line drawn at 36 degrees 30 across the territory acquired by the Louisiana Purchase, slavery was "forever" barred, Missouri to be the sole exception; south of the line it was permitted. The larger portion was retained for freedom but the South gained base areas favorable to cotton growing; nearly all the land, in fact, that could profitably be worked by slaves. Each side won its most important objective: The South retention of the balance of free and slave States in the Union, the North confirmation of the right of Congress to legislate on slavery in the territories. The South got the better bargain since admission of free and slave States in pairs had been merely a policy unilaterally proclaimed by her, whereas the Constitution itself explicitly states that "Congress shall have power to dispose and make all needful rules and regulation" respecting the Federal domain (Art. IV, Sec. 3). The clause, adopted with little discussion since the matter was considered settled, merely confirmed the authority of Congress to exercise the functions vested in its predecessor under the Northwest Ordinance of 1787. (The Ordinance went into effect while the Constitutional Convention was in session. It was formally reenacted by Congress in 1789.)

By all odds the most important legislation passed under the Articles of Confederation, the Ordinance followed in its essentials the "Plan of Government" drafted by Jefferson in 1784 for "the Western Territory"—the crown lands surrendered by Britain at the end of the War of Independence and "ceded or to be ceded by Individual states to the United States." Having been won "by the blood and treasure" of all 13 former Colonies, it was agreed (largely at Maryland's insistence) that these lands should be held as common property, the seven States having vague and overlapping claims thereto (based on colonial charters) promising to relinquish them (as, in due time, they all did). Congress appointed a committee (chaired by Jefferson) to provide for the temporary governance and eventual transition to statehood of this immense wilderness lying between the Appalachians and the Mississippi (an area almost as large as that of all 13 States combined). Ranked by many with the Declaration of Independence among Jefferson's greatest contributions to the American political system, his "Plan" provided for orderly and rapid passage through limited self-government to complete equality with the older States. Notable among the conditions it established for admission to the Union was exclusion of slavery (others were a minimum population, a republican form of government, assumption of a share of the Federal debt, etc.)

Jefferson's hope was that by barring slavery from the new States to come out of the Federal domain, it would in time disappear altogether, a hope widely shared at the time. It was taken for granted in the Constitutional Convention that Congress would apply the principles of the Ordinance to *all* Federal territories. James Wilson, of Pennsylvania, one of the most influential delegates (and a member of the Committee of Detail) assured the ratification convention of his home State (deeply disturbed by continuance of the slave trade for 20 more years) that "the new states which are to be formed will be under the control of Congress in this particular, and slaves will never be introduced amongst them."

But, in point of law, the Ordinance was not binding outside the area north of Ohio (the only Federal territory at that time, since as yet only Massachusetts, New York, Connecticut, and Virginia had surrendered their claims). The cessions subsequently made by the Carolinas and Georgia (from which Tennessee, Mississippi, and Alabama were formed) expressly specified that all the provisions of the Northwest Ordinance were to apply, *except* the slavery ban, while Kentucky was formed on land never ceded by Virginia, thus becoming automatically, as it were, a slave State. Its admission to the Union in 1792 made the Ohio River from the Virginia border westward the boundary between the free Northwest and the slave Southwest (as the Mason-Dixon line marked the boundary between the free North and the slave South).

There was thus a certain justification for the division of the Louisiana Territory along 36 degrees 30 in that this merely extended the existing demarcation westward at about the same latitude. But by permitting slavery to spread into areas to which no slave State individually had any claim, an area bought by the Nation and paid for out of general taxes, the Missouri Compromise opened a Pandora's box of troubles that would exacerbate the relations of the free and slave States for the next 40 years. News of the settlement aroused the 77-year-old Jefferson "like a firebell in the night," filling him "with terror." In sadly prophetic words, he wrote a friend: "I consider it at once as the knell of the Union. It is hushed, indeed, for the moment. But this is a reprieve only, not a final sentence. A geographical line, coinciding with a marked principle, once conceived and held up to the angry passions of men, will never be obliterated; and every new irritation will make it deeper and deeper."

In 1820, however, there was no way of avoiding the drawing of a "geographical line" across the territory Jefferson had bought from France. In conformity with international principles, the inhabitants of the settled part of the area (who held their slaves under Spanish and French law) had been guaranteed their property rights by the treaty of cession. Louisiana was therefore routinely admitted as a slave State (1812), with only the New England Federalists, a powerless minority in Congress, futilely protesting. The Ordinance of 1787, with its slavery ban, might have been made part of the Purchase Treaty insofar as the huge area not yet settled was concerned, but the opportunity was overlooked (both by Jefferson and the Congress of 1803). In consequence, there was no legal bar to subsequent extension of slavery into this territory, and the South had enough political power to make good her claim to a share of the newly acquired areas.

Grave issues, when postponed, grow harder to resolve. When disposal of the land ceded by Mexico in the Treaty of Guadalupe Hidalgo (1848) reopened the controversy over slavery in the territories, a compromise acceptable to both North and South proved extraordinarily difficult to work out, the positions of both having hardened in the interval.

Maintenance of the existing equilibrium between the slave and free States was rapidly becoming the *sine qua non* for continued allegiance of the South to the Union. As a minimum, she demanded that slavery be permitted in every new State to be formed of territory South of the 36 degree 30 line (which cut halfway across California). Meanwhile, resistance to any further extension of slavery was on the increase in the North. The Wilmot Proviso, introduced into Congress in 1846, provided that "as an express and fundamental condition" to the acquisition of any territory by negotiation with Mexico, "neither slavery nor involuntary servitude shall ever exist in any part of said territory." The Proviso remained under congressional consideration until the end of the war in 1848. Though it passed the House in two consecutive sessions (1846 and 1847), it was lost in the Senate. But the idea of a general ban on slavery in the territories was gaining ground outside the South; witness its inclusion in the party platform of the Free Soilers in 1848 (and subsequently of the new Republican Party).

One of the complicating factors in the crisis over the disposition of the Mexican war gains was that Mexico had abolished slavery in 1829, as had most of the former Spanish colonies when they attained political freedom. (Clay once remarked that in this aspect of progress our Southern neighbors were ahead of us.) If Southern demands were met, the raising of the American flag would bring slavery back to a huge territory (comprising half the land possessed by Mexico when she won independence, an area larger than France and Germany combined) where for a generation it had been banned by law—a prospect many in the North found unacceptable.

A story is told that when slavery was abolished in one of the Latin American countries, masters and slaves celebrated the day of emancipation by attending midnight mass together. Fact or fiction, it underlines the *comparatively* easier transition to freedom outside the United States. The South was not a colony for which the North could decree emancipation as England and other European colonial powers had done for their overseas possessions; neither could she be economically coerced, since she was a world trader and in no way dependent on the rest of the country. Slavery was a matter left exclusively to the jurisdiction of the States by the Constitution which would otherwise not have been accepted by the South. While elsewhere a law or decree sufficed, only a constitutional amendment could free the American slaves. There was no practical possibility that such an amendment would pass. The slave States were singularly impervious to the antislavery sentiments of the North and there were at all times enough to prevent adoption (even today it takes but 13 States to veto an amendment, and there were 15 slave States in 1850). In no other civilized country did it take a civil war to end slavery, but only by defeating the Southern States in war and reducing them to the status of conquered provinces could the 13th (as well as the 14th and 15th) amendment have been put through.

In 1850, slavery was being rapidly abolished throughout the Western World. That we in this country should have been less successful than others (often less gifted politically) in ridding ourselves of this incubus has long puzzled foreign observers. H. G. Wells may be right in claiming that North and South went to war because "the river steamboats, the railway, the telegraph, and their associate facilities, did not come soon enough to avert the deepening conflict of interests and ideas between the southern slaveholding States and the free industrial north." One might put it in more general terms and say that the *timing* of the Industrial Revolution was a significant factor in creating this conflict—that, if modern transport and communications came too late to bind North and South together, the almost simultaneous invention of the cotton gin in America and of spinning and weaving machinery in England came too early.

165

Slavery was a decaying institution when cotton gave it a new lease on life. Had the mechanization of ginning, spinning, and weaving the fiber been delayed a half century or so, slavery might by then no longer have existed in the South. For there is reason to believe she would eventually have followed the example of the North (where prompt steps were taken to end slavery), if not for humanitarian reasons, then because declining profits from tobacco and indigo (two of the principal plantation crops) and exhaustion of the soil would have made slave labor as unprofitable there as it was in the North. Before the development of cotton culture, wrote Woodrow Wilson, "slavery had hardly more than habit and the perils of emancipation to support it in the South."

But the Industrial Revolution made the exploitation of unskilled labor more profitable than it had ever been before, thus fastening slavery on the American South and bringing to the English Midlands those "Dark Satanic mills" whose horror has probably never been surpassed in any civilized country. Under conditions extremely harmful to health, children from 5 years on up labored 14–15 hours for little more than their keep; "apprenticeship" it was called, and destitute parents were denied aid from their parish unless they handed over their children to be indentured to a mill owner. Southern apologists never missed a chance to point out that in New England, too, free mill hands worked for little more than subsistence and lacked the slave's security against sickness and old age; that, in fact, a larger share of the planter's than the mill owner's profit went to labor.

The soil and climate of the Southern black belt (much enlarged by the Louisiana Purchase) were ideally suited to cultivation of short-staple cotton. The region's river system provided easy and economical transportation direct from plantation to seaport and from there to the mills of New England and the English Midlands. American cotton was not only the cheapest, but of all types the best suited to the new mechanized textile industry which came to depend almost entirely on the Southern crop. In response to rising demand, cotton growing expanded rapidly and the cost of slaves rose correspondingly. By midcentury, it was estimated that twice as much capital had been invested by the South in slaves than by the North in manufacturing plants. Land and slaves made up almost the whole of Southern wealth.

Fear for the security of this vast investment created the 1850 crisis. If the South were not allowed her share of the newly won territories, said Calhoun, free States would soon outnumber slave States and "the equilibrium which existed when the Government commenced" would be "effectually and irretrievably" destroyed. Already strained because of this conflict of interests, relations between the free and slave parts of the country were further exacerbated by the determined and vociferous agitation of Northern abolitionists—"men driven by the primary and unreasoning passion of pity."

The abolitionists were numerically insignificant, unpopular everywhere, and unsuccessful at the ballot box, drawing at the height of the movement only 2.5 percent of the popular vote (Liberty Party, 1844). Nor were they able to influence either of the major parties. (After 20 years of intensive anti-slavery propaganda, the Democrats—with a pro-slavery platform—carried all but four States in the 1852 Presidential elections.) They helped keep alive in the North a commitment to Jefferson's principle of excluding slavery from the Federal territories (witness its restatement in the Wilmot Proviso of 1846, and inclusion in the platforms of the Free Soil and Republican Parties, founded 1848 and 1854 respectively). But they also so alarmed the South that she hardened in opposing this principle and insisted on maintenance of the equilibrium between free and slave States, as the price of her continued allegiance to the Union.

What assurance did the South then have that the North, where abolitionist sentiments were gaining ground, would not force her to sacrifice this vast property in slaves? Secession feeling ran high throughout the South when the people of California—not having any slaves, nor being legally bound by the Missouri Compromise—voted 17 to 1 for a free State constitution and, without waiting for congressional action, set up a functioning government (even as Texas had done some years back, both these States having won their independence from Mexico without help from the United States). The South called a convention which was expected to lead to formation of a separate Confederacy.

Like minorities today, the South pushed the traditional worship of constitutional rights to a point which subordinated the whole American legal system (by Taney's court interpretation) to the needs of one peculiar and obsolete system of labor. This went far beyond the demands of South Carolina and Georgia in 1787. The interests of the South had come to demand the propagation of slavery as a constitutional right, if necessary in defiance of local opinion.

But for Clay's compromise, the South would have left the Union and most likely won her independence. Calhoun thought so and was filled with despair. The only future he could see for the South in the Union was one of diminishing influence and growing danger to her way of life. Calling on every last ounce of his waning strength, he wrote one more speech which he hoped would prevent adoption of the Compromise (someone else had to read it for him for Calhoun was at death's door). Clay, too, was feeble and in ill health but, returning from retirement, he ran for the Senate (and was elected in 1849) in order to try once more to hold the sections together. And again he was able to contrive a "reconciling" formula.

He proposed a series of separate measures, each balancing the demands of one section against those of the other—as his compromise for the District of Columbia which sought to appease the North by abolishing the slave trade and the South by retaining slavery until Maryland consented to its abolition. The most difficult problem was that the old line of 36 degrees 30 no longer offered an acceptable solution to the conflicting claims of North and South. Nothing could have induced California to divide herself into a free and slave section, while the other territories south of the line (Utah, New Mexico) were unsuitable for slave agriculture. Thus only Texas was left to the South in the game of matching free and slave States. Several slave States could have been cut out of Texas, thus assuring Southern equality in the Senate for some years to come, but her consent was unattainable. Only a more stringent fugitive slave law could win the consent of the South to Clay's compromise. The existing Federal law (passed in 1793) was being systematically evaded by a number of Northern States. The South had long demanded a new law that would hold them more strictly to their constitutional obligation to return escaped slaves to their owners upon request. This, Clay knew, he could not obtain without Webster's support.

Wracked by a painful cold, the 73-year-old Clay walked through a snowstorm to Webster's house asking for help. No compromiser by nature and all his life a strong opponent of slavery, Webster was moved by Clay's ardent plea that without the Fugitive Slave Law there could be no peaceful solution of the crisis and consented to speak in its favor (the law, however, proved unenforceable, public opinion having sickened of watching Federal marshals chasing escaped slaves through Northern streets).

The several measures constituting the Compromise of 1850 were passed by Congress. After the death of President Taylor who had been unalterably opposed, the bill was signed by his successor (Fillmore). Both political parties incorporated it into their platforms. Newspapers carried banner headlines "The Country is Saved," a 100-gun salute was fired on Boston Common, and the Nation gave a collective sigh of relief, certain the matter was now settled once and for all. Clay's Kentucky cherished him but Webster was bitterly attacked for his support of the Compromise, Horace Mann the educator calling him "Lucifer descending from Heaven."

Sometimes Clay thought himself a failure: his party condemned to minority status, his economic program failing of adoption, the grand prize he so eagerly sought eluding him (he was defeated in three presidential elections, twice failed of nomination). But success lay in another direction. He will always be remembered as the "Great Compromiser," the "Great Pacificator," the man who, by resolving the crises of 1820, 1833, and 1850 bought time—time that wisely used might have prevented the Civil War.

USS DANIEL WEBSTER (SSBN 626)

NAMED FOR Daniel Webster (1782–1852), foremost constitutional lawyer and the leading New England statesman of his time; a man of towering intellect, whose superb oratorical technique, commanding presence, and magnificent baritone voice gave compelling force to his arguments in and out of Congress. We have eyewitness reports that he held juries, judges, and assemblies of plain citizens spellbound for hours on end, his short, incisive sentences carrying them irresistibly along the logical path leading to the conclusion he wanted them to accept. In an age of great oratory devoted chiefly to the defense of regional interests, Webster did more than anyone else to fix in the minds of Americans a clear concept of the special nature of their "compact republic," and to awaken in their hearts a devotion to the Union that in time would take precedence over sectional loyalty.

Daniel Webster's parents were fourth generation New England farmers whose ancestors had come from England in the late 1630's. His father, Ebenezer, as a young man of 20 fought with General Jeffrey Amherst during the invasion of Canada (1759), rising from private to captain, and receiving 225 acres of bounty land in the wilderness of the upper Merrimack valley near what is now the town of Franklin, New Hampshire. He built a log cabin, cleared a farm, married, and had 10 children (by two wives). When the cabin got too small for his growing family, he built a frame house, thus inadvertently robbing his famous son of the important political asset of being born in a log cabin.

Ebenezer had received no schooling but taught himself to read and write. Dirt poor all his life and often in debt, he was yet a man of standing in the community. To wring a living for his large family from the meager soil of his farm, he had to work extemely hard, yet he found time to take an active part in public life. He helped found Salisbury, N.H. (Daniel's birthplace), and served it in many capacities: highway surveyor, moderator of the town meeting, town clerk, selectman, coroner, and, jointly with the town's lawyer and minister, founder of a circulating library, one of the first in the region. For a number of years, he was a member of the State legislature. As captain of militia, later promoted colonel, he fought through the whole of the Revolutionary War, returning occasionally to keep the farm going and his family fed, to help frame a constitution for his State, to enlist men and raise money for the war; hurrying back again to fight still another battle, until, after 8 years, freedom was at last won.

Twice he and his men guarded George Washington, and the General commended Captain Webster. His words were deeply cherished. It was a proud moment in Ebenezer's life when, as New Hampshire elector, he cast his vote for Washington in our country's first presidential election (1789). Like most New Englanders of his time, he was a Federalist; if nothing else, the war had taught him the value of a strong Central Government. From him, Daniel absorbed a deep devotion to the Constitution and the Federal Republic it established. He grew up midst talk of the great men and events of the Revolution by people who knew of them at first hand, especially after Ebenezer built a two-story house and opened a wing as a tavern for travelers along the main north-south highway that cuts through Salisbury.

That Daniel was unusually bright and ought to be given an education was obvious to his parents, as indeed to all who came in contact with the boy. But there was no chance of that until Ebenezer was appointed lay judge of the County Court of Common Pleas—his first *paid* public office. The small annual stipend would just suffice to have the boy prepared for college at Exeter Academy and put through Dartmouth, but Daniel declared that his brother Ezekiel, too, must have a college education. The two boys were throughout life as close as twins. They talked the matter over, devised a plan and brought it before a family council. Thus began the project to make "learned" men of two boys in a family that had never aspired to more than the status of independent farmers. Mutual help and sacrifice, unusual even in the most close-knit of families accomplished the project.

The parents sold their property, the sons promised to take care of them in their old age—which they did with tender care.

After admission to the bar, Daniel contented himself with a small village practice at Boscawen to be near his father and, upon the latter's death in 1806, made generous provisions for his mother and two sisters. The boys took turns studying and earning money. At times the going was hard. When Daniel's salary as a teacher would not stretch to pay off a family debt and keep Ezekiel at Dartmouth as well, he took extra work laboriously copying official documents far into the night. Four evenings' work earned him enough to pay a week's room and board. "This," he wrote, "appeared to me a very thriving condition." Meanwhile Ezekiel, after matriculating at Dartmouth, reported his total assets as one cent.

From this joint bootstrap operation they emerged with a sound general and professional education. Daniel was widely read and a good enough Latinist to have some of his translations of Horace's *Odes* published in the papers; he was fortunate enough to read law under Christopher Gore, one of New England's best lawyers. The two young Websters prospered; Ezekiel, lacking his brother's genius, on a more modest scale than Daniel who, once he was free to give all his energies to his own career, rose rapidly to the top of the profession and made a success in politics as well.

His life divides neatly into a New Hampshire and a Massachusetts half, the first in a way a preparation for the second. After his father's death, he turned the Boscawen practice over to Ezekiel and established himself in Portsmouth, N.H., then a thriving shipping and shipbuilding center. There, in competition with an unusually able bar, he sharpened his skills, won distinction, and built a profitable practice. From the start, he was involved in public affairs; championing, in speeches and writings, New England's trading interests which were being ruined as much by Jefferson's Embargo and Non-Intercourse Acts at home as by belligerent interference abroad. Portsmouth itself went into a decline as a result of the War of 1812 into which the country had been pushed by Western and Southern "war hawks" over New England's bitter protest. Elected to the U.S. House of Representatives (1813–17), Webster was harshly critical of Congress and voted against bounties to encourage enlistment, and taxes to pay for the war. Later his Southern opponents would accuse him of having been a nullifier, even a secessionist when his own region was being injured by Federal action, but Webster never went beyond verbal protests. "Resistance and insurrection form no part of our creed," he once said of his party. "By the exercise of our constitutional right of suffrage, by the peaceable remedy of election, we shall seek to restore wisdom to our councils and peace to our country." Faced with precisely the same situation that led Calhoun to advocate nullification—a protective tariff (1824) going counter to the free trade wishes of his constituents—Webster accepted the decision of the majority in Congress. "After a whole winter's deliberation, the act of 1824 received the sanction of both Houses of Congress and settled the policy of the country. What, then," he asked, "was New England to do?— Was she to hold out forever against the course of government?"

An unequivocal commitment to the Union was the signal contribution the short-lived Federalist Party made to the building of America. Continued by the Whigs (whom Webster later joined), it came down to Lincoln, the greatest Whig of them all, who was able for the first time to enlist mass support for a concept hitherto suspect because it was held by the country's educated and moneyed elite.

The declining commerce of Portsmouth boded ill for Webster's professional future. When fire destroyed his house and library, wiping out the savings of years, he moved to Boston where he rose almost at once to the pinnacle of his profession. He soon earned ten times more than in Portsmouth; even in periods of depression (when unskilled workers made half a dollar a day) his annual income seldom fell below $15,000. His brilliant performance before the U.S. Supreme Court earned him a national reputation. He won nearly all the great constitutional cases in which he appeared as counsel. Often the opinion of the court followed closely his own line of argument. Best known, perhaps, is the *Dartmouth College* case in which he defended his Alma Mater against the Governor and Legislature of New Hampshire.

The case turned on the question whether a State may without cause terminate the charter of a private college and transform it into a State institution. Webster seized unerringly upon the relevant point: Article I, Section 10 of the Constitution which declares that no State may pass a "law impairing the obligation of contracts." Doubtless the case would have been won on this clear-cut constitutional limitation of State power. But, having finished his presentation, he stood silent a moment and then added the poignant passage that has since become famous: "This, sir, is my case. It is the case, not merely of that humble institution, it is the case of every college in our land. It is more. It is the case of every eleemosynary institution throughout our country, of all those great charities founded by the piety of our ancestors to alleviate human misery, and scatter blessings along the pathway of human life. It is more...

for the question is simply this: Shall our State legislatures be allowed to take that which is not their own, to turn it from its original use, and apply it to such ends or purposes as they, in their discretion, shall see fit? Sir, you may destroy this little institution; it is weak, it is in your hands! ... It is, sir, as I have said, a small college,— and yet there are those who love it ..."

In *McCulloch* v. *Maryland*, he argued successfully for the right of Congress to charter a National Bank and against a State law taxing one of its branches. Again fixing on the crucial point, namely that the "power to tax involves, necessarily, the power to destroy," he declared: "it is essential to the existence and preservation of the government that Congress should be able to exercise its constitutional powers, at its own discretion, without being subject to the control of State legislation." In *Gibbons* v. *Ogden*, the Court accepted Webster's argument against a steamboat navigation monopoly granted by the State of New York, on the grounds that under the commerce clause Congress was supreme in all aspects of commerce and the States could not "assert a right of concurrent legislation." Generally held to have been Webster's most effective argument before the Court, it earned him the praise of Justice Wayne for having released "every creek and river, lake, bay, and harbor, in our country, from the interference of monopolies." Seward did not exaggerate when he said in the Senate that Webster's "unapproachable supremacy at the bar" was conceded by all "the fifty thousand lawyers in the United States," nor Justice Sprague of the Supreme Court of Massachusetts when he declared that "in consultation no man was ever more weighty; in trials at the bar no man was his equal."

Webster's public career, too, reached its apogee after his move to Boston. He was again sent to the House (1823–27) and served two terms as Secretary of State (1841–43, 1850–52), but it was as Senator from Massachusetts (1827–41, 1845–50) that for close on a quarter of a century he played a leading part in national affairs, his tenure coinciding with a period in our history more decisive for the Republic than any before or since: Sequel to the era of domestic harmony at the close of the War of 1812 (when nationalist sentiments and policies were in the ascendant); prologue to the tragic war that pitted the South against the Union, these were the years of growing alienation between the free and the slave States. Webster's was one of the mightiest voices in the Senate, then coming fully into its own as the principal forum for a continuing dialogue on the constitutional issues that divided the Nation.

Whatever the specific subject in debate might be, the controversy at bottom always turned on the nature of the Federal Union about which the Constitution makes no general or abstract statement, leaving it to be inferred from the specific grants of power and limits on power enumerated in that document. Was the Federal Government supreme within its assigned sphere of jurisdiction, or did the States retain the right to disavow Federal acts they deemed *ultra vires*? Was it, in other words, the government of a federated State, or merely the central *agent* of a league of sovereign entities? On this point, the South was moving into adamant opposition to the rest of the country. Webster's enduring service to the Nation was his devoted and skillful defense of the Union against the South's most eloquent orator-statesmen who, by whittling at essential powers, would have reshaped it in the image of the old Confederation (1781–89), "the wisest system," so it was now being said by many in the South, "which mankind had ever produced."

Yet the South had done as much if not more than any other region to bring the Union into being. Her statesmen had been among the first to recognize the inadequacy of the Congress functioning under the Articles of Confederation. In the chaotic years following attainment of independence, when the 13 ex-Colonies were about to fall apart, they had pressed hard for a more "efficient" Government. The Constitution was largely based on a Southern plan (Randolph's of Virginia). Jointly with their Northern colleagues in the Constitutional Convention at Philadelphia (1787), they had partnered one of the great political inventions — a "compact republic" empowered to deal with matters of common concern, capable of acting without the intermediation of its constituent parts, operating on the individual citizen. In that republic, the South had from the start exerted influence far out of proportion to her numerical strength (nine of our first dozen Presidents were Southerners, and so for over half a century was a majority of the Supreme Court).

But even as the Nation was celebrating the half century of independence (1826) — with no less fervor in the South than in the North — cracks were appearing to mar the edifice of Union. Slavery with its multifarious ramifications was driving a wedge between the free and slave parts of the Nation. In 1830, Webster could still speak with confidence of the affectionate regard in which Americans held their Union, having "seen their happiness, prosperity, and renown grow with its growth, and strengthen with its strength." A generation hence, North and South had grown so far apart that it was

175

almost impossible for the Federal Government to make laws satisfying both. Increasingly Congress was stalemated, with House and Senate taking opposite positions. Extremists North and South were moving to the conviction that, on balance, membership in the Union carried too high a price tag. During the crisis of 1850 (over disposition of the Mexican land acquisitions), survival of the Union was seriously in doubt. Calhoun, the acknowledged voice of the South, warned that the cords binding them were snapping and soon "nothing will be left to hold the states together except force."

As minority spokesmen are apt to do, Calhoun placed all the blame on the majority and expected it to make all the concessions. "The responsibility for saving the Union rests on the North, and not on the South," he declared. The North had a choice of but two alternatives: She must either reconcile herself to the permanence of slavery, cooperate in its protection (by dutifully returning fugitive slaves and putting a stop to the antislavery propaganda of the abolitionists), and concede the South such constitutional guarantees as would forever secure her political equality in the Union—or else let the slave States "part in peace." No majority as superior in population, wealth, and economic power as the North (now allied with the West) would anywhere at any time have accepted either of these alternatives.

"I hear with distress and anguish the word 'secession,'" said Webster. "Peaceable secession! Sir, your eyes and mine are never destined to see that miracle. The dismemberment of this vast country without convulsion!" It could not but lead to war. A glance at the map shows how unrealistic it was to expect the South could with impunity violate the oldest rule of international law—*pacta sunt servanda*—and walk out of the Union, taking the areas along which, having been won by common effort, had formerly been part of the Federal domain (Tennessee, Alabama, Mississippi, Louisiana, Arkansas, Florida); Texas alone had won independence on her own. Clay, who knew better than Calhoun what the river meant to Western farmers, warned that they "will never give their consent that the mouth of (the Mississippi) shall be held subject to the power of any foreign State." Only intense preoccupation with their own "grievances" can explain the delusion of Southern statesmen that the Northwest would accept a string of customs houses between the Great Lakes and the Atlantic.

No less unrealistic were the changes demanded in our political system; to guarantee an equal voice in Congress to the South (then holding 31% of the total free population) would have stood it on its head. "Absolute acquiescence in the decision of the majority," said Jefferson in his First Inaugural, is "the vital principle of republics, from which is no appeal but to force." It could only have been done by dismantling the Federal Republic and turning it back into a league of sovereign States, and for this the time had long since passed.

Webster replied to Calhoun in a speech so famous it is known in history simply by its date—March Seven. Pleading "out of a solicitous and anxious heart, for the restoration to the country of that quiet and that harmony which make the blessings of this Union so rich and so dear to us," Webster appealed to reason and mutual forbearance and history—to memory of the time when "there was no diversity of opinion between the North and the South upon the subject of slavery," both sections deploring it as a social and political evil. In conciliatory tones, without imputing blame, Webster traced the cause of the crises of 1850 back to the subsequent divergence of Northern and Southern attitudes towards slavery, rather than—as had Calhoun—to disputes over legal rights demanded or denied. The North grew "more warm and strong against slavery" while the South, reversing her previous stand, grew warmer and stronger in its support. "It was the cotton interest that gave a new desire to promote slavery, to spread it," changing "the whole nomenclature of the South on that subject," so that slavery had become a "cherished" institution.

As late as 1832, Thomas Jefferson Randolph (Jefferson's grandson) submitted a proposal for gradual emancipation to the Virginia House of Delegates where it was discussed at length. "Everyone spoke of slavery as he thought," said Webster; "very ignominious and disparaging names and epithets were applied to it . . . At that time Virginia was not unwilling or afraid to discuss this question." But already this was no longer permissible in the Lower South, now one enormous cotton field, regularly yielding a 10 percent profit without much effort or risk to its owners. From the cotton States, intense proslavery sentiments tolerating no criticism spread through the whole region. In 1832, the Richmond *Enquirer* had spoken of slavery as "a dark and growing evil"; in 1855, the paper called for revival of the slave trade.

Webster's remarkably perceptive and objective analysis of the alienation of North and South illustrates what William James years later was to call the greatest discovery of his time, namely, that men alter their lives by altering their attitudes of mind.

We embarked on the new and untried experiment of federated

self-government burdened by a common heritage of slavery. Nearly a fifth of the population were slaves, 90 percent of them concentrated in the South. Though some efforts were made in the South to translate antislavery sentiment into action, only the North — having fewer slaves and no real need of them — took steps to abolish the institution. In all but two Northern States (New York and New Jersey), it was on the way out when the Constitutional Convention met in 1787. Let another convention be called and let it meet 20,000 times, Hamilton said, it "will have the same difficulties to encounter, the same clashing interests to reconcile." In the diary he kept of the Convention proceedings, Madison noted that "the great division of interests in the United States . . . did not lie between the large and small States; it lay between the Northern & Southern," and resulted from the effects of "their having or not having slaves." For agreement to be reached, "mutual deference and concessions were absolutely necessary."

The divisiveness of slavery was well understood by most of the Founding Fathers. Speaking of his hope of eventual emancipation, Washington said that "not only do I pray for it on the score of human dignity, but I can clearly foresee that nothing but the rooting out of slavery can perpetuate the existence of our union by consolidating it in a common bond of principle." It was equally clear, however, that the matter must be left to the States. The South would not have accepted the Constitution, had there been the slightest chance of Federal intrusion. She demanded and obtained unequivocal guarantees protecting her slave interests (including over-representation in the House of Representatives). A minority section with only 40 percent of the total free population (48.7% if slaves were counted in) she held the stronger position, since the North was willing to accept a Union with slavery guarantees if the only alternative was no Union at all.

Said Charles C. Pinckney, reporting to the ratification convention of his home State of South Carolina: "We have obtained a right to recover our slaves in whatever part of America they may take refuge, which is a right we had not before . . . We have a security that the general government can never emancipate them"; this "species of property" has thus been made secure, despite "the religious and political prejudices of the Eastern and Middle States." The power to levy direct taxes has been circumscribed, said Abraham Baldwin of Georgia, so as to prevent "Congress from laying any special tax upon negro slaves, as they might, in this way so burthen the possessors of them as to induce a general emancipation." The demand that no impediments be put on the export of Southern plantation crops had been met by a flat prohibition of export taxes.

It was in the Constitutional Convention that the threat of disunion first proved its effectiveness as a weapon of the minority (down to the Civil War, it would be successfully used by the South to exact further concessions from the North). Paradoxically, the weapon proved equally effective within the South herself, where the strong desire of the Upper South for prompt cession of the slave trade was successfully frustrated by South Carolina and Georgia, though they held but 15 percent of the Southern (6% of the total) free population.

The Upper South had long been at one with—if not ahead of—the North in condemning the slave trade; Mason of Virginia called it "this infernal traffic," Martin of Maryland said it was "dishonorable to the American character." Jefferson's original draft of the Declaration of Independence contained a bitter remonstrance (elided by Congress) against King George for having "prostituted" his veto power over colonial legislation by suppressing all laws against importation of slaves. The Colonies were regularly denounced in the Privy Council for trying "to check or discourage a traffic so beneficial to the nation" (it would have been more correct to say "to the Royal African Company"). American statesmen, said Webster in 1850, ascribed the existence of slavery "not without truth, and not without some acerbity of temper and force of language, to the injurious policy of the mother country, who, to favor the navigator, had entailed these evils upon the colonies." One of the first acts of the Continental Congress was conclusion of an agreement to interdict further importation of slaves. Of the first four States outlawing the trade, three were Southern— Delaware (1776), Virginia (1778), Maryland (1783); only Pennsylvania among Northern States acted with comparable speed (1780), but all had done so by 1786. There was thus ample precedent for Federal proscription, and its approval would have been assured in the Constitutional Convention but for the opposition of South Carolina and Georgia. They were, as Madison wrote Jefferson, "inflexible on the point of the slaves," demanding that the slave trade remain within the jurisdiction of the States.

Holding out for more than 3 months, they won a 20-year postponement of Federal proscription. Moreover, instead of being mandatory as the majority in the Convention desired, Federal action was left optional. Thus no final settlement of this troublesome issue was achieved. It was reopened in the late 1850's when the cotton States agitated for revival of the trade—

even though Congress had declared it "piracy" (in 1808) and we were bound by the Webster-Ashburton Treaty with Britain (1842) to suppress it.

It was clear to the Convention delegates that South Carolina and Georgia would not have entered the Union had they been denied temporary permission to import slaves. It was this fear, of course, that gave the threat of disunion its force, persuading the Northern States, as well, to accept the slave trade compromise though they found it even more objectionable, seeing in it but another Southern stratagem to gain more power in Congress.

From the start, the South had been adamant in demanding that for purposes of apportionment of congressional seats (and hence of electoral votes), slaves be counted as "persons" (though in all other respects she regarded them as "property" to be specifically guaranteed by the Constitution). Courteous and forebearing gentlemen though they were, over this matter the delegates came close at times to losing their tempers. Their States would never be reconciled to "so much inequality and unreasonableness," declared one Northern spokesman. "Let us at once take a friendly leave of each other," said another; the Southern gentlemen "will not be satisfied unless they see the way open to their gaining a majority in the public Councils." Not so, protested a leading South Carolinian, he "did not expect the S. States to be raised to a majority of representatives, but wished them to have something like an equality." Persisting for weeks on end in his demand that all slaves be counted in, he finally consented to the "Federal ratio" which reduced the number to three-fifths but still gave the South overall one-third more voting power per citizen than the North.

Explaining the ratio to a member of the North Carolina ratification convention (who did "not wish to be represented with negroes"), one of the delegates pointed out that they had been duty bound "to acquire as much weight as possible in the legislation of the Union." Given Northern superiority in numbers, he said, this could only be done "by insisting that a certain proportion of our slaves should make a part of the computed population"—a concession not easily won. The delegates from New England in particular had been bitterly opposed, arguing that if slaves were counted, "their cows and horses were equally entitled to representation; that the one was property as well as the other" (some had been so impolite as to suggest the South be consistent and free her slaves if she wanted to use them to enhance her influence in the Federal Government).

It is clear from the evidence that the Southern members of the Constitutional Convention thought it eminently fair and just that their minority region be equally represented – perhaps because the slaveholding minorities in their own States wielded power far out of proportion to their numbers, but more likely because they feared for the security of their slave interests unless the South had enough power in Congress to prevent adverse legislation. In any event, without the three-fifth ratio the South would have gone her own way.

Once again, the North acquiesced, but the concession continued to rankle. It was brought up again during the crisis over admission of Missouri as a slave State (1819–20). "Equality of rights . . . is a vital principle in our theory of government" said Rufus King, a New England Federalist and enemy of slavery, who had fought the ratio in the Constitutional Convention. The principle had been disregarded as a "necessary sacrifice to the establishment of the Constitution," with the result that the slaveholding States held disproportionate power and influence in the Union. It was "an ancient settlement, and faith and honor stand pledged not to disturb it." To extend this disproportionate power to new slave States seeking admission would, however, "be unjust and odious" and he urged the privilege be reserved to the States already in the Union.

His proposal failed, but this and similar evidences of Northern restiveness deepened Southern misgivings which had been aroused by the unexpected intensity of feeling in the free States against extension of slavery into the wilderness areas of the Louisiana Purchase. The South won a substantial share of the territory and at least tacit acknowledgment of her self-proclaimed doctrine that no free State be admitted to the Union unless paired with a slave State. But in the end, slavery itself defeated her efforts to retain equality in Congress.

Each decennial census reduced her proportion of seats in the House (she had 30 out of 65 in 1789, 90 out of 237 in 1860), for she was steadily falling behind in population (in 1790, she had almost half the total population, in 1860, 40 percent; counting only her percentage of the free population, the figures were 40 percent and 30 percent respectively). The free States grew more rapidly because European immigrants (of whom over five million arrived here between 1830 and 1860) were unwilling to compete with slave labor and avoided the South. She held on to half the Senate seats from 1796 to 1850, but climate and soil decreed that there must in the end be more free than slave States, less than half the area we gained by purchase, war, or settlement being adaptable to slave agriculture. Nor could the South force every suitable territory to opt for slavery.

After almost a decade of the most determined effort to make Kansas a slave State, the 1860 census showed her with just two slaves, and in 1861 the people voted more than six to one for a constitution barring slavery. The South felt California ought by rights to divide along the Missouri line into a free and a slave State. A free State constitution was however adopted by the people (17 to one) in 1849, for which they were severely criticized by Calhoun. Neither would Texas, for the sake of the senatorial equilibrium, consider letting herself be carved into several slave States. In any event, their action merely hastened the inevitable (by 9 years) and fixed the ultimate number of slave States at 15 instead of 16 — not because of Northern injustice, as Calhoun averred, but because, in historian Herbert Croly's words, "the national domain contained more material for free than it did for slave states."

The Missouri debates seem to have first made the South aware that by sheer weight of numbers the Northern States must eventually exercise control over Congress. Seeking a legal basis for defense against the possibility of future Federal action inimical to slavery, the South in the 1820's turned to strict constructionism and to an extreme States' rightism, both directed toward holding Federal power to the lowest possible minimum. Quite innocuous measures desired by the North were voted down by her spokesmen in Congress, lest they set precedents that might threaten the institution around which she had built her economic and social life. Let the Constitution once be interpreted loosely, warned John Randolph in a speech denouncing a bill for federally subsidized post roads as unconstitutional, and thereafter anyone looking for authority to abolish slavery will be able to hook it "upon the first loop they find in the Constitution. They might take the preamble, perhaps the war-making power, or they might take a greater sweep and say . . . that it is not to be found in this or that of the granted powers, but results from all of them, which is not only a dangerous but *the most* dangerous doctrine." States' rightism took the form of the "compact" theory and its corollary, the nullification doctrine, stated with great precision and logic by Calhoun, and eloquently presented by a galaxy of talented Southern orators.

"Our system is a Union of . . . sovereign powers, under a constitutional compact, and not of a divided sovereignty between the States severally and the United States," declared Calhoun. To which Webster replied that the Constitution was not a compact, the Union not a confederacy of sovereign States, but that "the people created this government," that it is "the independent offspring of the popular will. It is not the creature of the state legislatures." Much given to the use of commercial terms, Calhoun argued from the "compact" theory that the Federal Government was but the joint agent of the States, hence its acts were at all times subject to disavowal by any of the sovereign principals, if deemed to exceed the powers granted by the Constitution. In a famous passage, Webster stressed the point often lost sight of by champions of States' rights, namely that, at every level, government in America derives its power from the people. "I hold it to be a popular government, erected by the people, those who administer it responsible to the people; and itself capable of being amended and modified just as the people may choose it should be. It is as popular, just as truly emanating from the people as the State governments. It is created for one purpose; the State governments for another. It has its own powers, they have theirs." As for Calhoun's thesis that the States had a constitutional right to veto enforcement of national laws deemed *ultra vires*, Webster made the telling point that "the main design, for which the whole Constitution was framed and adopted was to establish a government that should not be obliged to act through State agency or depend on State opinion and State discretion. The people had had quite enough of that kind of government under the Confederacy."

This is self-evident to modern Americans who cannot remember a time when the paramountcy of the National Government could be effectively challenged. But Webster was contending with serious threats to its very existence as a *viable government*. The compact and nullification doctrines were backed by the prestige of Jefferson, originator of both, though not in the context now being used. In 1833, South Carolina decided to offer armed resistance to enforcement of the tariff acts of 1828 and 1833, holding them null and void. Webster made short shrift of her claim that she was but using a constitutional remedy against unconstitutional national acts. Absurd dilemmas would face both State and Federal officials, ending in "direct collision between force and force," if nullification were put into practice. "To resist, by force, the execution of a law," he warned, "is treason."

It seems likely that Webster's speech (1830) had something to do with Jackson's toast a few weeks later at a Jefferson Day Dinner. Looking straight at the nullifiers he said, "Our Federal Union—it must be preserved," much to the disappointment of Calhoun and other Southern leaders who had pinned their hopes on him. Jackson was a Tennessean, a slave-owning planter, and an upholder of States' rights, but not to the point of accepting nullification which he recognized for what it was— a "practical absurdity" based not on a right of revolution against oppression, but on the untenable proposition that a State might remain in the Union, yet obey only such laws as it chose to consider constitutional. In his statesmanlike Proclamation to the People of South Carolina (1832) he branded nullification "incompatible with the existence of the Union, contradicted expressly by the letter of the Constitution, unauthorized by its spirit, inconsistent with every principle upon which it is founded, and destructive of the great object for which it was formed." A week later, he asked bluntly: "Disunion by armed force is *treason*. Are you ready to incur its guilt?" The words might have been Webster's.

In 1900, when a ballot was taken to choose candidates for New York University's Hall of Fame, Washington received 97 votes, and Webster tied with Lincoln for second place with 96. It is not often in modern times that oratory is awarded so high a prize. But Webster's place in history is with the Nation-builders. He taught his countrymen to think nationally, to place their Union at the apex of the American political system. The great debates in which he was involved illuminate the extraordinary difficulties of establishing and managing a Federal Republic. In comparison, popular government as such is a simple thing. The tenets of the Declaration of Independence are easily grasped and carry their own appeal. But the complex structure of our Federal Union was hard to understand, and apt to arouse popular mistrust rather than affection. The Federal Government had at first to function without the natural loyalty that attaches itself to old established political entities. It had to earn for itself a place in the hearts of the American people; some cherished local attachments had to be sacrificed. Above all, ringing words were needed to stir the soul to love of this vast new country. These Webster supplied in abundance.

He called forth a popular devotion to the Union such as neither the Revolution, nor the great debates over the Constitution had been able to arouse. Recitals of the most famous passages of Webster's speeches in countless commencement exercises implanted their patriotic sentiments in the American mind. A Union soldier told of keeping up his courage on sentinel duty by reciting the final and solemn sentence of Webster's second reply to Hayne (1830): "Liberty and Union, now and forever, one and inseparate." It may stand as a symbol of Webster, the Expounder of the Constitution, the Defender of the Union.

USS JOHN C. CALHOUN (SSBN 630)

NAMED FOR John Caldwell Calhoun (1782–1850): Congressman (1811–17), Secretary of War (1817–25), twice Vice President
of the United States (serving first under John Quincy Adams,
1825–29, then under Andrew Jackson, 1829–32), Senator (1832–
44), Secretary of State (1844–45), and Senator (1845–50). A man
of large capabilities, a prominent figure in American life
throughout his long career, Calhoun left his deepest mark as
a political theoretician. The influence his constitutional doctrines exerted was enormous, indeed incalculable in its effect
upon the course of American history.

Calhoun was born in the Abbeville District on the South
Carolina frontier, youngest but one of five children of a pioneer
farmer. His family was Scotch-Irish—part of that numerous
migration which reached our shores during the 18th century
and proceeded to come down the Piedmont Belt from Pennsylvania into Virginia and the Carolinas (the last great influx
into the South from abroad; later immigrants avoided the
slave States as these no longer offered poor but ambitious men
as much chance for advancement as was to be found in other
parts of the country). Calhoun's grandfather James arrived
(with two brothers) about 1733 and settled in western Virginia.
When Braddock's defeat (1755) left the frontier exposed to
savage Indian raids, James moved with some of his kinfolk to
the South Carolina uplands, founding the "Calhoun Settlement" near the Savannah River (where a party of marauding
Cherokees killed his wife).

In the 1780's and 90's, when Calhoun grew up, the region was
still primitive. Educational opportunities being limited, he was
sent to his brother-in-law's excellent academy in Georgia when
he was 14, but remained less than a year, his father's untimely

death calling him home. He stayed on at the farm for 3 years, evincing no interest in further schooling, but was finally persuaded by an elder brother to return to the academy and prepare himself for a profession. Rapidly making up the time lost, he entered Yale as a junior at 20 and after graduating with distinction, studied law at Tapping Reeve's School in Litchfield, Conn. (then probably the best of its kind in the country). By age 25, he was rapidly acquiring a substantial law practice in Abbeville and had made his first political speech. A year later, he was elected State assemblyman, thus following in the footsteps of his father, Patrick, who represented the district for years, first in the colonial, then in the State legislature.

Calhoun's political views later changed, but they were then essentially those imbibed at an early age from his father. Competent, and with decided political views, Patrick had been a man of some local importance. He acquired a score or two of slaves—unusual in an area where most men had to work the land themselves. Some of his kin went into the lowlands, there to gain wealth and social position; notably a cousin, his son's future father-in-law, who married into the Tidewater aristocracy. But Patrick himself was content to remain a back country farmer, never losing the sturdy republicanism so typical of men living on the frontier. Ardently patriotic during the Revolution, he shared his neighbors' mistrust of "distant" government had opposed ratification of the Constitution, fearing the people of his region would not have much influence on the new Federal Government; they had little enough influence on their own State government.

South Carolina had been chartered (1663) as a proprietary Colony and given a constitution (drafted by John Locke) envisaging a quasi-feudal social order with an hereditary nobility, a landed aristocracy, and a peasantry. Its early settlers were predominantly men of property, many of them planters from Bermuda and the British West Indies who acquired vast holdings in the fertile coast country where they grew rice and indigo with slave labor. Although proprietary rule ended in 1719 (the charter from the first proving unworkable), vestiges of its archaic institutions remained even after independence was won. The State constitution of 1778 perpetuated the high property qualifications for office holding of the colonial period, as well as a system of apportionment which grossly over-represented the lowlands, oldest and richest part of the State, and under-represented the more recently settled, poorer uplands (a situation worsening year by year since the back country, augmented by immigration, grew at a faster rate than the coast

187

country of slave plantations). As a result, the early history of the State was marred by bitter sectional strife, ethnic and religious differences exacerbating the political and economic cleavage. Most of the planters were of English descent and Anglician persuasion, while the upland farmers were Scotch-Irish or German in origin and dissenting in religion.

Calhoun took his seat in the State legislature in time to take part in the 1808 reform which gave his region, if not equality, a substantial increase in power. With the aid of a liberal lowland minority, the uplanders (now four-fifths of the population) were able to push through a constitutional amendment (1808) allotting them a majority of the seats in the lower house of the legislature where previously they held but 58 out of 202. The lowlanders (owning four-fifths of the State's wealth) were left in control of the upper house, thus retaining a veto on passage of legislation that might injure their special interests. Both sections found the compromise acceptable and mutual antagonism abated. (In 1810, the electoral system was further liberalized by removing all property restrictions on voting.) When presently the entire State went over to the cultivation of short-staple cotton—which, unlike rice and indigo, could be grown as well on up country family farms as on coast country slave plantations—a common economic interest consolidated the reconciliation effected by South Carolina's first major electoral reform. The new system of apportionment endured unchanged until overturned by the Reconstruction constitution of 1865.

Calhoun served in the South Carolina General Assembly (1808–10)—and never held another State office—but the experience was significant for his career. The formula which in 1808 established domestic harmony in his home State left a deep impress on his political thinking. His legislative tour convinced him that politics rather than the law was his true metier. He decided that as soon as this was feasible he would devote most of his time to public affairs. Marriage to his wealthy cousin Floride Bonneau Calhoun in 1811 gave him the necessary financial independence. He acquired a large plantation on which he later built a mansion—Fort Hill—which still stands as a memorial on what is now the campus of Clemson University. Giving up his law practice, he ran successfully for Congress and, except for a few months in 1845, was not out of national office for the rest of his life.

He entered Congress as a leader (second only to Kentucky's Henry Clay) of the young "war hawks"—a combination of land hungry Southerners and Westerners bent on ousting Britain from North America by force of arms, believing her to be the principal obstacle to their aim of rapid westward expansion. As acting chairman of the Foreign Relations Committee, Calhoun brought out the report of June 3, 1812, which recommended that war be declared. With Clay, he steered it through the House over the determined opposition of the maritime States of the Northeast. So strong was the wave of disapproval engulfing what New Englanders derisively called "Mr. Madison's War," that their resistance (continuing throughout the hostilities) came at times close to nullification of the war effort.

Calhoun labored prodigiously for military success—"the young Hercules who carried the war on his shoulders," he was called by Alexander J. Dallas, Madison's Secretary of the Treasury. Ending inconclusively, gaining us none of our objectives, the war (1812–15) revealed all too clearly our military weakness and economic dependence on foreign products and markets. Spurred to continued efforts in furtherance of national strength and unity, Calhoun rallied the "war hawks" behind Clay's legislative program (the "American System"). Thanks in part to Calhoun's parliamentary skill, most of the program was enacted in a single year (1816)—the charter for a Second Bank of the United States, the first protective tariff act, the largest naval appropriation bill to that date. Haunted by fear that America's size exposed her to "the greatest of all calamities, next to the loss of liberty . . . *dis-union*," Calhoun asked for funds to subsidize internal improvements. "Let us," he pleaded, "bind the Republic together with a perfect system of roads and canals." Congress responded, but Madison vetoed the bill. Under Monroe, Calhoun served as Secretary of War, proving himself an exceptionally able administrator and innovator of organizational reforms. John Quincy Adams wrote in his diary that Calhoun was a man "of enlarged philosophical views, and of ardent patriotism," standing "above all sectional and factious prejudices, more than any other statesman of this Union with whom I have ever acted." This was in 1821.

Before the decade drew to a close, Calhoun completely reversed his political stand. The ardent nationalist became an equally ardent sectionalist at midpoint in his public career. He had been taking a broad view of the powers vested in the Federal Government, now he called for strict interpretation of the constitutional grant. He had sponsored legislation enhancing the military and economic strength of the Nation; now he denounced such legislation as contrary to the interests of his region and pronounced them unconstitutional. During the early part of his political life, his objective had been to unify the country. During the latter part, his actions served to divide it, albeit that was not his intent.

In thus reversing himself, Calhoun was responding to the wishes of his constituents whose attitude toward the Union was changed radically by the Missouri and tariff crises of the 1820's. He was at first a reluctant convert to their altered viewpoint, but soon became convinced that the Southern States had no choice but to fall back on the rights they had reserved to themselves when they entered the Union, if their most vital interests were to be protected against injurious Federal acts. The South—as the term went—became a "conscious" minority.

Such political reversals were not uncommon at that time. The four decades during which Calhoun held public office spanned the so-called "middle period" of our history, the turbulent years when—independence won, the Federal Government established, and foreign intervention averted—the young Republic faced as its most serious problem a divisive regionalism periodically threatening to dissolve the Federal bond so carefully and laboriously wrought by the Founding Fathers. With his usual perception, de Tocqueville noted (in 1835) that the country's three major geographic sections—the commercial Northeast, the plantation South, the homesteading West— were behaving like rival nations. Lining up two to one on nearly every important national issue, they pursued their parochial interests in a triangular power play, their spokesmen in Congress forming temporary combinations in furtherance of specific objectives. Thus matters elsewhere settled by the ordinary legislative process were resolved through regional coalition politics, inherently a more divisive proceeding. Not only were Federal laws apt to be regarded as regional victories, defeats, or compromises rather than measures agreed upon for the benefit of the Nation as a whole, their constitutionality was also more likely to be questioned, the regions shifting position depending upon whether they were at the moment in the majority or in the minority. In control of the Government, they were ready enough to stretch Federal power if this served their particular interests and needs, but outvoted they were inclined to denounce like action by the majority as unconstitutional usurpations of power.

When the 13 Colonies achieved independence, the South was roughly in equilibrium with the rest of the country (her population somewhat smaller, but her area much larger than the Northeastern and the Middle Atlantic States combined). The unexpectedly rapid growth of the West upset this equilibrium almost at once, producing the triangular pattern of the "middle period." Nevertheless, for decades the South more than held her own in the Nation's councils for she was almost continually part of a majority coalition. Her natural ally was the West. The two agricultural sections shared a common viewpoint, usually opposed to that of the Northeast; they supported each other's expansionist aims and were bound by economic ties, the South buying much of her food from the West. Easily accessible by inland waterways (the only cheap and convenient means of transport for bulky goods in the early days of the Republic), she was the best, indeed the only large-scale market for Western farm products.

As long as she could count on the support of the West, the South felt secure in the Union, certain that she had sufficient influence to prevent passage of Federal acts damaging her special regional interests. But once aware that she faced the prospect of losing the support of the West, she could find security only in her own ability to place constitutional restraints on the majority.

The 19th century revolution in transportation loosened the economic ties that bound the West to her. New markets for Western products opened in the East and in Europe with the coming of canals and railroads in the 1820's and 1830's. Not only ease of transportation but also superiority of credit and banking facilities offered by Eastern institutions soon diverted much Western commerce from the Mississippi and New Orleans to the great Atlantic ports of the Northeast. From there it moved on the shorter North Atlantic shipping lanes to Europe, the replacement of sail by steam having lessened the natural advantage of the Gulf Stream and the trade winds which heretofore favored the Southern ports.

Along the new trade routes, industrialization spread inland. While the South remained purely agrarian, the West diversified her economy. By 1860, she had one-quarter of the country's woolen mills and the output of her grist mills almost equaled the total value of the Southern cotton crop. These new interests drew her away from the South and into the Eastern orbit (on such matters as the tariff and subsidies for internal improvements). Politically as well, a wedge was being driven between the two old allies. They still shared a common determination to wrest the continent from the Indians and any foreign power laying claim to portions of it, no matter how well founded in law these might be, but they no longer saw eye to eye on the disposal of newly acquired territories. Southern opposition frustrated

191

every effort of the West to obtain free distribution of public land for homesteaders. But nothing so alienated the West as Southern insistence on the geographic extension and national protection of slavery. Westerners looked upon *all* the as yet unsettled parts of the continent as the exclusive patrimony of the homesteader, to be kept free of slaveholders, slaves and freedmen alike; the South demanded an equal share of the territories jointly acquired (by conquest or purchase). This, more than anything else, hastened the gradual merging of East and West into a solid North from which she—the South—could in the end no longer detach her old partner. Her consequent reduction to permanent minority status in the Union (not yet completed before he died but clearly foreseen and greatly feared by him) was the decisive factor in shaping Calhoun's evolution as a political thinker.

It was then that the South grew more adamant in demanding maintenance of the equilibrium between free and slave States. With slavery under constant attack, she came to regard equality in the Senate (giving her a veto over laws injurious to her interests) as the indispensable condition of remaining in the Union. (Garrison, the most influential abolitionist, rejected the Constitution as a "convenant with death and an agreement with hell.") In a matter so vital to her, the South was not prepared to let herself be outvoted. Had the Constitution not left slavery to the jurisdiction of the States, and protected slave property by requiring the return of fugitive slaves, the South would not have consented to transformation of the old Confederation into a Federal Republic.

"It was slavery, of course," Woodrow Wilson said, "which made the South unlike the rest of the country," an anachronistic 18th century island in a Nation moving swiftly into the modern industrial age. With its manifold ramifications, this tragic heritage of our colonial past cut so deep a fissure in the body politic that in the end regionalism triumphed and the Union broke in two. Washington clearly foresaw this. "Nothing but the rooting out of slavery can perpetuate the existence of our union by consolidating it in a common bond of principle," he warned (thus anticipating the thrust of Lincoln's "House Divided" speech of 1858). Yet neither in the colonial period, nor while we fought for independence, loosely allied under the Continental Congress, had slavery been a divisive issue; it became so only when we undertook to organize ourselves into a Federal Republic.

Slave labor—long since extinct in the mother country—was accepted as an economic necessity in all 13 Colonies (indeed, in all the colonies of the New World—Portuguese, Spanish, Danish, French, Dutch, as well as English), the reason being a lack of free labor to develop the vast riches of the new lands, even merely to produce the exportable staples needed to pay for essential imports from Europe. A ticket to America was then beyond the financial resources of workingmen (and remained so until the 19th century revolution in maritime transport reduced the cost). Those who had the wherewithal to pay for their passage found economic independence within such easy reach that few would work for others, despite wages three to four times higher than at home. As for the Indians, they preferred the freedom of their primitive existence to employment by the alien intruder. Enslaving them was legal in all 13 Colonies but they could seldom be bought (the North American tribes not being in the habit of selling their war prisoners), they were difficult to capture and, if captured, they usually ran away. Indian slavery made hardly a dent in the prevailing manpower shortage. Relief came through importation of indentured labor from the British Isles and the Continent (chiefly Germans and Swiss) and of African slaves. More than half the men, women and children (some estimated three fourths) coming here during the colonial period were indentured servants; about one fifth were slaves.

Indenture was introduced by the Virginia Company of London shortly after the founding of the first English settlement at Jamestown, Virginia, in 1607. Indentured servants worked the land the company reserved for its own use. To encourage their importation by individual colonists, the company devised a system of land tenure based on so-called "head rights," i.e., the granting of 50 acres free (at first 100 acres) to anyone paying his own passage or that of another. Not a few of the great plantations were built up by successive importations of indentured servants. The labor exacted from each usually sufficed not only to develop the 50 acres his master received for having brought him here, but generated enough capital to finance the immigration of another indentured immigrant whose arrival added another 50 acres and so on.

Similar systems of land tenure were adopted in a number of other Colonies (Southern and Mid-Atlantic) where large-scale agriculture was feasible; they were not used in New England, though indentured domestic servants were widely employed. However, to guarantee the expenses of the English merchants who financed their venture, the Pilgrims who came to Plymouth in 1620 bound themselves to a sort of group indenture, agreeing that the fruits of their labor should be held in common for

7 years and only enough for subsistence drawn therefrom until final settlement of their obligations. (Industry and thrift allowed them to end their bondage at the end of 6 years by settling all the claims of the original investors.)

Modeled on the traditional apprenticeship system, indenture was a contract enforceable by penal sanctions, involving a term of servitude (usually 4 years for adults, up to age 21 for children) in return for maintenance and passage to America. The indentured servant's lot was not an enviable one. Often sold at auction, he was subject to his master's almost total authority. Some were worked harder than slaves, and the mortality from bad food, crowding and infectious diseases on the longer North Atlantic voyage at times exceeded even the average of 13 percent who died on the notorious "middle passage" from Africa. But having completed his term, the indentured servant merged easily with the general population, no stigma attached to his previous conditions of servitude. Moreover, indenture was the only way agricultural, general, and domestic laborers could come to what from the start was hailed as "the best poor Man's Country in the World."

The majority came voluntarily, making their arrangements with a shipmaster, immigration broker or employer, but so great was the demand for their labor in America and so high a price were employers willing to pay (up to £20 sterling at the close of the colonial period), that many were lured by false promises and not a few were kidnapped by criminal gangs for sale to unscrupulous shipmasters who would pay 1 or 2 pounds and thus make a good profit on each kidnap victim. (Life was hard for the poor, especially for young men venturing into the port cities—if not kidnapped for indenture to the Colonies, they might well fall prey to His Majesty's press gangs and be forcibly inducted into the Navy.) About 50,000 of the indentured persons brought here were convicts (debtors and felons) who chose "transportation" to the Colonies and 7–14 years of servitude in preference to imprisonment or even execution; a few hundred were political prisoners condemned to serve for life.

For several decades, indenture remained the principal, indeed the preferred source of manpower on Southern plantations, but with the spectacular growth of tobacco culture, demand outran supply and European indentureds were first supplemented, then replaced by African slaves. Virginia had 2,000 slaves and 6,000 indentured servants in 1681; by 1720, slaves outnumbered those indentured in every Colony south of Maryland. Oddly enough, slavery (both Indian and African) was first sanctioned not in the South but in Massachusetts (1641), Virginia following 20 years later and the remaining Colonies at the end of the 17th century. (On the other hand, Massachusetts was the first State to eliminate slavery entirely. When the 1790 census was taken, she alone reported not having a single slave.)

Slavery in America is discussed almost entirely in terms of the struggle for its abolition; slavery elsewhere might hardly have existed. We should therefore be reminded that white slavery was then as institutionalized as black, surviving in some places even into the late 19th century. Yet such is the sense of guilt induced by slavery that it is often forgotten that this was at one time a universal condition, and white victims were uprooted and enslaved as ruthlessly as blacks.

Indigenous to Africa, slavery had been brought to the Western Hemisphere a century and a half earlier by the Portuguese and implanted in every European colony. Some 400,000 slaves were carried to the North American Colonies prior to 1776; several times as many to the West Indies and to Central and South America. Almost no one protested this commerce in human beings; African chiefs were as eager to barter their slaves for guns, rum and trinkets as Arab slave traders to march them in shackles overland to the seacoast and European shipmasters to buy them for sale in the American market. Not until the late 18th century did the people of Western civilization turn first against the slave trade, then against slavery itself.

The antislavery movement was almost exclusively a middle class phenomenon, in part motivated by the ethical rationalism of the Enlightenment, in part by the compassion for all victims of human cruelty which animated such religious sects as the Quakers, the Evangelicals, the Jansenists. It worked through a new political invention, the private pressure group espousing some particular cause — a band of men of substance and influence dedicated to the disinterested objective of collecting and disseminating information about their cause and arousing public opinion on its behalf in the hope of forcing the authorities to decree reform. Abolition of slavery was one of the first of these causes and England the country where mobilization of private philanthropic sentiment for public action was most effectively used.

The first official statement branding slavery a moral and political evil intolerable in a civilized nation appears to have been made by Lord Mansfield, Chief Justice of the King's Bench, *Sommersett's* case (1772). At issue was the status of a West

195

Indian slave whose master had taken him to England. Sommersett ran away, was caught, and forcibly placed on board a ship for return to his owner. Through the good offices of two prominent abolitionists, he was released on habeas corpus and brought before the Court. Declaring slavery "so odius that nothing can be suffered to support it, but positive law," and there being no statute to overcome this presumption, Mansfield set him free. The judge reportedly said that English air was too pure to be breathed by a slave — perhaps in analogy of the medieval maxim, "city air makes free," which made any serf a free man after residing in a town for a year and a day.

Thousands of slaves taken by colonials to Britain were liberated as a result of *Sommersett's* case (and a similar decision by a Scottish court in 1778). But abolitionist attempts to extend these decisions to the Colonies failed for there slavery had the sanction of positive law. So powerful were the West Indian planters both in the colonial governments and in Parliament that emancipation by statute seemed at the time unattainable. The abolitionists therefore decided to concentrate first on the slave trade, forming a Committee to this end in 1787. It took 20 years of intense agitation to move Parliament, for the financial sacrifice was great. The trade, which Britain dominated through the 18th century, was one of the most lucrative branches of her foreign commerce and vital to the West Indian colonies since these depended on continuing imports to maintain their existing slave labor force. As finally passed, the bill provided that no vessel could clear out for slaves from any British port after May 1, 1807, and no slave be landed in any British colony after March 1, 1808.

The demand for slaves was so great however, that despite strong measures by the British Government they continued to be smuggled into the West Indies. Recognizing that the trade would not end until colonial slavery itself ceased to exist, the abolitionists reorganized as the English Anti-Slavery Society (1823). Their years of agitation now bore fruit. Strongly supported by public opinion, Parliament in 1833 provided for gradual and partially compensated emancipation, effective 1838. Other countries followed rapidly. By midcentury all major trading nations had outlawed the slave trade (English taxpayers contributing £300,000 to compensate Portugal and £400,000 to compensate Spain), and slavery itself was rapidly disappearing in the countries of Western civilization. The United States, Brazil and Spanish Cuba were the only important exceptions.

How different the history of our country would have been had the timing of American independence and English abolition of slavery been reversed. To eradicate it proved far more difficult in our Federal system with its division of political powers between the Federal Government and the States than in England with its all-powerful Parliament.

Ironically, it was the virtual autonomy in *local* matters granted the settlers by Britain that was a root cause of our difficulties. Imperial rule was largely confined to the *external* affairs of the Colonies. Though the mother country retained veto power over colonial legislation, she rarely exercised this right unless imperial interests were at stake. Federalism, no less than slavery, was a heritage of our colonial past.

Britain regulated Indian affairs, kept peace among the Colonies, defended them against foreign enemies, controlled their foreign and domestic commerce. She appointed the royal governors but left them dependent on the colonial legislatures for their salaries. In fact, if not in law, the Colonies managed their internal affairs with little interference from the government in London and none from their colonial neighbors. Slavery was considered a domestic matter to be dealt with by each Colony as it saw fit; in contrast, the slave trade (largely in the hands of the Royal African Company of London) was under imperial control—which explains in part why the Convention which drew up the Constitution in 1787 was able to reach agreement making it possible for Congress to abolish the slave trade (which was done as of Jan. 1, 1808), while no one even raised the question of granting the Federal Government authority to emancipate the slaves.

It was Britain's attempt, at the end of the Seven Years' War (1763), to alter this traditional relationship with the Colonies and subject them to novel restraints that brought on the Revolution. Having won independence, the 13 former Colonies emerged as sovereign States acknowledging no political superior. When they agreed to constitute themselves as a Federal Republic with a Central Government that would be paramount within its carefully circumscribed domain (leaving the States sovereign within theirs), the States were loathe to relinquish to this government any of the rights they had possessed when they were Colonies. A quick look at Article I of the Constitution shows that few of the powers delegated to Congress (sec. 8) had ever been exercised by them as Colonies, and most of the restraints put on the States (sec. 10) had previously been imposed on them by the mother country.

There was much antislavery feeling at the time of the Revolution, both North and South, but only the Northern States (having few slaves and no real need of them) translated senti-ment into action. No Southern State seriously considered emancipation by law, though some for a time encouraged individual manumission. When the Constitution was being written, 700,000 out of a total population of just under 4,000,000 were slaves, 660,000 of them concentrated in the six States south of the Mason-Dixon line, 40,000 in the North. Of those in the North, 32,500 were held in New York and New Jersey where slavery was still legal in 1787, though its abrogation was expected in the near future (it came in 1799 and 1804, respec-tively). The remaining 7,500 lived in New England and Penn-sylvania, under laws providing for the gradual emancipation (so gradual that not until 1840 did slaves disappear entirely from the census rolls of these States).

Slavery was thus legal in all but one third of the 12 States represented in the Constitutional Convention of 1787 (Rhode Island having chosen to remain absent)—as indeed it was nearly everywhere else in the world at that time, the only exception being Europe west of what is now the Iron Curtain. Many of the Northern delegates considered slavery destructive of popular government and inconsistent with the genius of republicanism, a view shared by not a few of their Southern colleagues *individually*. All were however sensible of having been sent to the Convention by their home States, not to draw up a political manifesto on the order of the Declaration of Independence, but a practical plan of government that would meet with their approval (the Convention having decided on July 23 that the mode of ratification of the Constitution should be by ratification conventions elected in each State for this specific purpose). Without their approval, as Hamilton noted, "nothing could have been done; for the Convention had no power to establish, but only to recommend a government."

The delegates of the Constitutional Convention reached an early agreement, James Wilson told the Pennsylvania rati-fication convention, that "in drawing the line between the national and the individual governments of the states," they would follow the principle that "whatever object was con-fined in its nature and operation to a particular State ought to be subject to the separate government of the States; but what-ever in its nature and operation extended beyond a particular State, ought to be comprehended within the federal jurisdic-tion." In specific cases, the application of this principle caused much controversy, but not in regard to slavery.

No one doubted that Southern States would have rejected the Constitution, had the slightest attempt been made to limit their traditional jurisdiction over slavery within their territorial domain. Nor was any objection made when their delegates demanded inclusion of a Fugitive Slave clause in the Constitution, in order that—as Charles Pinckney put it—the property of the Southern States in slaves be protected as securely "as any other kind of property in the Eastern States." A similar clause covering fugitive indentured servants had been part of the short-lived New England Confederation (1641–84) so the provision was not without precedent. By unanimous vote and without debate, the "comity clause" (which bound the States to mutual rendition of escaped criminals) was extended to include runaway slaves.

Thus, abolition of slavery was far more difficult in this country than in England. As the legislature of a Government of limited powers, Congress operates under legal restraints unknown to Parliament which, so the saying goes, can do everything except turn a man into a woman (and vice versa). While Parliament could disregard the opposition minority and decree abolition, once a majority of its members decided to end slavery, Congress could not. The Fugitive Slave clause, moreover, precluded Northern courts from following *Sommersett's* decision (besides making it illegal for the free States to grant asylum to slaves seeking refuge). Because of it, the American judiciary was denied the authority possessed by the British to emancipate slaves setting foot on "free soil."

That jurisdiction over their slaves must remain with the States was taken for granted in 1787, but the continued influx of additional slaves was not. Federal prohibition of the slave trade had overwhelming support in the Convention. If anything, the Upper South was more anxious than the North to end slave imports (having a sufficiency of slaves and no vested interest in the trade). As early as 1761, the Virginia Legislature had tried to limit such imports by raising the duty, only to have the law vetoed by the Crown.

One of the first acts of the Continental Congress was negotiation of an agreement among the States to interdict slave imports. With Delaware (1776) and Virginia (1778) leading the way, 10 of the States had by 1783 enacted laws prohibiting such imports (and North Carolina had placed a heavy tax on them). This was long before any European colonial power took similar action (the first being Denmark which decreed in 1792 that the traffic should cease after 1802). When the Constitutional Convention met, only South Carolina and Georgia had as yet failed to act.

They had not outlawed slave imports because, unlike the Upper South where slaves already were overabundant, they had a shortage. Last of the Colonies to have been settled, much of their land remained uncleared and slaves were used for this task. As Colonies, they had never been denied the right to import them. They were not prepared to yield this right to the new Federal Government. Pressed to abide by the wishes of the ·majority in the Constitutional Convention that Congress end the slave trade forthwith, the delegates of South Carolina and Georgia pointed out that to do so would be of no avail since their home States would reject the Constitution if this matter were removed from the exclusive jurisdiction of the States. "The nature of our climate, and the flat swampy situation of our country, obliges us to cultivate our lands with negroes," declared Charles C. Pinckney, "without them South Carolina would soon be a desert waste." "Georgia will not purchase the Union by yielding to national powers" the abridgment of what he termed "one of her favorite prerogatives," said Roger Baldwin, one of her delegates. Putting it more bluntly, Rutledge of South Carolina reminded the Convention that "religion and humanity had nothing to do with this question. Interest alone is the governing principle with nations. The true question at present is whether the Southern States shall or shall not be parties to the Union."

They had only 6 percent of the total free population in the country, but being sovereign States they could not be coerced by the majority. Their consent was finally won—as part of an overall adjustment of conflicting Northern and Southern demands—but with the proviso that congressional action be postponed for 20 years and left optional (instead of mandatory, as the majority wished).

The compromise satisfied the Lower South but had rough going in the Constitutional Convention and in the ratification conventions of a number of States. The 20-year postponement aroused the greater resentment at the time, but proved to have been the lesser evil.

As their delegates had promised the Convention if the matter were left to the States, South Carolina and Georgia themselves enacted laws forbidding slave importations long before 1808— the former at once, though she revoked the law in 1803 as being "unenforceable," the latter for good in 1798. The fact that Congress was merely *authorized* to end the slave trade 20 years hence (instead of being *commanded* to do so) had more serious consequences, for the optional character of the constitutional provision precluded achievement of a final settlement of this divisive issue. The Federal acts passed in 1808 and 1820 outlawing slave trading and declaring it "piracy" punishable by death could—like any other legislation—be revoked at a future date. Indeed there were some in the cotton States who wished to reopen the issue in the decade preceding the Civil War! And this despite the fact that we were bound by the Webster-Ashburton Treaty with Britain (1842) to join her in suppressing the slave trade against which England was mobilizing the world. Doubtless fear of offending Britain, as well as Virginia, accounts for the fact that agitation for revival of slave imports ceased after secession. (The Constitution of the Confederacy prohibited the slave trade, while confirming the legality of slavery.)

Unless their demands had been met, South Carolina and Georgia "would not have entered into the Union of America," Madison told the Virginia ratification convention. "Great as the evil is," he argued, "a dismemberment of the Union would be worse. If these States should disunite, they might solicit and obtain aid from foreign powers." (The area lost to the Union would have been larger than that of all the Northern States combined, for under their colonial charters the territory of these two States then included large parts of what is now Tennessee, Alabama, and Mississippi.)

In 1787, Americans did not underestimate the danger that, pushed too hard by the majority, States in the minority would go their own way, leaving the Union so weakened that it might not be able to preserve its independence—a danger that did not come from the South alone. "I will not confederate on this plan" was a cry wrung from others who believed that too great a sacrifice was being demanded of their home States. The records of the Convention show that no delegate—however national his outlook—would have agreed to a plan of government placing his own State or particular group of States into a permanent position of inferiority in the Union.

That the Constitution must be equitable toward every part of America was the most pervasive sentiment in the Convention. For the small States, this meant equality in the Senate, to prevent a coalition of large States from depriving them of their political liberties; for the large States, numerical representation in the House, to prevent a coalition of small States from depriving them of their wealth by imposing excessive taxes; for the Southern States, safeguards in the Constitution, to prevent the free States (individually or through coalitions in Congress) from depriving them of their slaves by judicial or legislative fiat.

Yet, determined as they were to retain control in this matter for their home States, the Southern, no less than the Northern delegates took the *eventual* demise of slavery for granted.

Lincoln often cited the remark of a Southern Congressman that in the Convention "it was the belief of no man that slavery would long continue." Ellsworth of Connecticut gave voice to the general view when he said that "as population increases, poor laborers will be so plenty as to render slaves useless. Slavery will not be a speck in our country." It was thought that, unable to compete with free labor, it would fade away — even as indentured servitude was then disappearing rapidly (except in one or two places where it lingered on until the 1820's).

Already slavery was being questioned by some in the South on economic, not just on moral grounds; it had been introduced a century earlier because wage labor was unavailable. In cost and efficiency, it could not compete with free labor unless slaves were employed the year round and produced goods of exceptionally high value for which there was an assured demand. The principal slave-grown crops — tobacco, rice, indigo — were hard hit by loss of the protected market and the bounties they had enjoyed before independence. In the Upper South — where most of the slaves were held — their numbers were increasing more rapidly than profitable employment could be found for them. Soil erosion further hastened the decline of tobacco culture in the Lower South. The most important American crop at the time — indigo culture — did not survive till the end of the century.

Competent planters, like Washington, quickly got out of tobacco and into grains and mixed farming, but the profits were less and they were hard put to recoup the higher cost of their slaves. The value of slaves was decreasing, the number of manumissions increasing. Meanwhile the slave population was increasing rapidly. Forty-two percent of Washington's slaves were children, a percentage not uncommon in Virginia and Maryland. "Were it not that I am principled against selling negroes," he wrote in 1794, "I would not in twelve months be possessed of a single one as a slave."

He provided in his will that after the death of his wife, all his slaves should be freed, those no longer able to work to be cared for and the children taught to read and write and to be brought up to some useful occupation. It was not unreasonable to expect that manumission would gradually reduce the slave population.

But whatever chance there may have been of a gradual end to slavery in the South was lost when Eli Whitney invented the cotton gin in 1793.

Short-staple cotton, hitherto of little commercial value, suddenly became a highly profitable crop, with worldwide demand generated by the newly mechanized textile industry. By 1830, the output of cotton, which could be grown as far north as Virginia, increased 150-fold; by 1860, 1,000-fold. As the Cotton Belt west of the old Lower South extended westward into new territories, the demand for slaves increased and their value rose rapidly. By 1830 it had almost quadrupled; by 1860 it had risen 10-fold. The supply came chiefly from the old Upper South. "Never in history, perhaps, was an economic force more influential upon the life of a people," wrote Frederick Jackson Turner, for slavery was "resuscitated from a moribund condition to a vigorous and aggressive life." At the very moment in history, when the rest of the Western World turned against this ancient evil, slavery became the very foundation of the economic, political and social life of the South.

But even when the great majority of slaves were put to cotton growing, they were outnumbered by the free farmers and their families who raised cotton as a cash crop of their homestead. However, Southern beliefs, mores and policies were set by the small but capable and determined planter minority. And so cotton perpetuated slavery, and slavery precluded economic diversification.

Slavery also created a moral rift between the South and the rest of the country, and it placed her outside the mainstream of American economic life. She alone could not participate in the industrial growth getting underway throughout the rest of the country. She lacked the capital (all her assets were tied up in land and slaves, hence not readily convertible) and skilled labor (her slaves could not be trained for factory work and free men would not come to work in Southern mills).

The Southern States, wrote Calhoun in 1828, because of their "soil, climate, habits, and peculiar labor," were destined to be and always remain "staple States." However, the successful industrialization of the *modern* South shows that slavery alone was the insuperable obstacle foiling her earlier attempts to establish industries. Having chosen to retain this archaic labor system, the South found herself locked into the position of an underdeveloped enclave imperfectly integrated into a progressive national economy. Southerners, of course, saw their situation in a different light. They took pride in producing staples for which the demand was so great that (unlike Western grain growers) they had no competitors in the world market, and (unlike Northern manufacturers), they needed no tariff protection in the domestic market; nor, for that matter, federally subsidized internal improvements, being blessed with a magnificent system of natural waterways.

Because of the importance of cotton in the world, the South was that rarity, a minority economically independent of the rest of the country. By the same token, she was a minority whose economic interests were at odds with those of an ever-growing majority.

The late 1820's saw the irreversible parting of ways that led in the end to secession and Civil War. Previously, North and South agreed *in principle* that slavery was an evil thing; now Southern opinion veered from the position of deploring it theoretically while accepting it as a practical necessity, and there began the long-drawn and tortuous effort to present it to a disapproving world as the *only* practicable form of labor if cotton, now acclaimed the indispensable fiber, were to be produced at all. A "positive good" Calhoun would call it, although as a young man he had regarded slavery as mere "scaffolding."

An additional factor separating the South from the rest of the country was the protective tariff. As he observed the jockeying by other regions for special tariff advantages which drove duties steadily higher, Calhoun reached the conclusion that the protective principle was divisive. In 1827, he privately expressed the fear that this would promote political plundering and in the end "make two of one nation." By then he had begun to see the South as an entity with interests *permanently* opposed to those of the rest of the Union.

These interests could therefore never coincide with those of the majority of States in respect of the commercial policy of the country. As a permanent minority, they had a right to expect Congress to keep strictly to the letter of the Constitution when enacting tariff and other commercial laws.

The sole purpose of the protective tariffs, ran his argument, was to secure the home market for industries unable to compete with European manufactures. They were a Federal tax levied for the exclusive benefit of the industrialized regions and therefore manifestly unfair to agricultural regions such as the South — an unjust financial exaction imposed on the minority by a "tyrannical" majority. They were also clearly unconstitutional, for the authority granted the Government to regulate foreign commerce did not include the right to use tariffs as a means of extending privileges to favored sections.

We are used today to the imposition of Federal taxes to provide subsidies for particular sections of the population and to the enactment of Federal laws designed to raise prices for the benefit of particular economic interests, but in the 1820's Calhoun's argument carried weight. And indeed the records of the Constitutional Convention bear out his assertion (made in a speech a few years later) that "our Union rests on justice, on the equal distribution of its advantages and burdens."

In 1828 he drew up a severe and powerful indictment of protective tariffs as grossly unfair sectionalist legislation. This attack reflected his new conviction that—as he expressed it—in respect of the commercial policy of the country, the advantage of the Southern minority could never coincide with that of the Northern majority. This indictment, his "Exposition," was his first State paper precisely depicting the dissimilarity of the slave and free economies—a dissimilarity Calhoun and most Southerners believed was fixed and unalterable—the first to analyze in detail the political consequences of his dichotomy. No one saw the issue more clearly and stated it more courageously than he in the "Exposition" and subsequent letters, addresses and speeches.

Written at the request of a committee of the South Carolina Legislature while he was Vice President (and not acknowledged as his work until the final break with President Jackson in 1831 which led to his resignation in 1832 and immediate election to the Senate), it marked Calhoun's abandonment of some of the nationalist policies he had heretofore supported but which he now judged prejudicial to his State and region.

The specific conflict discussed in the "Exposition" was economic, but his line of reasoning had broader implications which he would later develop into the doctrine of "concurrent majorities," and the demand for an "equilibrium" between the Southern minority and the Northern majority in the Union. The idea of a profound division of interests was subsequently carried by Calhoun into every aspect of commercial legislation and into the vexing issue of slavery in the territories.

Here was the germ of the thesis underlying all of Calhoun's subsequent constitutional doctrines, namely that the discontent of but one region (even if it represented a minority of people) must in the end destroy the Federal Republic (either by political separation of the minority from the majority or by subjugation of the former by the latter). One of the "great defects of our system," he declared, was that "the separate geographical interests are not sufficiently guarded." All the more important was it then, in the case of regional conflicts, to avoid stretching Federal authority beyond the strict letter of the Constitution, as well as to recognize that when Federal legislation exceeded the bounds of the constitutional grant, any State of the minority had a right to suspend the operation of an unconstitutional act within its own territory.

This line of reasoning brings to mind the years of anarchy which followed victory in the Revolutionary War and the bitter protracted debates over adoption of the Constitution in 1788. Later advocates of this course merely shifted base, attacking not the charter but its clear intent to establish a National Government.

More farseeing than most of his contemporaries, Calhoun had thus reached the logical conclusion as early as 1828 that her divergent interests must inevitably place the South in opposition to the majority of the States in the Union in all matters of economic policy. His views in this matter proved fatally decisive for the country.

The basic issue between North and South became evident when the country was faced with the nullification crisis of 1832–33, which proved to have been a rehearsal in many ways of the Civil War. Henry Clay found a way to compromise the issue but for a brief moment the rift between North and South was revealed in all its frightening depth and intensity.

The South now came to regard preservation of equality in the Senate (and hence her veto on abolitionist legislation) as the indispensable condition of her continued allegiance to the Union. What the South feared was that a Northern majority under abolitionist influence would compel emancipation by constitutional amendment or unconstitutional Federal legislation.

When Calhoun entered Congress (1811), it was dominated by a coalition of Southerners and Westerners. When he died, the coalition had become one of Northerners and Westerners, the South being in the minority.

After 1828, the search for a "reconciling formula" that might keep the growing North-South antagonism from destroying the Union occupied his mind, and he devoted all his energies and considerable talents to the formulation of constitutional safeguards for his region. The 1808 reform in his home State had been based on the idea of "balance" or "equilibrium" between sections representing the minority and the majority of the population, respectively. The requisite constitutional device was the principle of "concurrent majorities." Since each section controlled one of the two legislative chambers, neither could impose its will on the other. Hailed at the time as a "fair" resolution of sectional conflict, it was, of course, a profoundly "undemocratic" one. Democracy accords the minority rights but exacts correlative duties as well—the right to plead its viewpoint, the obligation to abide by majority decisions. To protect the minority against "the tyranny of the majority,"—one of Calhoun's favorite phrases—can be called "fair" only if one is prepared to submerge the individual in his particular group, to reduce the principle of "equal rights" to "group rights," a procedure reminiscent of the prerevolutionary French *Etats-Generaux* and other feudal institutions combining a broad suffrage with the most blatantly unequal weighting of votes. Thus in France, for example, the First Estate, representing 100,000 clergymen, was equal to the Second, representing 400,000 nobles, and the two together had a voting power equal to that of the Third Estate which represented everybody else (i.e., 96 percent of the French people).

The South Carolina arrangement was, of course, nothing like so discriminatory. In the upper house, it did however give a four to one advantage (on a per capita basis) to the minority section, which is why the device of "concurrent majorities" is on occasion resuscitated by other minorities seeking to escape the operation of the democratic process.

The success of the constitutional compromise he helped bring about as a member of the South Carolina Legislature left an impress on his political thinking. Sectional strife was the dominant theme, so to speak, of his entire career, but it was in the last two decades of his life that it absorbed his energy and talent to the exclusion of almost everything else. Searching for a constitutional solution of the growing conflict between the Southern minority and the Northern majority in the Nation, he returned to the formula of 1808 which had restored domestic harmony in his home State by establishing an "equilibrium" between its minority and majority. He seems to have been unaware or at any rate undisturbed that, if nationally adopted, this concept would have nullified the Declaration of Independence and the Constitution and turned the Nation back into the ineffective league of sovereign States it had been under the Articles of Confederation.

Calhoun eventually carried the "equilibrium" idea to its logical (and wholly impractical) conclusion, devoting all his energies and considerable talents to the formulation of constitutional safeguards for his region. In his posthumously published *Discourse on the Constitution and Government of the United States* he maintained that the Union could not be preserved unless the South were given ironclad guarantees against passage of congressional acts injurious to her vital interests. He recommended an amendment to the Constitution providing for two Presidents, one elected by the North, the

207

other by the South, the assent of both to be required for validation of all acts of Congress.

But Calhoun's ingenuously wrought doctrine—which on the surface appears logical—ran into the increasingly national outlook of the majority of Americans. Northern opinion slowly reached the conclusion that it would not permit the American political system to be designed primarily to give local protection to slave property, in the process denying the North the necessary legislation for a diversified economy and imposing on it the obligation to protect the slave owner and the slave property he brought within its borders.

A statesman and political theoretician of note, he loved the Union and wished to preserve it. Built with impeccable logic upon premises ultimately rejected by the majority of his countrymen, his doctrines became the political platform of his region. His dogma that "united the South and divided the Union" in final analysis made conflict inevitable.

Toward the end of his life, he had an inkling of the coming tragedy. Virtually the last words he spoke were "The South, the poor South." Regionalism triumphed and the Union broke in two because we knew not how to prevent a continuous widening of the deep fissure in our body politic that was the tragic heritage of our colonial past. It is a sobering thought that ours was the only modern union to be destroyed by secession and put together again by force of arms in the bloodiest, longest fratricidal war ever fought by a civilized people.

As the tides of history swept the country toward the war, called by William H. Seward an "irrepressible conflict of opposing and enduring forces," the issues dividing North and South were being laid bare in the Senate and argued out with great skill and eloquence. Speaking extemporaneously (a piece of paper cupped in hand on which a few key words had been written), great orators held audiences spellbound for hours on end, sometimes days. Fully reported in the press, their speeches were widely read.

Among them, no three were greater than the famous triumvirate of Calhoun, Clay, and Webster. No other contemporary public figures devoted such great and prolonged efforts as these three to abatement of the centrifugal forces that were tearing the Union apart. Each offered a different solution; together these represented *every* feasible option *then* open to the country. Calhoun hoped to preserve the Union—though with diminished power and effectiveness—by placing it on a new constitutional basis. Clay sought to stave off a final breakup by judiciously balanced compromises, hoping that in time the Union would command such strong loyalty that no region could destroy it. Webster sought to arouse a sense of loyalty to the Union by expounding the Constitution and making the people aware of its manifest glories and benefits.

Their contests, wrote Charles A. Beard, were "worthy of a place in the annals of oratory beside the noblest intellectual tourneys of ancient and modern times," not only because of "the eloquence and cogency of their arguments," but also because of "the results that flowed from their deliberations." Nor were there among contemporary political leaders any who equaled them in their intense and prolonged efforts to find a way to hold the Union together.

It is doubtful whether we get as clear an insight today into our political system and the processes of our Government from the bland messages of the mass media as Americans of that day gained from the interplay of ideas of men of brilliant intellect and formidable forensic skill. Yet frank and full discussion could not prevent secession and war—dismal proof that keeping a "dialogue" going will not necessarily resolve profoundly divisive issues.

Calhoun, the Southerner, Clay the Westerner, Webster the New Englander—writing in 1888, James Bryce author of that classic *The American Commonwealth* called them "the ornaments of their generation, not indeed rising to the stature of Washington or Hamilton, but more remarkable than any, save one, among the statesmen who followed them." Yet the prize each coveted—the Presidency—was denied them all. Less able men were preferred; men who were "safer" because they straddled the issues dividing the Union instead of facing them and trying to tackle them, at the risk of becoming "controversial."

There was a curious parallelism in their lives. All three were of the second generation of American leaders, those who had no adult experience of life in a Colony. Calhoun and Webster were born the year we attained independence (though peace had not yet been formally concluded), Clay 5 years earlier. Their terms in the House and in the Senate coincided closely; they died in harness within 2 years of one another. Regardless of previous views, they all ended their careers as nationalists. They knew that unless every part of the country felt that its most vital interests were met by merging them with those of the Nation as a whole, the Union was in jeopardy. Yet they did not attain the principal objective to which each in the end gave his greatest efforts—reconciliation of the rival sections of the country so that the Union might continue to live.

It was natural that when the Senate appointed a committee (chaired by Senator John F. Kennedy) to select the five greatest senators, they should all three have been included (Robert La Follette and Robert A. Taft were the others). Their portraits are on the walls of the Senate Reception Room.

USS ABRAHAM LINCOLN (SSBN 602)

NAMED FOR Abraham Lincoln (1809–65), 16th President of the United States and, next to Washington, best known and most cherished of all who have held that lofty position. More has been written about Lincoln than about any other President, yet we cannot be certain of having taken the full measure of the man. He is hard to appraise objectively; the affection he inspires gets in our way. We have trouble disentangling him from the legend built by popular adulation. The thought of what he might have achieved had he not been struck down by an assassin's bullet intrudes when we attempt to evaluate what he actually accomplished. Walt Whitman perhaps came closest to the truth in his brief elegy to the slain President, calling him "the man, gentle, plain, just and resolute, under whose cautious hand . . . was saved the Union of these States." The essence of Lincoln is encompassed in these few words—the man he was, the aim he sought and attained, and the manner in which he pursued his objective.

He was the most American of our Presidents; no other country could have produced him or would, in Lincoln's day, have elevated a man of such lowly origins to the highest office in the land. To use his own words, he had been born "in the most humble walk(s) of life," of parents who were poor and came from "undistinguished families," his birthplace a small backwoods cabin on what was known as the "Sinking Spring Farm" in Hardin (now Larue) County, Ky. Of his forebears Lincoln knew little but genealogists have since traced them back to Samuel Lincoln of Hingham, England, who came to Massachusetts in 1637. Samuel's descendants moved westward, settling for a generation or two each in Pennsylvania, Virginia and Kentucky, where Lincoln's grandfather was killed by Indians while laboring to open a homestead in the wilderness. His father, orphaned at 6, roamed from one newly broken farm to another in Kentucky, Indiana and Illinois (another branch of the family migrated into Tennessee and Ohio). These were aimless wanderings that led to no change in fortune. The new farm hacked out of virgin forest might briefly yield bigger harvests but was seldom a lasting improvement over the one left behind; the new cabin was no more comfortable than the old one; every move meant discomfort and extra work. When Lincoln's father—never much of a planner—took the family to the wilds of Indiana, they arrived too late in the season to build a house and had to spend the winter in a rude shelter open on one side, with poles and brushwood enclosing the other three, a so-called "half-faced camp." In the spring, when Lincoln was but 7, "an ax was put into his hands" and for the next 15 years he remained bound to the endless round of cutting trees, burning stumps, planting corn, building cabins and fences—the hard, unskilled labor from which six generations of his family had never managed to extricate themselves. "It is a great folly to make anything of my early life," Lincoln said to a campaign biographer when he was running for President in 1860. "It can be condensed into a single sentence you will find in Gray's Elegy—'The short and simple annals of the poor'."

The circumstances of Lincoln's childhood and youth were indeed common enough in frontier America. What is significant is that he was able to surmount them, to get away from what James Truslow Adams called "the poverty, ignorance, lack of ambition, shiftlessness of character, contentment with mean things and low aims which kept so many thousands in the huts where they were born." Neither luck nor a helping hand eased Lincoln's way; his life was not cut to the Horatio Alger pattern. He advanced by removing every obstacle himself, the first being illiteracy; no small achievement for a boy living on an isolated frontier farm—"in an unbroken forest," as he remembered it—with parents who could not read or write. "There was absolutely nothing to excite ambition for education," he once said. Such schooling as he could get (all told a year or so) was obtained a few weeks at a time under a succession of uninspiring teachers who had no qualifications other than mastery of the three "R's." Lincoln was almost entirely self-taught. From his stepmother who gave him affection and support (his own mother died when he was 9) we know of his lying before the fire at night, reading or doing sums on a piece of wood as a slate; of his walking miles to borrow a book; of the handful of well-read volumes stored on a

212

rude shelf that made up his own tiny library. What spurred him was intellectual curiosity, an innate hunger for knowledge. How he came by these traits nobody can tell, but they showed themselves early in life and both puzzled and annoyed his unambitious father who is quoted as saying, years after his son had left home: "I suppose Abe is still fooling hisself with eddication. I tried to stop it but he had got that fool idea in his head, and it can't be got out."

To an unlettered community, his pursuit of knowledge might have seemed odd, but it did not set Lincoln apart. All his life, he had in marked degree the ability to be completely himself, yet at one with people in general and well liked by them. Withal, he was no bookish lad nor looked like one. Tall and exceptionally strong, mighty with an ax even as a boy and locally famed for his feats as "rail-splitter" (a nickname that followed him into the White House), he could outrun, outlift, outwrestle anyone in the county. His life was one of hard outdoor labor (only the nights were free for study), differing *outwardly* in no way from that of the people among whom he grew up, whose company he enjoyed even though he had interests they did not share. It is doubtful he was aware of *inwardly* growing beyond them. One of Lincoln's attractive characteristics was a sense of humor that kept him from taking himself too seriously or being overly impressed by his own achievements. "When I came of age I did not know much," he wrote years later. "Still, somehow I could read, write, and cipher to the rule of three, but that was all"—not much perhaps but enough to escape from life on a pioneer farm. And when Lincoln discovered that to make his way in the outside world he needed some special skill, this little "store of education," as he called it, was the essential tool with which he was able to build a professional career.

At first, nothing went right. The jobs he could get either petered out or barely sustained him; he helped build a flatboat and navigate it down the Mississippi to New Orleans; then settled in the village of New Salem (Illinois) working as clerk, manager of a mill, postmaster. He ran for the legislature and was defeated (1832). He volunteered for the Black Hawk War, was chosen captain by his militia company, but arrived too late and saw no action. (Jefferson Davis who commanded a company of Regular Army in that war is said to have administered the oath of allegiance to him.) His first and only business venture—part ownership in a grocery store—ended in disaster. The partner died leaving a debt of $1,100 that Lincoln felt honor bound to assume, though a staggering sum for him; it took 15 years of painful scrimping to pay it all back. In desperate need of a better paying job, he borrowed a book on surveying, quickly mastered its content, and was appointed deputy county surveyor, a job that he said "kept body and soul together" while with some more borrowed books, he taught himself law in the evenings. At 27, he was a licensed attorney. Having meanwhile won his second bid for the legislature, he moved to Springfield, the State capital and opened an office in partnership with a capable lawyer. So poor was he still that on leaving New Salem his surveying instruments were attached for a debt and he made the journey on a borrowed horse, all his possessions fitting easily into his two saddle bags. But he now had the winning combination: law as profession and politics as avocation; a combination virtually guaranteeing advancement in a pioneer State rapidly filling with people (in the generation since admission to the Union, Illinois grew 20-fold).

The striking thing about Lincoln's career as a lawyer-politician is that for nearly two decades such success as he had was in no way out of the ordinary. Nothing he said or did before he reached the age of 45 presaged what he would achieve in the last decade of life. True, he rose to prominence in the bar and party of his State, but so did scores of contemporary frontier leaders whose names have long since been forgotten. Some, born with no greater advantages than he, advanced faster and prospered more; in land speculation alone fortunes were to be made by able lawyers. Lincoln was one of the few who did not take this, then the surest road to wealth and influence; he was 40 before his practice earned him a comfortable living. An active party worker, an effective organizer and canvasser, he had, by his midforties, become the leading Illinois Whig. But in a normally Democratic State, there was little chance of making an outstanding record in public office. His 8 years in the State legislature (1834–42) brought him no special distinction; his single term in the U.S. House of Representatives (1847–49) lost him the support of the people of his district, the only time this happened to Lincoln who had respect for his "sovereign" in the very marrow of his bones (he did not stand for reelection). In this instance, he got out of step by opposing the Mexican War which to him, as to most northern Whigs, seemed but a scheme to gain more slave territory. Pondering the issue of slavery — torn between rejecting it as a moral evil and intensely disliking the tactics of the abolitionists — Lincoln came to the conclusion that, if there was no constitutional way to end it in the States where it existed, slavery must at least be kept from engulfing any more land. He joined the congressional Whigs in their attack on President Polk for having

214

"unconstitutionally and unjustly" begun the war, only to find himself accused of treason by his constituents who were expansionist to a man and divided in their views on slavery. Illinois, settled by migrants from both South and North, had prior to attaining statehood (1818) been part of Indiana Territory whose inhabitants in 1803 petitioned Congress for relief from the slavery prohibition of the Ordinance of 1787. Their plea was rejected; Randolph of Virginia pointing out that slave labor was neither necessary to "prompt the growth of the settlements" nor economically feasible, being "the dearest that can be employed," advantageous only "in the cultivation of products more valuable than any known in that quarter of the U.S." The authority of Congress to regulate slavery in the Federal territories and the propriety of banning it in the Northern areas were not questioned at that time. Had this view prevailed half a century later, Lincoln's career might well have continued its routine course. The turning point came in 1854, its proximate cause the bitter controversy on this very issue which broke out following passage of the Kansas-Nebraska Act. Lincoln's approach to the problem, expressed in a series of powerful speeches, won him national attention — ultimately the Presidency.

Strange to say, the controversy had its origin not in the slavery issue per se, but in sectional rivalry over location of a government subsidized transcontinental railroad; a rivalry all the more intense in that only one such railroad was deemed feasible. Nor was this last great slavery crisis of the South's making, though Southern intransigence prevented a peaceful solution. It was precipitated by Connecticut-born Stephen A. Douglas, leading Illinois-Democrat and Lincoln's great political rival (for the Senate, 1858; the Presidency, 1860). The Kansas-Nebraska Act was his handiwork; its object, to get the projected railroad routed centrally across the country from Chicago (where Douglas had bought up land in anticipation of the city's growth as a rail terminal). Earlier attempts had foundered on Southern opposition in the Senate. The South was pushing its own route for which the Government had already been induced to buy a strip of desert from Mexico (Gadsden Purchase) for direct passage to the Pacific. To secure the railroad for his own section, Douglas was willing to pay a high price; nothing less than the opening to slavery of areas from which it was excluded by the Missouri Compromise of 1820. Except for the newly acquired Utah and New Mexico Territories, there would have been no more land left from which another slave State might have been carved.

Declaring for congressional noninvolvement in the Federal territories and the principle of "popular" or "squatter sovereignty," the Kansas-Nebraska Act revoked the Missouri Compromise explicitly, the Compromise of 1850 by implication. It thus demolished the carefully constructed system of mutual concessions which had so far preserved the Union by definitively settling for every acre of American soil whether it was open or closed to slavery; the fate of large areas that were to have been "forever" free was now left to local option, virtually insuring that there would be internecine struggles between pro- and antislavery forces whenever a new State was formed ("bleeding Kansas" was a portent of things to come). Rightly termed the worst legislative blunder in American history, it so exacerbated relations between the free and slave parts of the Union that the national parties broke apart. The Whigs disintegrated in 1854; the Democrats put up rival presidential candidates in 1860; the rift between Northern and Southern members was now unbridgeable. If the North was angry at having been swindled of contractual rights deemed hardly less sacrosanct than the Constitution, the South felt cheated when the areas newly opened to slavery proved unsuitable for slave agriculture, and Kansas, earmarked as a slave State, voted six to one for freedom (despite pressure from the Federal Government).

The South had pushed the traditional worship of the Constitution to a point which subordinated the American legal system to the needs of one peculiar and incongruous institution. The aggressive theories and politics of the Southerners made the moderate opponents of slavery realize it was wrong for the beneficiaries of that institution—about 350,000—to claim that there could be no cotton without slaves. These opponents saw that, unless checked, the Southern planters would succeed eventually in nationalizing slavery by appropriating the national domain in its behalf. A body of public opinion was gradually formed which looked to denationalize slavery by restricting its expansion. This body was finally organized as the Republican Party (1854). In the North, anti-Nebraska groups sprang up spontaneously, most of them eventually merging with the newly formed Republican Party—so named because its platform called for exclusion of slavery from *all* territories, a policy dear to Jefferson's heart (though never officially adopted by his own Republican Party).

This new party can be considered the first truly national party in the sense that its ideas and policies had national import. There were three Republican wings: the radicals, opposed to all compromise with the South; the moderates, including Lincoln, in agreement with many of the radical aims but willing to make temporary concessions provided slavery would be restricted; and the conservatives, who favored compromise and were more interested in the economic and social principles of their old parties than in the antislavery commitment of the new. The moderates prevailed with increasing difficulty during the war; though ultimately the radicals, being the most active, set the Republican Party line, bringing about, after Lincoln's death, the excesses of the Reconstruction period.

Astonishingly successful in the 1856 and 1858 elections, the Republicans made certain of winning the Presidency in 1860 by passing over the leading contender, an Easterner (William H. Seward), nominating Lincoln who alone could carry the crucial States of Pennsylvania, Ohio, Indiana, and Illinois (the rest of the free States were deemed safe whoever the candidate). Faced with the prospect of a "Black Republican" in the White House, the South saw no alternative to secession, if slavery and its distinctive way of life was to be preserved. It did not matter that the Republican nominee was Lincoln, even though his voice for the past 6 years had been the sanest and most conciliatory heard in the land.

Lincoln stated the issue dividing the Nation in simple terms that cut through the legalistic arguments with which North and South tried to bolster their case. The Union was a house divided against itself because of the presence of an institution that could not be squared with the Nation's commitment to the principles of the Declaration of Independence. To endure, it must become either all slave (and cease being a democracy) or all free (thus realizing the promise of the American creed). Divided it could not stand. This was the dilemma politicians and people alike had refused to face since the founding of the Nation. The division was not one of constitutional interpretation, but a "difference between the men who think slavery wrong and those who do not . . . The Republican Party think it wrong . . . Because we think it wrong, we propose a course of policy that shall deal with it as a wrong." As with any wrong, what needed to be done was to keep it from spreading, so that "in the run of time there may be some promise of an end to it." For the first time it was clearly understood that American nationality was a living principle rather than a legal bond; that in a democratic nation, local and individual rights could not be made the excuse for national irresponsibility. The people of the North finally understood the issue and supported the man who more than any other political leader had properly defined the issue for them.

Neither Lincoln nor the Republican platform went beyond this moderate demand. "I have no purpose, directly or indirectly, to interfere with the institution of slavery in the States where it exists," he declared in his First Inaugural speech. "I believe I have no lawful right to do so, and I have no inclination to do so." A few days before war broke out, Congress adopted, with Lincoln's approval, an amendment that would have made this irrevocable. Nor did Lincoln deny the South's constitutional right to demand return of fugitive slaves, provided only that "all the safeguards of liberty known in civilized and humane jurisprudence" be preserved, "so that a free man be not in any case surrendered as a slave." The South could have held on to its peculiar institution until such time as Southern public opinion would have joined that of the rest of the civilized world in condemning human bondage as a barbaric custom. Two years into the war, Lincoln still hesitated before issuing the Emancipation Proclamation. He did so in the end chiefly to prevent Europe from recognizing the independence of the Confederacy. It had the desired effect abroad but the Republicans suffered a setback in the midyear elections.

Lacking the selfrighteousness of the true reformer—he liked people too well for that—Lincoln's antislavery policy was without hatred of the slave owner, even sensible to his problems. "I surely will not blame them for not doing what I should not know how to do myself," he said in 1854. "If all earthly powers were given me, I should not know what to do, as to the existing institution." He was adamant, however, in rejecting Southern assertions that slave owners had the constitutional right to take their property wherever they wished and demand it be legally protected. If conceded, this would make slavery "national," freedom "sectional," said Lincoln, in his masterly dissection of the Dred Scott decision (1857)—the worst blunder in the history of the Supreme Court. Disregarding John Marshall's wise policy of never meddling in political issues (for which obviously there can only be political solutions), the court flatly denied the right of Congress to bar slavery from the Federal territories—a practice going back to the Ordinance of 1787 and believed authorized by the Constitution (Art. IV, sec. 3). As Lincoln pointed out, the two instruments were drawn up in the same year and by virtually the same persons. Like Jefferson and Jackson, he would not accept what to him, as to most Northerners, was not only a judicial error but a blatantly partisan decision to boot (five of the six Justices who declared the Missouri Compromise unconstitutional, including Chief Justice Taney, were Southerners). Lincoln saw ominous implications in the novel and unduly broad interpretation given by the court to the "due process" clause (Fifth Amendment). What was to prevent it at some future date from stretching the clause still further so as to deny to the States as well, the right to bar slavery (as via the 14th amendment the Court in later years restricted State action in matters clearly reserved to them under the Constitution)? We might wake up some day, he warned, and find "that the Supreme Court has made Illinois a slave state." Unlike bad laws that can be repealed—the people having but to throw out their perpetrators in the next elections—judicial errors can only be corrected by amendment— impossible in this case since adoption would have been blocked by the 15 slave States. It is a sobering thought that they could have prevented adoption even had the Union then consisted of 50 States as today, instead of only 31. Lincoln's remarks on this situation in his First Inaugural Address remain relevant: "If the policy of the Government upon vital questions affecting the whole people is to be irrevocably fixed by decisions of the Supreme Court, the instant they are made in ordinary litigation between parties in personal actions the people will have ceased to be their own rulers, having to that extent practically resigned their Government into the hands of that eminent tribunal."

Lincoln came to the Presidency with no experience in the management of large affairs, civilian or military, no personal knowledge of the world or even of his own country beyond the frontier region where he had spent all his life. He took office at a time of extreme peril. Greater demands were made upon him than on any previous President and he had fewer resources to meet them—his party composed of heterogeneous groups not yet properly fused and therefore tending to quarrel; the Congress largely made up of new men who had little experience in statecraft, much of the talent having left for the South; his Cabinet was often rent by discord. Yet Lincoln was one of our ablest war Presidents, a better strategist than most of his generals, a more skillful statesman than his civilian advisers, and at times the only man to see the realities of the contenders' war potential. Yet he never faltered in his conviction that the North would win.

Lincoln's competence saved the Union but he is best remembered as the most humane leader ever to guide a country through a bitter fratricidal war, towards a peace he intended to be without vengeance. Towards "our late friends, now adversaries" (as he liked to call the Confederates) Lincoln felt no rancor, even when his armies suffered humiliating reverses. No sooner was victory in sight than he prepared a plan that would speedily restore the Southern States to "their proper practical relation with the Union" (Proclamation, Dec. 6, 1864), demanding no more of them than abolition of slavery and return to the Union. When Booth shot Lincoln, the plan died with him; his successors did not have the strength to prevent Congress from imposing a Draconian peace. It does not bear thinking what this senseless crime of one unstable egomaniac, fancying himself in the role of avenger of the South and slayer of tyrants, was to cost the Nation.

American history abounds with instances of men who rose from obscurity to eminence (more than one President was born in a log cabin), but Lincoln was *sui generis*. It has been said that he solidified the American ideal. He was living proof that the American dream has substance, not only on the obvious level of material success or fame—rags to riches, log cabin to White House—but in its deeper implication which postulates that neither obscure antecedents nor poverty or lack of formal schooling limit man's capacity to grow in his competence and humanity, if only he be sufficiently determined. Lincoln had a fine mind but he was not a genius, nor did he have some special talent that needed only to be developed to raise him above his humble beginnings. Yet he made himself intellectually candid, concentrated and disinterested, as well as morally humane, magnanimous, and humble. These qualities were not possessed by the average or even by the exceptional American of his day— they were generally ignored or undervalued. Yet high intelligence, humanity, magnanimity, and humility are precisely the qualities which Americans, to become better democrats, should add to their strength and to their homogeneity.

One must assume that during the uneventful middle years, he used the meager opportunities at hand to develop within himself the qualities he was to need as President. Much of his law practice was circuit riding. As he jogged along in his one-horse buggy on the 400 mile round of the Eighth Illinois Judicial District, he was able to indulge his habit of reading and of thinking hard and to a purpose (contracted as a boy while he taught himself the rudiments of knowledge). The law itself disciplined his mind, taught him to grasp the essence of a case and argue it in simple, lucid language; his words were marvels of dry vigor and control. He was wont to say: "If I can strip this case of technicalities and swing it to the jury I'll win it." Just so did he strip the legalistic brushwood from the issue of slavery and Union, swinging it to the jury of his compatriots and winning them to his view that the Union stood for human liberty—for Government of, by and for the people—and that it was worth fighting for.

During his mature years, he rarely proclaimed an idea which he had not mastered, and he never abandoned a truth which he had once thoroughly achieved. He had the wisdom and empathy that makes for effective leadership within the democratic process. Unpretentious, he understood and respected the thoughts and feelings of plain people, had the patience to wait until they caught up with the ideas and actions he advocated. Because of his close rapport with the popular mind, he could act resolutely yet remain within the limits of public consensus. By the manner in which he conducted the Presidency in the most perilous years of the Nation's history, he vindicated the democratic faith of the American people. In a sense, he became the patron saint of that faith.

To restore the Federal Republic was Lincoln's single aim as President; everything he did served this objective. He found it rent in two when he took the oath of office, the sundered parts angrily disputing territory won in a century of common effort. When he died 4 years later, the parts had been rejoined, the Union made "indestructible," its paramountcy so firmly established that it was never again questioned by any State or region. This achievement ranks with the winning of independence and the founding of the Union in which Washington took the leading part. Popular judgment is sound when it pronounces the "Savior of the Union" and the "Father of his Country" the two great American Presidents; for each, at his moment in history, was indispensable to the very existence of this Nation.

USS STONEWALL JACKSON (SSBN 634)

NAMED FOR Thomas Jonathan Jackson, known to history as "Stonewall" Jackson, Confederate general and strategist and one of the South's most illustrious heroes.

Third of four children, he was born at Clarksburg, in what is now West Virginia, January 21, 1824. When Thomas was 2, his father died leaving the family penniless. Called early to help support his mother, he had few opportunities for education. His mother died 5 years later and he was then raised by a succession of relatives, ending up as a ward of his uncle. While still a teenager, he worked as a schoolmaster and constable. In 1842, at the age of 18, he was appointed to the U.S. Military Academy.

A poor boy from a rural town, Jackson found himself at a disadvantage in competing against his classmates, many of whom had prepared for the Academy at better schools. Through sheer effort and hard study, he rose from 51st in his class at the end of his first year to 17th at graduation.

When Jackson and his classmates received their commissions in June 1846, the United States was at war with Mexico, and the young lieutenant of artillery was immediately sent to join the front. He participated in the campaign against Mexico City and distinguished himself at the Battle of Chapultepec. After brief tours of duty at garrisons in the East and in Florida, he resigned from the army to become Professor of Natural and Experimental Philosophy and Artillery Tactics at the Virginia Military Institute in Lexington, Va. At VMI, Jackson was an indifferent teacher and his marked eccentricities made him the butt of many student jokes. Shy and with few close friends, he found comfort in religion which became something of an obsession during his years at Lexington. A devoted and hardworking member of the Presbyterian Church, he regularly donated a 10th of his income to the church, and established at his own expense a free Sunday school for the children of Negro slaves and freedmen in which he served as the principal teacher.

Lincoln's election and the subsequent secession crises presented Jackson with a cruel dilemma. Like his fellow Virginian, Robert E. Lee, he opposed secession and believed that, "It is better for the South to fight for her rights in the Union than out of it." After Fort Sumter, he felt he had no choice but to remain loyal to his native State.

At the outbreak of the war, Jackson was appointed a colonel of Virginia Volunteers. His first assignment was command of the arsenal at Harpers Ferry, the northern outpost of the Shenandoah Valley, later to be the scene of his famous exploits. At the Battle of Bull Run on July 21, 1861, Jackson, now a brigadier general, commanded the 1st Brigade of General Joseph E. Johnston's Army of the Shenandoah. At the height of the battle, as the Confederates were beginning to buckle under the weight of the Union attack, a neighboring brigadier general, Bee, rode up to Jackson with the cry, "They are beating us back!" "Then, sir," came the quick reply, "we will give them the bayonet!" Encouraged by this answer, Bee rallied his own retreating troops and cried, "Look, there is Jackson standing like a stone wall!" The Union attack was repulsed and Jackson had acquired his famous nickname "Stonewall."

After Bull Run, Jackson was promoted to major general and sent to the region of the Shenandoah. When a new Northern army under General George B. McClellan again moved to capture Richmond, Jackson was in command of a small force near Strasburg, Va. Convinced that most of the Federal troops in his area had gone east to join McClellan, Jackson advanced, with barely 3,000 men, and captured Winchester. At Kernstown, he was repulsed by a Federal Army under General Shields which outnumbered his own by more than two to one. So bold and vigorous was Jackson's attack, that the Northern commanders believed that he was in command of a much larger force.

Alarmed at the threat to Washington posed by Jackson's supposedly large army, President Lincoln ordered a large Federal force under General Banks back to the Shenandoah Valley and retained an additional 30,000 men at Washington to defend the city. All of these troops were thus prevented from joining McClellan's attack on Richmond. As Jackson's biographer, Colonel G. F. R. Henderson, has observed, "It is seldom

223

that a battle so insignificant as Kernstown has been followed by such extraordinary results."

Kernstown, however, was only the beginning of Jackson's remarkable campaign in the Valley. On April 21, with Richmond menaced by more than 100,000 Federal troops, General Lee called upon Jackson to take some of the pressure off the besieged Southern capital by a diversionary campaign in the Shenandoah. Jackson responded brilliantly. Before General Banks could be attacked safely it was necessary to check the advance of the Federal troops from the west, which would threaten Jackson's rear.

On May 8th, reinforced to 18,000 men, he drove the enemy back into the mountains of western Virginia, then turned on General Banks at Front Royal and Winchester, driving him back to the Potomac. Jackson then found himself menaced by three armies: General Fremont's to the southwest, General Shields' to the east, and Banks' across the Potomac. By skillful and lightning movements and before they could combine, he defeated his opponents separately. By June 10th Jackson was safely out of the Valley and on his way to join Lee at Richmond. With 18,000 men, he had checkmated Northern forces of over 70,000, thus depriving McClellan of needed reinforcements and giving valuable time to Richmond's defenders.

In the Seven Days' Battle, Lee succeeded in repulsing the Union attack on Richmond, and McClellan's army began withdrawing from the vicinity of the capital. Meanwhile the Federal forces in the Piedmont, Va., area were consolidated into a single "Army of Virginia" under Major General John Pope.

In order to crush Pope before he could be joined by McClellan's forces, Lee dispatched Jackson with almost half the Confederate Army to march north and then east so as to get behind Pope's forces. In 2 days of forced marches, Jackson covered 54 miles, fell upon and destroyed the Federal advance base at Manassas Junction. In the campaign of Second Bull Run which followed, he played a masterful role and, together with Lee, drove Pope back upon the defenses of Washington.

By this time Jackson had become almost a legend in the Confederacy. After the Antietam campaign in which he again saved the Southern cause from disaster, he was promoted to lieutenant general and given command of the 2d Army Corps of the Army of Northern Virginia.

A soldier, an incurable breaker of regulations, confessed when brought before Jackson for punishment, that his offenses were committed with the intention of "getting a good look at the General."

Jackson, however, remained detached and unmoved by his growing fame. "Don't trouble yourself about representations that are made of your husband," he wrote to Mary Anna Jackson shortly after his promotion to lieutenant general, "These things are earthly and transitory . . . Let us follow the teaching of inspiration. 'Let another man praise thee and not thine own mouth: a stranger not thine own lips.'"

In April 1863, a new Federal invading army of more than 120,000 under General Joseph Hooker advanced against the Confederate positions on the Rappahannock near Chancellorsville, Va. Hooker planned to use his superior force, which outnumbered Lee by almost two to one, to envelop the Confederate left flank. Jackson and Lee conferred on a strategy. They determined, in one of the boldest gambles of the war, to send the bulk of the Confederate Army under Jackson on a wide swing around the Union right flank while Lee, with only 14,000 men, would hold the front.

In the predawn darkness, Jackson's men moved out on still another of the legendary forced marches. Twelve hours later, at sunset, they were in position at right angles to, and preparing to attack the Union line which was still unaware of their presence.

The attack was devastating. The entire right wing of the Union Army was demoralized and routed. In the gathering darkness Jackson was severely wounded by the fire of his own men. He died a week later. "Could I have directed events," Lee wrote him, "I should have chosen for the good of the country to be disabled in your stead."

His body lay in state in the House of Representatives at Richmond not far from the spot where, 2 years earlier, a puzzled legislator had asked "Who is this Major Jackson?" when his name had been put forward for a commission in the Virginia Volunteers. He was buried in the simple cemetery near Lexington, Va., where he had spent his happiest years.

Jackson's death was a fatal blow to the Confederacy. The Army of Northern Virginia was never again the same pliant instrument it had been when he was alive; never again did Lee have a subordinate who at once grasped what was in his mind and brilliantly executed his plan.

Jackson was the ideal lieutenant, never called upon to command a large force independently. A tactician and leader of the first order, his Valley campaign remains a classic of what a small force can accomplish when led by a resolute officer who understands the use of mobility and secrecy. In brilliance of planning and boldness of execution he has had few American equals. Although his career as a general lasted but 2 years, he left his mark as one of our great soldiers.

USS ROBERT E. LEE (SSBN 601)

NAMED FOR Robert Edward Lee (1807–70). Born in the Tidewater area of Virginia where the Nation had its beginnings and to a family whose military heritage went back to the Crusades, Lee distinguished himself as one of the great generals of the Confederacy. He left his mark on American history in his impact on men, even more than on events. His contemporaries spoke of him as the perfect American soldier. In every situation confronting him, whether on parade ground, at command post, or on field of battle, he demonstrated extraordinary ability in leadership. His men responded with fervor to his indomitable will when he took command of the Army of Northern Virginia on June 1, 1862. Within that army, he developed discipline and morale that remain models to this day. Although in the end he surrendered to an overwhelming force, his generalship continues to be studied by all dedicated to the profession of arms. The student of Lee cannot help but be impressed by him as a living embodiment of "determined self-reliance." He had the capacity to make do with what he had and to make the most out of available resources.

Faced with adversity throughout much of his life, he learned to develop a rigorous code of daily conduct. A truly Christian gentleman, humility, patience, kindness, and faith were innate traits which seldom failed him in his relations with his soldiers and superiors. Self-control was second nature to him, and he was able to follow up a rare outburst of temper by a gracious act to the victim of his rage. Those who served with him discovered his inability to act disrespectfully or scornfully toward stubborn incompetents or to anyone who provoked his wrath. Because of compassion for others, he consistently avoided placing blame, acting with consideration to the problems of his associates, thus gaining the respect even of those who resented his authority. "Excessive consideration for the feelings of others," his principal biographer wrote, "explained this weakness."

He came of a family with a great record of public service. His father, Henry Lee, was famous in the Revolutionary War as a leader of Washington's cavalry, earning the sobriquet "Light Horse Harry." The founder of the American branch of the family, Richard Lee, who migrated to Virginia during the reign of Charles I, became secretary of state and a member of the Privy Council of Virginia, and helped hold the Colony for Charles II. Two Lees (Richard and Henry) signed the Declaration of Independence.

Robert was the fifth child of Henry and Anne Hill Carter Lee. "Stratford" on the Potomac in Westmoreland County, Va., patrician home of the great Lee family, was his birthplace. His father, following a distinguished military career, became Governor of Virginia, but wrecked his brilliant prospects through excessive land speculation. In 1811 Lee's father gave up Stratford and moved the family to Alexandria, Va., where they were able to live on the modest trust left by Mrs. Lee's father.

At 11, Robert, without fully knowing the reasons for his father's declining fortune, had to take over the responsibility of caring for his ill mother. He worked hard at his studies, displaying considerable talent in mathematics, which later helped him gain admittance to the U.S. Military Academy in 1825. Better prepared in his schooling and more mature than most of his classmates, he excelled in academics and achieved high proficiency in the military requirements. He graduated with a distinguished record, standing second in the Class of 1829 and receiving a coveted commission in the Corps of Engineers. Before the Mexican War in 1846, Lee had already demonstrated his ability and officer-like qualities.

In 1831, he married Mary Ann Randolph Custis, great-granddaughter of Martha Washington, and heiress to the Arlington estate which overlooks Washington. Thus by birth and marriage, Lee was connected with the leading Virginia families.

During the war with Mexico, Lee won high praise for his service on the staff of a fellow Virginian, General Winfield Scott. In 1852, against his wishes, he was named Superintendent at West Point. Not only did he improve the curriculum but he also devoted much time to the individual cadets, thereby earning the respect of Secretary of War Jefferson Davis and General Scott. Both advanced his career by giving him command responsibilities rather than staff assignments, first in command of a cavalry regiment and then as Department of Texas commander. But duty at distant posts and the stress of long absence from home led him to consider resigning from the army. He spent many tedious hours with courts-martial details, an experience which would later prove useful in dealing with wayward soldiers and officers. In 1859, while in Washington, he was sent to Harpers Ferry, where he quietly though firmly ended John Brown's insurrection. Thence he returned to the Texas border only to be summoned to Washington in February 1861, to meet the crisis of his career.

During President Buchanan's administration (1857–61) tensions over extending slavery into the territories mounted. After John Brown's raid, the Nation ran its fateful course toward disunion, and Abraham Lincoln's election triggered the secession of seven Southern States. Lee held no sympathy toward rebellion. Condemning slavery as morally repulsive and economically unsound, he had, in common with many landowners of Virginia, liberated his slaves. But he considered it would be a still greater evil to eradicate slavery by force.

On April 12, 1861, Confederate batteries fired on Fort Sumter, starting the Civil War. This action removed many constitutional difficulties from Lincoln's effort to preserve the Union, and he moved quickly to suppress the rebellion by calling on the militia from all the States, including the eight slave States still in the Union. The President's decision to coerce the Confederacy moved Virginia to secede and join the Confederacy.

While Lee believed in the Union, he felt even more strongly that the authority of the Federal Government had been voluntarily conferred on it by the several sovereign States which therefore had the right to secede if they wished. On the eve of the crisis he wrote, in words echoing Calhoun, "I can anticipate no greater calamity for the country than the dissolution of the Union. . . . Secession is nothing but revolution. . . . In 1808, when the New England States resisted Mr. Jefferson's Embargo Law and the Hartford Convention assembled, secession was termed treason by Virginia Statesmen; what can it be now? Still a Union that can only be maintained by swords and bayonets, and in which strife and civil war are to take the place of brotherly love and kindness, has no charms for me. If the Union is dissolved and the Government dispersed I shall return to my native State and share the miseries of my people and, save in defence, will draw my sword no more."

On April 18, Lee declined General Scott's offer to make him

the Union's overall field commander. The next day, learning that Virginia had passed an ordinance of secession, he submitted his resignation. He did not tell the Virginia leaders, hoping he could avoid participating in a war he condemned. Nevertheless, asked by the Governor to take command of Virginia's forces, he accepted, throwing all his energies into his State's defense. A month later, Scott sent Union forces into northern Virginia, where they occupied Arlington Heights, Lee's home. At Richmond, Lee became Davis' informal military adviser with the rank of general, his mission being to mobilize Virginia's volunteers. To this extent he finally identified himself with and sanctioned the political aspirations of Virginia's leaders. Having led an apolitical life, he did not analyze the fine points in Calhoun's arguments for States' rights as against those for Federal Union. To him, Virginia was the ultimate expression of local sovereignty; he gave his sword and his person as a means to preserve her rights.

For over a year Lee remained in the background, having to steer a difficult course between Jefferson Davis and the senior military commander of the Confederate forces, General Joseph E. Johnston. He observed the sudden ups and downs in morale of the Confederate troops in Virginia, as well as General Scott's astute tactics in attempting to isolate the Confederacy by the use of seapower and by invading along the rivers of the trans-Appalachian area. On May 31, 1862, destiny called: Johnston was wounded and Lee took command of the troops defending Richmond and the rest of Virginia.

The Army of Northern Virginia was his first field command. Responding to his drive, it became a formidable fighting machine. Lee faced General McClellan and his 100,000 men within 7 miles of Richmond and in the Shenandoah Valley, breadbasket of the South, where three separate Union forces were trying to corner General "Stonewall" Jackson. Lee knew exactly the course to take and acted quickly. With General Jackson he worked out the tactic of dividing and destroying the Union forces. In several maneuvers Jackson drove the enemy from the field and then, according to plan, joined Lee before Richmond.

During June 1862, Lee resuscitated a sagging army, coped patiently with politically appointed officers, assigned capable officers to top commands and overcame the administrative deficiencies and staff jealousies he had inherited from General Johnston. He reorganized his army in the field while it was fighting a larger, better equipped enemy. He learned his enemy's weaknesses and fought General McClellan to a draw.

The Peninsular Campaign brought out Lee's dormant greatness. During July, August, and September of 1862, he forged a highly mobile army that soon gained victory after victory, achievements that generated in the Army of Northern Virginia an *esprit de corps* unexcelled in modern military history.

Upon assuming command on June 1, 1862, Lee had found four handicaps: First, there were no underpinnings of a Regular Army organization within the Virginia—or any other Confederate—volunteer force. Second, there was no time to create a disciplined force by means of leisurely drills or routine garrison life. Virginia had been lucky at Bull Run in July 1861, and at Ball's Bluff in October 1861, because of the blunders by the untrained enemy. Third, capable leadership in the Army of Northern Virginia existed only at its top command. Company and regimental officers were often influential politicians from rural Virginia, owing their positions to election by the very men they led. A gap existed between those loyal to the State government and those loyal to provincial dignitaries. Fourth, Lee knew that the Army of Northern Virginia considered itself a voluntary association of gentlemen organized for the immediate purpose of driving out what it considered overbearing and greedy Yankees. Such disparate attitudes created a barrier to discipline and morale.

Conscription had to be accepted by the Confederates; this had forced General Johnston to reorganize the entire army in order to hold the line of the Potomac. The conscripts elected new field grade officers, the inevitable result being to force out many promising officers who had begun to prove themselves as leaders after Bull Run. For this reason, the training process was making little headway. The new enlistees, coming from isolated rural areas, were vulnerable to diseases which they caught from one another. During the winter and spring of 1861–62, most spent their first months in the makeshift field hospitals. Medical officers were often more familiar to the men than were their company commanders.

The high morale achieved after Bull Run had been impaired by mismanagement of the quartermasters and commissaries. Food and clothing rarely reached the soldiers on schedule. When Lee first started correcting these faults, his colleagues treated him as an outsider, one not of General "Joe" Johnston's caliber.

Within 3 months, he accomplished something few commanders are able to achieve. In quick succession he established order in an army that was growing daily while facing the enemy. He established a fair and rapid system of courts-martial that handed out punishment in hours instead of weeks. He learned the importance of issuing food and clothing on schedule; that the quality of rations is not as important to the soldier as the regularity of issue. Even when cornered at Appomattox, Lee was still trying to eke out daily rations to his men.

While facing McClellan in front of Richmond, Lee took measures to improve morale. The word "morale" and the phrase *"esprit de corps"* defy dictionary definition. Lee left no written formula. He ended favoritism in the ranks, which had grown endemic since Bull Run, by insisting that assignments be placed on a fair basis; that those who had drawn soft duty behind the lines in return for voting for company officers be sent to the front. The spirit of the officers and soldiers improved, and he soon had them won over. Unable to do away with the entrenched system of politically appointed officers at the regimental level, Lee concentrated on selection and assignment of the best as brigade, division, and corps commanders. These, in turn, rooted out the weak officers at company level, and young, capable officers were soon in command. A most important action was to require his soldiers to dig entrenchments to protect the right of his Richmond front, so that he could strike with his left. The soldiers hated dirt digging; it was "slave work," unheard of for Southern volunteers. Lee drove his men to this manual labor, not only because of the need for protective works, but also because they needed muscle-building and the experience of working together on an assigned mission.

During July and August 1862, he was able to turn his attention from what he called corrective morale measures to concentrate on the long-range problems facing his army. He had assumed command of the Richmond campaign, distrusted by nearly all under him except Jackson. Armies are rarely better than their staffs. After the Battle of Malvern Hill, improvement in their work was notable. His headquarters and subordinate staffs were soon working out complicated offensive plans envisaging a dual sweep out of the Richmond bowl toward the protective shield of the Alleghenies, then down the Shenandoah and a quick end to Pope's new army around Manassas. The timing and supply of the August battles around Manassas and the September invasion into Maryland owed their success to this staff work of Lee's lieutenants. He stressed the gathering of intelligence, every bit of which he screened himself; he demanded that information be "early and accurate." He underscored the words, for one without the other results in lost opportunity. Study of Lee's battles and the movements of his army—always inferior in numbers and supplies—reveals that his main reliance was based on superior strategy. His basic principles of war were two: surprise and economy of force.

In the summer of 1862, he gave the Army of Northern Virginia its greatest heartening—victory. The army's morale grew, so much so, that after Chancellorsville it considered itself unbeatable. Unfortunately, Lee also became victim of this delusion. After Gettysburg, he explained his defeat by saying: "I thought the Army was invincible; I expected too much of it. Well, it was not, it fell back!"

Gettysburg brought to light the inherent defect in the South's ability to carry on the war. Although seasoned veterans retained spirit, their losses became irreplaceable; there was no replacement for Jackson; the brigade commanders had improved, but the number of experienced ones had been reduced. Longstreet as a corps commander was seriously wounded and out of the line. Ewell was barely able to stay active. Forced to use green corps commanders, Lee himself had to lead his army in 1864. This brought him into close personal contact with individual Southern soldiers and made him accessible to them. On several occasions he threatened to lead a charge, but his men seized his horse and led him to the rear.

In General Grant, Lee faced an opponent with stubbornness and willpower equal to his own, as demonstrated in the Wilderness campaign. The Army of Northern Virginia showed the effects of Lee's 2 years in command by their high morale in standing steady at Spotsylvania Court House, along North Anna, at Cold Harbor, and in the trenches at Petersburg and Richmond. His men continued to have faith in Lee because he called on them only when it was necessary, held them to a minimum of losses, and promised them success up to the last days of the war.

In the end, at Appomattox, Lee had but 8,000 men with muskets in hand, and two batteries of artillery with only enough ammunition for 2 more hours, yet his ragged troops, unfed for 6 days, came running to Lee, saying: "General, is it true we have surrendered? . . . say the word and we will go at them again!" This was the final tribute to a great leader.

If he did nothing else Lee proved to the world that once aroused and believing in a cause, the American soldier can be a tough fighting man; in peace, the most forgiving.

After the war, Lee set himself to heal the wounds of his people, taking no part in the numerous controversies which the war aroused. Although in financial straits, like most Southerners, he refused to write his account of the great events in which he had played a leading part. He accepted the presidency of what is now Washington and Lee University where he spent his last years teaching by example and precept, constantly urging his students (many of whom were veterans of his army) to work hard, keep the peace, and restore the South.

Lee's chief characteristics were his rapid grasp of a military situation, his skillful use of interior lines of communication, his capacity to guess the mind of his opponents and understand their weaknesses. Few commanders have equalled his power of arousing devotion in their men. His contribution to the art of war was his use of field defenses in aiding maneuvers. He was ahead of his time; not until the 20th century were his methods understood and applied.

He died October 12, 1870. The news of his passing was mourned throughout the Nation. Historian Douglas Southall Freeman wrote: "No American has ever had an influence on the people of the Confederate States comparable to his. In all matters on which he expressed himself, he is still regarded as the final authority. In him the South still sees the embodiment of all its best ideals."

USS ULYSSES S. GRANT (SSBN 631)

N AMED FOR Ulysses Simpson Grant (1822–85), General of the Armies, Secretary of War, and 18th President of the United States.

Born April 27, 1822, at Point Pleasant, Ohio, Grant came from a long line of hardworking Puritans. Matthew Grant was the first of the family to reach these shores, settling in Massachusetts in 1630. One of Grant's grandfathers was a captain in the American Revolution and later emigrated to Ohio.

It was his father's idea for Ulysses to go to West Point. He graduated in 1843, standing 21st in a class of 39. This was not high enough for the engineer or artillery corps; he became a first lieutenant in the infantry.

In September 1845, Grant's regiment became part of General Zachary Taylor's forces in Mexico. Later, in the march on Mexico City, he served with General Winfield Scott, one of America's leading soldiers. He did well in combat and his gallantry was recognized. His assignments in Mexico also included that of regimental quartermaster and commissary, which made him responsible for rations, clothing, forage, and equipment. He disliked these duties, preferring action in the field, but performed them well and they gave him a background that later stood him in good stead.

After the war, he married Julia Dent; it was a singularly happy marriage. For a while he was stationed in California and Oregon but the separation from his wife and the boredom of army life were too much for him. He resigned his commission in 1854 and spent the next 6 years at various jobs without much success. In later years he recalled this time of hard work and close association with his family as one of the happiest periods of his life. When the Civil War broke out, he was a clerk in his father's store in Galena, Illinois. He was commissioned colonel of the 21st Illinois Regiment and brigadier general soon afterwards.

Because of the part Grant was to play in the conflict, it is useful to consider the problems facing Lincoln at the outbreak of hostilities. There were three: the military front, the domestic scene, and foreign affairs. In each he acted cautiously, seeing what had to be done, then waiting for the time and the proper instruments to attain his goal of preserving the Union. Of the three, the most important was the military. Thanks to Scott, the Union had retained most of the enlisted strength of the Regular Army at posts extending from the New Mexico Territory to Kansas. These troops quieted the territories and kept the vast Western region in the Union. On the domestic front, the most crucial problem was to hold the border States for the Union. Lincoln was able to keep Maryland, Kentucky, and Missouri sided with the North. His success in keeping the British and French from intervening was the work of shrewd diplomacy but it, too, depended upon the fortunes of war.

The very nature of the conflict forced on Lincoln a strategy that called for the overthrow of the Confederacy. The implementation of this strategy was profoundly influenced by the geography of the region. Along the seacoast and the Mississippi, the Navy established an effective blockade which, starting at St. Louis, Missouri, went to New Orleans and thence around Florida to Point Lookout, Md. This "Anaconda" strategy, conceived by General Winfield Scott, was Lincoln's way to ensure that the Confederacy would be isolated and forced to rely on its own resources. Strategy for the land war was far more complex. Fundamentally, there were two main theaters—to use a modern term: the area east of the Appalachians in which lay the capital cities of Washington and Richmond; and that to the west of the Appalachians—the broad valley of the Mississippi. Success in the East would mean capture of Richmond; in the West, cutting the Confederacy in two, making possible an invasion of the most southern of the seceded States. Neither theater could be considered in isolation from the other.

It was in the West that Grant first won fame. Despite hindrance from the inept strategical views and the ambitions of General Henry W. Halleck, who commanded the Department of the Mississippi, Grant achieved a series of victories that heartened the Union. Acting closely with the Navy, he captured Fort Donelson and Fort Henry (where 15,000 Confederates capitulated) on the Cumberland and Tennessee Rivers in February 1862. The "unconditional surrender" terms he demanded were clear evidence of his determination and of his feeling that this war would demand new and stern measures to bring it to an end. Two months later he was surprised at Shiloh, but the dogged courage of his men and his own refusal to panic saved him, though with high casualties. Halleck, however, then intervened and, through slow movement and the dispersal of his forces, lost the opportunity Grant had gained. By the spring of 1863, Grant was again in command. In a brilliant campaign which showed a superb grasp of strategy and tactics, he captured Vicksburg (taking more than 29,000 prisoners)—one of the most important victories won by the Union in the entire war. With its fall, the entire length of the Mississippi was in Union hands. Abraham Lincoln commented, "The Father of Waters again goes unvexed to the sea."

After Vicksburg, Grant, now a major general in the Regular Army, wanted to march on Mobile on the Gulf of Mexico where he would establish a supply base and then move north into regions of the Confederacy yet untouched by the war. Again Halleck interposed, dispersing his troops to hold fixed positions. The situation, moreover, was complicated by the intervention of the French under Napoleon III in Mexico. This period of indecision and lost opportunities ended when, after the Army of the Cumberland under Rosecrans was defeated at Chickamauga and forced into Chattanooga, Grant assumed command of the Military Division of the Mississippi, comprising three departments and their field armies. His presence turned a beaten army into a winning one. From November 23–25, he fought the Battles of Lookout Mountain and Missionary Ridge; victories that drove the Confederates from Tennessee, and opened the road to Georgia.

At Chattanooga many of the South's veteran units had been destroyed. Grant saw that the Confederacy's last chance for a military victory had passed. By now he had seasoned armies in the West, experienced commanders, and a competent staff and supply organization. Viewing the Confederacy as a whole, he evolved a grand design to end the war. This involved splitting the Confederacy east of the Mississippi in two by driving to Atlanta and by denying Lee the use of the area's railroads, hence of supplies. He predicted that Lee's end would come on the railroad lines in Virginia or in northwestern North Carolina.

Lincoln appreciated Grant's logic, but for the moment deferred action. The real importance of this strategic thinking was Lincoln's acceptance of him as General in Chief and his confidence that Grant could bring unity of command to the Union forces. What Lincoln had lacked throughout the war was a field commander who could integrate all the field armies and conceive and conduct a theater of war strategy. In Grant he had found his man. On March 9, 1864, Lincoln made him a lieutenant general — a rank Congress had only recently revived — and Grant assumed command of all the Union armies. His friend and comrade, William T. Sherman, was given the Western Command to carry out the new plans that Grant would develop.

As General in Chief, he reported directly to Lincoln and to Secretary of War Stanton, keeping them informed of the broad aspects of his strategic plans. He removed himself from Washington, the political seat of Government, to avoid becoming another McClellan. Henceforth, his headquarters accompanied the Army of the Potomac. Though he was prepared to go quickly to troubled spots, Grant elected to accompany Meade's Army of the Potomac so he could assess, first-hand, Lee's moves and their effects on other parts of the Union Army. To tie together his far-flung armies totalling more than one million men, while maneuvering against a great captain and a veteran army in a field of war, he employed a vast 15,000 mile telegraph system. By rail or steamboat, Grant was never far from Lincoln and, in turn, the President visited Grant frequently.

In the spring of 1864, he began his advance in Virginia. Lee checked him in the tangled forests of the Wilderness, but each time Grant, instead of falling back, side-stepped and pressed forward once more. "I purpose to fight it out on this line if it takes all summer" was his message from the battlefield of Spotsylvania. Lee never again escaped to sweep north. Inexorably, through bloody struggles such as Cold Harbor, the Union armies pressed closer until Lee's forces were hemmed in at Richmond and Petersburg. Despite the loss of 72,000 men, Grant kept the full support and confidence of Lincoln. Finally, on April 9, 1865, Lee surrendered at Appomattox.

Largest and longest conflict of the 19th century, save for the Napoleonic struggle, the American Civil War has been argued and analyzed for over a hundred years. It continues to excite the imagination because it was full of paradox. Old-fashioned, in that infantry attacked in the open in dense brigade formations, it also foreshadowed modern total war. Though not all the elements were new — railroads, telegraph, steamships, balloons, armor plate, rifled weapons, machine guns, wire entanglements, the submarine, torpedoes, large-scale photography — all were used extensively and the lessons learned were soon employed by foreign military forces.

At war's end, Grant found himself embroiled in political

struggles of which he had little understanding. After Lincoln's assassination, Andrew Johnson became President and briefly considered harsh punishment for Lee and other Confederate leaders. Grant intervened successfully. Johnson later appointed Grant Secretary of War but, as political disputes between the President and the radical Republicans of Congress erupted, Grant resigned. Bitter quarrels with Johnson led him into the camp of the radical Republicans. With their support, he was elected President in 1868 and again 4 years later.

In the general decline of public morality during his Presidency, corruption reached close to him although he himself was innocent. A simplicity of nature, combined with the tendency to believe that nothing could be wrong with those who shared his friendship, made him ill-fitted to cope with the situation. In his two administrations, the 15th amendment to the Constitution (providing that suffrage should not be restricted because of race, color, or previous condition of servitude) was adopted; inflation was checked; an agreement was reached with Britain over claims for damages resulting from ships built in England for the Confederacy and used against Northern shipping; and civil rights were restored to all but a few Southerners.

Returning to private life in 1877, Grant and his wife traveled around the world and, in 1880, returned to Galena. Later he moved to New York where he fell into financial difficulties by giving his confidence to unworthy people. This left him penniless just when he was beginning to suffer from the disease which caused his death. To recover financially, he wrote his memoirs. Much of it was written while he was suffering from cancer of the throat; he finished the manuscript only a few days before his death. Its writing was an act of heroism comparable with those he showed as a soldier. The work was like the man himself, modest, frank, and unassuming. It ranks as one of the best military biographies.

It is Grant the soldier who is remembered and who personifies the Union Army as Lee did the Confederate. A comparison of the two men is fascinating. Lee came from a patrician background; Grant had a more common origin. Lee graduated with honors from West Point; Grant's academic career was undistinguished. Lee was the embodiment of Southern landed aristocracy, which—although he personally detested it—was based on slavery, and he upheld the political doctrine of local sovereignty as the best way to maintain a traditional way of life. Grant is harder to capture but, over the years, his reputation has grown as the better strategist.

239

In many ways the two were alike. As cadets at West Point, both liked mathematics. As young officers in the Mexican War, both shared great promise, and both disliked the routine of the peacetime army. Each was devoted to his family and could not bear the thought of lonesome frontier duty. Both were good officers, understanding the dry-as-dust details behind the pounds of rations per man per day, and could take in a battlefield with the sweep of the glasses. Finally, both generals understood the privations of the man in ranks, and both in their own way won the loyalty of the fighting man.

Grant was a modern soldier. He learned rapidly on the field of battle. In the West he worked well with the Navy, using the ironclad river gunboats with vigor and imagination. Also in the West, where distances were great, he grasped the importance of railways, lines of supplies, and the telegraph. He recognized, too, the economic foundation of warfare.

As historian Charles Francis Atkinson has said, "There were soldiers more accomplished, more brilliant, more exact; but it would be difficult to prove that these generals or any others in the service could have accomplished the task which Grant brought to complete success. Singleness of purpose, and relentless vigor in the execution of the purpose, were the qualities necessary to the conduct of the vast enterprise of subduing the Confederacy. Grant possessed or acquired both. He had the most important qualities of a great captain; courage that rose higher with each obstacle, and the clear judgment to distinguish the essential from the minor issues of war."

USS MARIANO G. VALLEJO (SSBN 658)

NAMED FOR General Mariano Guadalupe Vallejo (1808–90), a highly esteemed and influential public figure who served his native California with distinction during the crucial years when its future was being shaped.

At the time of Vallejo's birth, California was a sleepy outpost lying on the periphery of Spain's colonial empire. It was part of the seas, lands, coasts, and islands in and around the Pacific that Spain asserted were hers "now and for all time, while the world lasts, and till the day of judgment." This was in 1513 when Balboa discovered the Pacific.

Having thus posted a "no trespass" sign, Spain took no further action to make good on her claim to California until other countries, chiefly England and Russia, showed an interest. Sir Francis Drake, an old enemy, one of the admirals in the fleet that defeated the Armada in 1588, was her first challenger. He sailed the *Golden Hind* into the bay that bears his name and took title to the region north of the Golden Gate for Queen Elizabeth I, naming it New Albion. Spain responded by sending Vizcaíno to explore and carefully map the entire coast of California. Next came the Russian explorers of Alaska, more feared than the English because of Russia's proximity to North America. In 1769, Spain responded by occupying California.

Since she lacked the resources to populate the land and administer it properly, Spain contrived a colonization scheme requiring few genuine settlers and a minimum of government services. She called upon the Franciscan order to undertake the task of Christianizing the Indians and putting them to work producing crops and tending livestock. A sixth of the land was turned over to them. On this land they built 21 missions, spaced a day's journey apart, between San Diego and Sonoma.

Out of the skill of the frairs, the docility of the Indians, the fertile soil and ideal climate, there evolved a flourishing pastoral economy. Food was abundant and enough surplus meal, wine, oil, hemp, hides, and tallow were produced to buy all other necessities from the mother country. Spain provided virtually no government services except defense. To protect the missions against the unconverted, often hostile Indians, forts or presidios were built and manned with garrisons of professional soldiers. In time, small towns (pueblos) arose in the protection of the presidios. However, colonists, other than friars and soldiers, did not become numerous during the half century of Spanish occupation.

Vallejo, eighth of 13 children of a sergeant, grew up in the Monterey Presidio and chose presidio service for his career. He joined the garrison as a cadet at 15, put down his first serious Indian rebellion at 19, and at 26 was sent to Sonoma to establish a military post and serve as its commandant with responsibility for keeping all of northern California pacified. He proved himself a first-rate organizer of frontier defenses and established complete control over the Indians, handling them with a judicious combination of firmness and kindness, qualities he possessed to an unusual degree.

The end of Spanish rule enlarged Vallejo's prospects in life, as it did for most of his abler young compatriots. Mexico's generous land grant policy enabled virtually every Californian to have his own well-stocked ranch, large or small. Vallejo, himself, received an enormous grant when he was made Commandant of the Northern Frontier and given the responsibility to direct and encourage colonization in that area. Then, too, as citizens of Mexico, the Californians enjoyed for the first time a measure of self-government, as well as representation at the capital. Vallejo was elected a member of the local assembly or *disputacion* in 1830 and a delegate to the Mexican Congress in 1834.

Nevertheless, Mexico never gained the complete allegiance of the Californians. They had taken no part in her revolt against Spain, remaining loyal and never doubting the mother country would win. Paradoxically, the success of the insurgents in severing communications between Spain and her distant colony had the unexpected result of changing what had been docile colonials into troublesome citizens extremely critical of the Mexican Government when it assumed jurisdiction in 1822 as the legal successor to Spain.

What changed them was their sudden exposure to the world

from which Spain had kept them isolated by forbidding foreigners to enter California or even trade with the inhabitants. When Spanish imports were cut off, these restrictions could no longer be enforced. Foreign trading vessels were welcomed, bringing not only the goods the people needed, but also news and ideas that greatly impressed them. They brought such news — and it was "news" to many of them — as the successful revolt of the American Colonies against England and the rise of the United States whose flag flew over many of the vessels now entering their ports; ideas never before encountered — such as democracy, government by and for the people, individual freedom. In the light of these ideas, Mexico appeared as an exploiter interested only in collecting customs dues and finding lucrative positions for her officials, while neglecting to provide the public services to which citizens of a civilized country were entitled. Mexico, herself in turmoil for decades, could not or would not grant such reasonable requests by Vallejo and others as that she send trained and properly paid soldiers to garrison the presidios instead of the unpaid convicts she had been using, or that she provide a reliable mail service. Nor would she appoint Californians to the governorship, even though the Mexicans she sent, almost to a man, were chased out of the country. In 1836, the Californians rebelled and made Vallejo's nephew, Alvaredo, governor and Vallejo, himself, top military commander. But, after a few years of virtual independence, sectional and personal jealousies brought Mexico back into control.

While the Californians quarreled with each other and with Mexico, increasing numbers of foreigners settled in the country, wrote glowing reports home, and kindled the interest of their respective governments in the possibility of acquiring this desirable land. Most foreign observers agreed Mexico would lose California, and annexation by some other power — England, France, or the United States — was inevitable since the Californians were too few in number, too inexperienced in self-government, too riven by traditional animosities between northern and southern towns, northern and southern families to establish a viable independent state. It was fortunate that, at this critical moment, they had in Vallejo a leader with a firm grasp of the limited options open to them and the bearing of these on California's true long-term interests.

Vallejo was the most powerful man, if not in the whole country, at least in the northern half. He had held high positions since the age of 22. Though of Spanish heritage, he was a true *hijo del pais* whose devotion had always been centered not on the larger Spanish or Mexican empire but on his native land.

His views therefore carried weight when he formally stated them at a meeting of the California Assembly in 1846, during a long debate on the possible choices before the country. Opinion was divided on whether to accept a foreign protectorate and, if so, by which country, or try to set up as an independent State. All agreed Mexico's rule must end.

Vallejo began his speech by declaring that, as a free man, he could not endure the idea of dependency on a European monarchy. "We are all republicans — badly governed and badly situated as we are — still we are all, in sentiment, republicans." And he asked, "Why should we shrink from incorporating ourselves with the happiest and freest nation in the world, destined soon to be the most wealthy and powerful? Why should we go abroad for protection when this great nation is our adjoining neighbor?" He concluded with the prophetic words: "When we join our fortunes to hers, we shall not become subjects, but fellow citizens possessing all the rights of the people of the United States . . . We shall have a stable government and just laws. California will grow strong and flourish, and her people will be prosperous, happy and free."

Vallejo lived to see all this happen. Elected to the constitutional convention of 1849 and subsequently to the State senate, he helped give California its first democratic government. He lived long enough to witness the extraordinary transformation of a pastoral land where people lived simply but well by barter (it is estimated that there was but $25,000 in cash in the whole country), into a bustling American State moving rapidly into the front rank of modern industrial societies. In his lifetime, a few thousand settlers grew into 1,200,000. He also saw the reckless destruction of much of its beauty and natural wealth, as well as the countervailing growth of a strong conservation movement. In the year of his death, a large part of the Sierra Nevada was withdrawn from private use and three national parks were created. To this day the destruction goes on and the efforts at conservation continue.

The story of Vallejo's life might well serve as a reminder that what we call "progress" has its good and its bad sides. In our current efforts to preserve what is still left of the natural beauty of our country, the California of Vallejo's youth might serve as a vision — a vision of an earthly paradise, blessed by fertile soil and clear skies; where wildlife was fantastically abundant, the flora varied, and the mountain slopes were covered with the world's most beautiful and gigantic trees.

USS THOMAS A. EDISON (SSBN 610)

NAMED FOR Thomas Alva Edison (1847–1931), one of the most fertile inventors of all time. A sampling of his more than 1,000 patents shows the wide range of his technical interest. Some were for improvements, big and small, of existing artifacts (the quadruple telegraph repeater for simultaneous dispatch of several messages over a single wire, transmission developments for the telephone, a separator for extraction of low-grade ores); others were for original inventions of major importance, such as the phonograph (1877) and the incandescent lamp (1879). There were devices concerned with the telegraph, the telephone, the electric dynamo, the electric locomotive, the storage battery, the kinematic camera; there were processes involving production of very thin sheet metal, of photographic film for motion pictures, for constructing concrete buildings, for making plate glass; there were his complex system for electric transmission of power (designed in conjunction with his incandescent lamp) and his railway signal system. There were an electric pen, a microphone, a device which later developed into the mimeograph, and many, many more. When Congress awarded him a gold medal in his 81st year, a rough estimate of the value of his inventions was put at over $15 billion.

European honors had come to him long before. France made him a Chevalier of the Legion of Honor when he was but 31, and a Commander 11 years later; Italy, a Grand Officer of the Crown when he was 42. Britain gave him the Albert Medal of the Society of Arts when he was 45.

Possibly his greatest single invention was the art of inventing itself, through systematic teamwork as at his Menlo Park and East Orange industrial laboratories (the first of their kind in the world). Edison was the first great organizer of inventive effort and one of the last to keep the enterprise in his own hands, from original idea through the long process of experimentation leading to the desired product and its commercial marketing. A technical man himself, he understood that inventiveness—whether individual or collective—flourishes best in an atmosphere of freedom, where the productive men are protected against interference by nontechnical "administrators." After Edison, invention became a virtual monopoly of huge private and public bureaucracies managed by nontechnical "organization men," overfond of administrative charts and regulations. Edison's staff of scientists and technologists worked their heads off because he worked with them and harder than any of them, and because he made invention a challenge and an exciting adventure. Compared to modern industrial laboratories, his were crude and seemingly unorganized, but their per capita output of original ideas and products has never been equaled.

The story of Edison the inventor with its triumphs and defeats (there were almost as many of the latter as of the former) is interesting enough, but less so than the story of Edison the poor, severely handicapped boy who did a man's work from age 12 onward, yet found time to educate himself entirely on his own. His was a Horatio Alger story with the element of luck left out, for Edison earned every good thing that came his way. It was also a case of fact preceding fiction. It has been suggested that Horatio Alger patterned his young heroes after Edison who was then already a legend—the "Wizard of Menlo Park" who could invent absolutely everything and whose inventions were easily understood and appreciated by everybody. Unlike "pure" scientists who produce speculative theories whose values are rarely evident to the general public, Edison was a genuine folk hero, revered for the benefactions his inventions bestowed on mankind. Despite his later wealth, he seemed close to ordinary people; much of the story of his life was of a kind they could seek to emulate.

Born in Milan, Ohio, part-Dutch, part-English by descent, Edison came of a numerous clan of hardworking, long-lived, extraordinarily prolific farmers and tradesmen; skilled workers, enjoying modest prosperity when times were good, relapsing into near poverty when they were bad. Of education they had little, but to a man they took an interest in public affairs and were noted for independence of mind and rebelliousness of spirit. Twice in three generations they crossed the Canadian-American border as political refugees. Great-grandfather

John, who had been brought from Holland to New Jersey by his widowed mother in 1730 (when he was 3), remained loyal to the English King during the American Revolution. He was one of the 30,000 Loyalists who fought as bravely for England as the revolutionaries fought for independence. John served under Howe, was condemned by a Revolutionary court to be hanged as a traitor but released upon intervention of relatives on the Revolutionary side. Together with 80,000 other Loyalists, he was resettled by Britain in Canada. Father Samuel took part in the ill-starred Canadian rebellion *against* the King (1837) and had to run 80 miles to find refuge in the United States, pursued by the King's men and Indian guides and dogs. Twenty-five years later, Samuel was again on the run, this time from a mob of Unionists in Detroit whose anger he had aroused by his outspoken opposition to Lincoln and the Civil War. Edison himself grew up in a community of Jacksonian radicals. Though later in life he voted Republican, he never became as tractable as the Eastern capitalists who financed his inventions would have liked him to be.

He was the first of his family to rise in the world. The Edison individualism and determination, not to say obstinacy, were as important to his success as his own mechanical genius. He had need of a stout heart and a determined spirit, for deafness, poverty, and lack of formal schooling (especially in higher mathematics and theoretical science) proved frustrating handicaps to a career as inventor. Poverty may have aggravated his loss of hearing and certainly deprived him of higher education.

The deafness is believed to have been caused by scarlatina followed by severe middle ear infections which received no medical attention but were treated by home remedies and patent medicines. Though Edison bore his affliction cheerfully and managed his life so that he could do without normal hearing, he sadly wrote in his diary, "I have never heard a bird sing since I was twelve years old."

It was bad luck that he contracted scarlatina at the very moment (1852) when the family finances suffered total collapse, as did those of virtually everyone else in their home town. Milan was typical of many American communities which existed only to serve a single commercial enterprise, in this case the Erie Canal. With the coming of the railroad, the canal was shut down for it could not compete with this new form of transportation. Father Edison, who had been doing quite well (they owned a sizeable house and property) moved promptly to the nearest railroad depot, Port Huron, Mich., but he was never again able to achieve the modest prosperity the family had enjoyed in Milan.

His illness delayed young Edison's enrollment in school until he was 8. Already an "experimenter" in miniature who had to see the reason for every new item of knowledge before he was prepared to accept it; he could not respond to the rote teaching typical of one-room rural schools. To an unimaginative teacher, a bored child will often seem stupid. One day, the boy overheard her call him "addled," whereupon he ran home in anger, declaring firmly he would never return to school. In this decision he was backed by his mother who recognized her son's unusual reasoning power and undertook to teach him herself. Nothing better could have happened to young Edison.

The daughter and sister of Baptist ministers, Nancy Edison had received a somewhat better than average education and had briefly taught school before marriage. Mother and son were in such close rapport that she instinctively found the right methods for arousing his interest in the subjects she taught him. Better read than most women of her time, she passed on to him her love of good books, reading to him at elementary age the English classics from Shakespeare to Dickens and the historical works of Gibbon, Hume, and Sears. At 9, the boy read such books himself. His mother had given him what formal schooling so often fails to give: the necessary tool for continued self-education.

Even today, books are for those who love them and have good minds; the best and cheapest and most easily accessible "teaching machines." Edison later told how at 15 he became a member of the Detroit Public Library and found there a refuge in the loneliness that came with growing loss of hearing. "I started with the first book on the bottom shelf and went through the lot, one by one. I didn't read a few books. I read the library"—from Victor Hugo's *Les Miserables* to Newton's *Principles*, from Burton's *Anatomy of Melancholy* to the *Penny Library Encyclopedia*. This random sampling of the whole range of literature saved Edison from the narrow outlook that so often afflicts men of specialized talent who have had no formal schooling.

His mother even started him on the road that led to the career for which he had so eminent a talent and where he was little handicapped by deafness. He was 9 when she found for him an elementary textbook outlining experiments in chemistry and physics that he was able to copy in a little laboratory he built in a corner of the cellar. Thereafter he never ceased experimenting—as child and youth, in manhood and in high old age.

Books and experiments were his pleasure as well as the means to his spectacular worldly success. "My mother was the making of me," he often remarked. Indeed, she guided him well. Few men are fortunate enough to discover a career that totally absorbs their interest and thus by itself gives them a full and happy life, regardless of external circumstances.

What neither his mother nor random reading of books could give him, however, was knowledge of higher mathematics and of theoretical science, for these are rarely acquired without the discipline of formal schooling, or at least of reading under expert direction. For lack of this knowledge, Edison had needless difficulties with many of his experiments but, as with all his difficulties, he simply redoubled his efforts and in the end overcame them.

Having taught him all she knew, Edison's mother continued as his close confidant and wise counselor in the small business ventures he now began to undertake. His first, at 11, was a fairly profitable market garden where he and a friend raised vegetables which they peddled around town in a hired horse-cart. At 12, his working life began in earnest. He took the job of newsboy and candy concessionaire on the daily mixed passenger and freight train leaving Port Huron at 7:00 A.M. for the 3-hour ride to Detroit, where the train lay over until evening, returning to Port Huron at 9:30 P.M. It was a long day for a small boy, but he had little choice. On trains people raise their voices, so he could hear them. What other job would have given him this advantage?

As he was paid no wages, Edison's income depended on his business ingenuity. He made a little extra by carrying a variety of farm products on the train (free of charge) which he sold at way stations. Since his margin of profit on the sale of newspapers was minuscule, it was important that he gauge correctly how many he could sell. Even at that early age he was a clever entrepreneur as is illustrated by the following story:

Having noticed that news of major Civil War battles sold papers like hot cakes, he made it a habit to check with the composing room of the *Detroit Free Press* for advance information received there by telegraph before ordering his daily supply. He was there the day the news of the Battle of Shiloh came in over the wire and, as he later described it, saw at once that "here was a chance for enormous sales, if only the people along the line could know what happened." He rushed to the telegraph operator and proposed that a short bulletin be wired by the Detroit train dispatcher to the telegraphers at every station enroute to Port Huron, asking them to post news of the battle on their bulletin boards. Then he bought (on credit) five times his normal supply of papers and sold them as "extras" at a greatly increased price per copy, netting what for him was a fabulous profit. "It was then that it struck me that the telegraph was just about the best thing going," he wrote later, "for it was the notices on the bulletin boards that had done the trick. I determined at once to become a telegrapher."

And so he did, though not before he had detoured into successful journalism by purchasing a secondhand press and some type (with part of the Shiloh windfall), writing, editing, and printing a small local paper, the *Weekly Herald* which had a circulation of 400 among the railway personnel and sold at 8 cents a copy. Though his grammar and spelling were distinctly individualistic, he had a flair, and might have become a good journalist had his interest not shifted to telegraphy, to the exclusion of all else.

His discovery of telegraphy was a major turning point in Edison's life, for it provided him with a means of livelihood while he taught himself during his free time how to become an inventor. To his great joy he found that "deafness did not prevent me from hearing the clicking of a telegraph instrument." He even thought deafness "an advantage to a telegrapher" since it cut out distracting sounds. Every evening he now practiced on an instrument he himself made. He had gone about as far as he could on his own when a Horatio Alger incident gave him the chance to learn the art properly. By quick thinking, he rescued the stationmaster's child from an oncoming train, whereupon the grateful father offered to give him free instruction.

From age 16 to 22, Edison was a member in good standing of the nomadic tribe of telegraphers. There was then a romantic aura about the telegraph which by 1861 had spanned the continent—8 years before the railroad—and the operators of this mysterious apparatus. For the most part footloose, carefree, young men, well paid but usually out of pocket, they drifted from job to job across the country, heroes in the eyes of most American boys who thought theirs a delightfully adventurous life. For Edison, the adventure soon wore thin under the strain of living a double life—telegrapher at night, experimenter in the daytime, with very little time out for sleep, often going shabby, cold, and hungry to buy needed laboratory materials. His very success increased the tension. As ever more new ideas for inventions absorbed his interest—all needing to be carefully tested out—he came to begrudge every moment he had to give to the routine job to which he was chained because it alone kept him alive and made it possible to continue experimenting.

But the day finally came when he dared resign his job and set up as an independent inventor. He was 22 then and the going was rough at first. But a year later he sold his first profitable invention (a stock printer) for $40,000, a princely sum in 1880. From then on he was on the road to certain success. Frustrations and reverses were still to come his way in great number but the years when he had often no more than a dollar to his name were definitely over.

The reason for Edison's success has frequently been asked, and it has never been satisfactorily answered. A "scientific" reply might be that one of the prerequisites of originality is the art of forgetting, at the proper moment, what we know. Without this art the mind remains cluttered with ready-made answers and is not forced to ask the proper questions. For a special type of mind, ignorance in a limited sense gives the advantage of having freedom from certain types of constraint.

To Faraday, his ignorance of mathematics was an asset; Edison benefited from his ignorance of science. As a child, "his demands for explanations of what seemed obvious to his elders created the belief that he was less than normally intelligent. As his head was abnormally large, it was thought that he might have a brain disease." At a time when his inventions were transforming the pattern of life, his ignorance of scientific theory raised criticism and opposition, especially among highly trained scientists and engineers without inventive talent. He is said to have carried the art of forgetting to such extremes, that on one occasion, when he had to queue at New York City Hall to pay his taxes, and an official suddenly asked him his name, Edison could not at the moment remember it, and lost his place in line.

As with all men who win out in the face of adversity and frustration, Edison himself was frequently asked the "secret" of his success. For people who accomplish little in life, genius is the facile explanation, but Edison would reply that "genius is 99 percent perspiration and one percent inspiration." This, of course, holds true for everyone.

What we are endowed with at birth is the one percent to which we must add 99 percent in effort, perseverance, and courage if we wish to reach the limits of what it is "possible" for us to achieve. Nor is it likely that by some magic the 99 percent of effort will some day be eliminated; that science and technology will somehow progress to a point where man will be spared the labor of developing *himself;* or that society as a whole will painlessly do it for him.

We are each and every one of us, as was Edison, the shaper of our own life. This is the lesson his story teaches us.

USS GEORGE WASHINGTON
CARVER (SSBN 656)

NAMED FOR George W. Carver, a botanist and chemurgist renowned in the annals of American scientific agriculture. The child of slaves, he did not know the day of his birth. Even the year is not certain, but he thought it was 1860. Where he was born, however, is not in doubt. In 1943, shortly after he died at Tuskegee Institute, Ala., both Houses of Congress passed, without a dissenting vote, a bill authorizing erection of a national monument at his birthplace in Diamond Grove, Mo. In fourscore years, George W. Carver had come a long way and accomplished a great deal.

None of it had come easy. His start in life was most inauspicious. A sickly infant, orphaned before he was a year old, it seemed unlikely he would survive. He lost his father in an accident and soon after was kidnaped, together with his mother and sister, by marauding nightriders. Those were lawless times. Stealing slaves for sale to plantations in the Deep South was not uncommon. But George Carver was such a puny baby that the kidnapers had no use for him, and so his master was able to get him released in return for a race horse valued at $300. Of mother and sister nothing was ever heard.

Hard as it was to be a slave child without kith or kin, by great good fortune his master Moses Carver (from whom he took his surname) was not a typical planter but a plain farmer, one of the so-called "Black Republican abolitionist Germans," or "lop-eared Dutch," as they were contemptuously called, who had migrated to Missouri in the 1830's. He was opposed to slavery, but he and his wife were childless and middle-aged; they needed help and servants were not to be had. So Moses bought a slave girl from a neighbor for $700. After she had been abducted, he took it upon himself to raise her small son.

Slavery ended when the boy was 4 years old but he remained with the Carvers and was treated much as any other farm boy. There was a lot of work to be done and George was expected to do his share. He was an especially apt pupil in all the domestic chores around the house and showed early that he had a way with growing things. People called him "plant doctor" for he could cure any ailing plant; he seemed to know instinctively what it needed in order to grow.

The boy was born with a keen mind, fantastically clever hands and so great a thirst for knowledge that no obstacle could bar him from obtaining an education. Of rebuffs he suffered many, but he was also often given a helping hand. The free school nearby was barred to him, whereupon Mrs. Carver gave him an old blue-back speller and with her help he taught himself to read and write. Thereafter he was hardly ever without a book in his hand. He would prop it up while he washed and ironed, these being some of the chores that earned him a living while he gradually accumulated school credits.

At 10 he decided he must find a school and so he left the Carvers, all his possessions in a small bundle over his shoulder. Thus began an odyssey that was to take him in short stages northward geographically and upward educationally. At several critical times during his 30-year quest for an education, luck or his pleasing personality, or perhaps a combination of both, brought him into contact with warmhearted childless couples who gave him the concern and care usually found only in one's own family. With a few he stayed but he was never a burden. He earned his keep for he was a prodigious worker, determined never to accept charity.

George Carver literally inched himself up the educational ladder, working his way not just through college but through grade and high school as well, working all the time to support himself. He was 20 before he got to high school, 25 when he graduated. Highland University accepted his credentials but when he presented himself, he was told negroes were not admitted. He was 30 when he finally entered Simpson College in Iowa. A year later, he entered Iowa State University, graduating with a Bachelor of Science degree in 1894. Invited to become a member of the staff in charge of systematic botany, the bacteriological laboratories and the greenhouse, he continued his studies and received a Master of Science degree in 1896. That year, he was invited by Booker T. Washington to organize and direct a new agriculture department at Tuskegee Institute in Alabama. There he remained the rest of his life.

254

From earliest childhood, Carver had the habit of rising at four and walking about the countryside for an hour or two. Soil, plants and trees interested him intensely; he wanted to know how they were put together, what made them fruitful. Nature was both a consolation and a challenge. In Tuskegee, he found the land exhausted from one-crop cotton culture, robbed of its mineral content, eroded from lack of plant cover, treeless and sun parched. The campus was bare earth, dusty in dry weather; a sea of mud when it rained. He went about looking for ways to restore the overworked earth and found it in green manure and the growing of nitrogen-producing legumes—pod bearers such as vetch, peas, clover, peanuts—plants which enriched the soil. Crop rotation which European peasants had practiced for a thousand years had to be relearned by Southern tenant farmers who knew no other crop but cotton. Carver went among them preaching diversification; he urged them to grow peanuts and sweet potatoes. Those who heeded his advice rode out the disastrous invasion of the boll weevil.

On the experimental farm he developed at Tuskegee, he evolved a cross between the short-stalk and the tall-stalk cotton known as "Carver's Hybrid," as well as three other new strains. With green manuring, he grew enormous potatoes, cabbages, onions, watermelons and cantaloupes. He instituted a visiting day each month for neighboring farmers to show what could be grown with scientific methods. They were most impressed with his new cotton strain which carried 275 huge bolls on a single bush, and yielded nearly a bale and a quarter per acre, in contrast to the usual one-third of a bale most tenant farmers produced.

To bring the message of scientific agriculture to those who could not come to Tuskegee, Carver loaded a wagon with tools, boxes, jars and packages of seed and set out every Friday evening after class to give demonstrations to meetings of farmers. In 1906, with money donated by Morris K. Jesup, a member of the Slater Foundation, he designed the so-called Jesup Wagon which served as a movable farmers' school and was adopted in other countries.

Carver's skill as soil scientist and plant breeder was to him but a means to help raise the standards of the Southern farmer, not just in productivity, but in his whole way of life. It was obvious to Carver that the prevalent diet of pork, meal and molasses lacked the vitamins and minerals necessary for good health and stamina. So he urged farmers to grow more vegetables and fruits, showed them that many common weeds, properly cooked, were edible and nutritious, taught their

255

women how to prepare them. His own boyhood had been spent on a multipurpose farm where everything the family needed was grown and processed, only sugar and coffee being bought. He called this "living at home" and preached it throughout the land. By avoiding store purchases, a little could be saved each week and eventually a piece of land bought. This, he said, was the way out of poverty. Tenant farmers lived in drab cabins. Noticing the beautifully colored clay in which Alabama abounded, Carver developed a simple method of making color wash and demonstrated how much even the shabbiest cottage could be improved by a paint that cost not a penny.

Carver is best known as a pioneer "chemurgist"—a word, coined by Dr. William J. Hale in 1934, which means chemistry at work. In his book *Pioneers of Plenty*, Christy Borth called Carver "the first and greatest chemurgist." Carver made paper from Southern pine "at least a quarter of a century before Dr. Charles H. Herty tackled the problem," and synthetic marble from wood shavings "years before a rocklike plastic made from wood waste became a chemurgic promise." He saw promise in the peanut when it was still a lowly weed growing along fences and tolerated by farmers only because their children liked its taste. From the peanut and the sweet potato, Carver developed more than a hundred different products, including plastics, lubricants, dyes, medicines, ink, wood stains, face creams, tapioca and molasses. He developed these in his laboratory at Tuskegee which he had put together out of odds and ends salvaged from scrap heaps.

When he had first arrived to take up his post, he discovered there was no money to equip a laboratory. In the course of his life, necessity had made him a genius at making do out of nothing. He and his students made the rounds of the rubbish heaps on campus and in town. They collected bottles, cut their necks off evenly and turned them into beakers. A thick, chipped tea-cup became a mortar, a piece of pipe the pestle. An old ink bottle with a wick made of string stuck through a cork became a Bunsen burner. Pieces of tin were punched and became sifters. Reeds served as tubes to transfer liquids. Carver had brought with him the one indispensable and costly thing not to be found on scrap heaps: a microscope. It was a parting gift from colleagues at Iowa State.

The products of his laboratory made his name known and brought him tempting offers of positions in industry, and checks for advice that had been sought from him. He politely declined the positions and returned the checks. He had no interest whatsoever in money and could not be bothered with the problem of marketing his inventions. His head was too full of ideas for new products. Advice, he thought, should always be free. He hoped it would reflect favorably on people's attitude toward his race if he helped others with their problems. His own needs were minimal. Indeed, out of a salary of $1,500 a year at Tuskegee, he saved $33,000 which he donated to the Carver Foundation for creative research in chemistry.

Many people from all over the world sought out this shy and retiring man, wanting to talk to him and to observe his work. Edison, Henry Ford, Theodore Roosevelt, and other important men became his friends. Honors and honorary degrees came his way. One was the Roosevelt Medal for distinguished service in the field of science (1939). He was introduced to the dinner guests in Theodore Roosevelt's New York home with these words which are a summing up: "I have the honor to present not a man only, but a life, transfused with passion for the enlarging and enriching of the living of his fellowman."

USS GEORGE BANCROFT (SSBN 643)

NAMED FOR George Bancroft (1800–91); author, educator, literary critic of note and America's foremost 19th century historian; a man whose keen mind applied itself as fruitfully to problems of politics, administration and diplomacy as to the pursuit of truth in the realm of pure intellect. His preeminence as a scholar was matched by able performance while serving his country as Secretary of the Navy and as minister to London and Berlin.

Navy men know Bancroft best as the founder of the Naval Academy. He was appointed Secretary of the Navy by Polk in 1845, at a time when the crisis with Britain over the Oregon boundary, and with Mexico over admission of Texas to the Union, called for an effective combat-ready Navy. Bancroft found the Navy disorganized, rent by dissension, the politically appointed officers inadequately trained for their duties. With a fresh mind, unbound by naval traditions, he set about the necessary reforms. It was clear to him that the basis of a first-rate Navy must be a first-rate officer corps. Since we lacked the reservoir from which the English drew their officers – an educated upper class with a long tradition of public service – he felt we must have an academy where young men from all walks of life received schooling that would shape them into well-educated, technically competent officers. But Congress, mistrusting the idea, had twice voted down proposals for a naval officer school. In view of the urgency of the problem, Bancroft decided to act on his own.

As assets he could count the existence of two small schools where, during brief periods ashore, midshipmen were taught mathematics and navigation; also of a small number of teachers posted to the larger ships to give instruction at sea. Using the best of the teachers as the nucleus of a permanent faculty, he was able to house them in an abandoned Army post—Fort Severn. Since he had the authority to order midshipmen ashore, he assigned them to the school as ships reached port. By stringent economies, he found enough money to finance the first term; he also succeeded in getting an able man (Commander Buchanan) appointed as head. Under him, standards of discipline, deportment and academic performance soon exceeded anything previously seen. Faced with a *fait accompli*, Congress was won over and appropriated funds for continuance of the Naval Academy.

During his year and a half term as Secretary, Bancroft also took steps that brought the solution of the Texas problem appreciably closer. He gave orders that led to the occupation of California and sent Zachary Taylor into disputed territory between Texas and Mexico. Years later, when serving as minister at Berlin, he was instrumental in bringing the Oregon dispute to a satisfactory conclusion. At his behest, the German Emperor was induced to act as referee. So ably did Bancroft argue our case that the award went to the United States.

He was equally successful in performing the principal task entrusted to him at Berlin—to resolve the long drawn-out conflict between the United States and Prussia over the status of nationalized citizens of German origin. The views of the two countries were diametrically opposed. As a country of immigration, we held it was the right of anyone to change his nationality; we therefore granted nationalization to qualified aliens without regard to claims upon them asserted by their countries of origin. Prussia, as most other European countries, maintained that a citizen could not escape his civic duties, especially military service, by emigrating and becoming nationalized abroad. Whether returning for brief visits to relatives or for prolonged redomicile, German-Americans in large numbers were seized and put into the army. England's impressment of American sailors—one of the causes of the War of 1812—was justified by her on a similar conception of nondivestible nationality.

Bancroft, who knew his Germans, appealed to Bismarck's sense of family solidarity, arguing that maintenance of ties between German-Americans and their relatives was desirable from every point of view, and their visits to Germany ought not therefore be rendered hazardous by the threat of military impressment. He succeeded in obtaining acceptance of the principle that an individual has the right to renounce his nationality, Prussia being the first European power to acknowledge this novel American idea. In his turn, Bismarck won his point that such renunciation must be bona fide; that Germany could not permit her citizens to visit America briefly, become nationalized and then return and resettle in Germany, thus demonstrating the ease with which one might escape his military duties. Agreement was reached that American nationalization after 5 years of residence would be accepted by Germany as proof of genuine American citizenship, provided the former national did not return to Germany with intent to settle there permanently, a visit of less than 2 years being considered permissible. The Bancroft formula proved acceptable to most European countries and became the basis of numerous consular and nationalization treaties; it was also incorporated into our own laws of nationality, tempering the previous custom of granting citizenship without any requirement that naturalized citizens continue to demonstrate a sincere desire to accept full citizenship responsibilities.

Bancroft's personal popularity was important in the success of his mission to Berlin. He was one of the first American college graduates to study at a German university and obtain a doctorate, graduate education then not being available in the United States. He spoke the language, and had translated German books and written informed and sympathetic articles interpreting German literature to America; moreover, he was a scholar of world renown and thus enjoyed the respect Germany customarily accorded eminent savants. His success as a scholar made him a more effective diplomat; conversely, his diplomatic position enabled him to ransack European archives for primary sources for his historical writings.

Bancroft's claim to fame rests chiefly on his monumental *History of the United States* in 10 volumes (later condensed by him to six) which he was 40 years writing. At the University of Göttingen he had observed the meticulous scholarship for which Germany then was world famous. This he applied to his History, achieving an authenticity not found in contemporary American historical writings. In his methods of research, his rigorous effort to base the book on documentable evidence, he was modern. But the fact that he wrote history as literature, and that he conceived of American history as an "epic of freedom and democracy" obsoletes his work in the eyes of many "science-oriented" historians today.

Bancroft did not observe and report the doings of his historical figures with the detachment of a scientist describing the movements of atoms or neutrons. As his biographer Nye wrote, "the guiding principles beneath his historical writing lay in his conviction that history was but the record of a divine plan manifested in the past, and that the divine plan proved that mankind was intended by God to progress toward a future state wherein principles of truth, justice, beauty, and morality—perceived intuitively through the Reason—might guide and raise it." Bancroft was a fervent patriot, deeply committed to democracy and imbued with the transcendentalist view that man must inevitably progress through the use of his divinely given reason. He had become acquainted in Germany with the ideas on which transcendentalism was based and they permeated everything he thought, wrote and did. Whatever we may think today of this 19th century faith in the dignity of man and the inevitability of progress, the transcendental viewpoint from which he wrote the History was in tune with his time. As they came off the press, the volumes were at once translated into German, French, Italian, and Danish and read widely abroad as well as here; it is said that one-third of all New England homes had a copy of the History. In those days a scholarly book could be a best seller! In fact, it made its author wealthy.

Bancroft was born in a poor New England parsonage but grew up in an atmosphere of books, ideas and high principles. That in his eighties he could still work long hours in his study and go horseback riding daily, Bancroft ascribed to the austerity and hardiness of his youth. But more than his physical vigor, he valued the spiritual and intellectual debt he owed his upbringing. His father's insistence that his children acquaint themselves with all sides to any question before making up their own minds, his refusal even to advise them in religious controversies where he might have considered himself an authority, developed self-reliance and independence of spirit.

The father had himself broken the tradition of five generations of his family—all farmers, all strict Calvinists, all deacons of the church—to become the first Bancroft to be educated at Harvard, the first to become a minister, the first to espouse a more liberal form of Calvinism—Unitarianism. Just so did his son George later break with the political tradition of Whiggism to become a Jacksonian Democrat. Courage was needed in both cases, for New England looked with disfavor on nonconformists.

Edward Everett Hale described life in the parsonage as "plain living and high thinking with a vengeance." It proved a good recipe for success in life. Most important of all, perhaps, was the atmosphere of keeping an open mind, of continuing to learn throughout life. In the son was amply fulfilled the father's plea at the end of his daily prayer: "Give us a teachable temper."

USS THEODORE ROOSEVELT
(SSBN 600)

N AMED FOR Theodore Roosevelt (1858–1919), 26th President of the United States. Scion of a distinguished family of Dutch, Huguenot, and Scotch-Irish stock, Roosevelt was born in New York City. He went to Harvard, made Phi Beta Kappa, and after graduation enrolled in Columbia Law School, but soon discovered that his interest lay not in the law but in literature, natural history, and above all, politics.

Public service was in the family tradition. His father's ancestors had been active in the affairs of New York for centuries; his mother's family had produced men who gave notable service to Georgia and the South. Roosevelt himself was only 23 when he was elected to the New York State Legislature (1881–84). Thereafter, his public offices were many and varied: member of the United States Civil Service Commission (1889–95); Head of the New York City Police Board (1895–97); Assistant Secretary of the Navy (1897–98); Governor of New York State (1898–1900); Vice President for a few months and, after the assassination of McKinley, President of the United States (1901–09). He also ran unsuccessfully for Governor of New York State in 1886 and for President in 1912. When the Spanish-American War broke out, he resigned from his secretaryship of the Navy, organized the First U.S. Volunteer Cavalry regiment (the "Rough Riders") and, at their head, stormed San Juan Hill. In the "private intervals" of his busy life, he en-

The USS THEODORE ROOSEVELT (SSBN 600)
as she is about to be launched on October 3, 1959.

joyed the great outdoors as a western rancher, African explorer and big game hunter. He also found time to write several books.

No bare listing of his activities can give an inkling of the fantastic energy with which Roosevelt threw himself into every task he undertook. The "only life worth living," he once said, was "a life of effort." Indeed, effort—hard, intelligent, continuous exertion—was the hallmark of his life and the secret of his success.

As a child he had been sickly, much troubled by asthma. He was only 12 when his father told him bluntly that he was a sorry physical specimen and something had better be done about this. A gymnasium was installed, and here the boy worked out with a punching bag, dumbbells, and horizontal bars. Later he took boxing lessons, learned to hunt, and became proficient in other sports. By dint of extraordinary perseverance and iron determination the sickly child transformed himself into a man of exuberant health and vitality, and of above-average athletic competence.

Though favored by fortune in having parents who gave him the right mixture of love and discipline and, above all, constant encouragement and guidance, Roosevelt was truly a self-made man and proud of it. Only a few, he used to say, are born with superior endowments, but anybody who wants to make the necessary effort can achieve a level of competence that allows him to stand beside the exceptional man and do his duty with equal efficiency.

He could prove this in his own person, for he was a politician and statesman of renown, though lacking most of the attributes that win easy popularity; a persuasive speaker, though his voice was not good; much loved by the American people, though anything but handsome. He won their affection by his sincerity, his devotion to the public good, his love of adventure, his enjoyment of life. He had a singularly attractive personality because he was in harmony and balance within himself; heart, mind and body, had all been brought to their highest potential. Though he said, "I am just an ordinary man without any special ability in any direction. In most things . . . just above the average, in some . . . a little under, rather than over," this surely was too modest an assessment. His intellect was very much above the average, though it is true that he achieved greatness not because he was a genius. He did, however, receive a rigorous liberal education and remained, all his life, intensely interested in a broad range of subjects. This breadth of knowledge and interest enabled him to see national issues clearly and from a long range point of view. He therefore often understood better than the experts the very problems that fell within their particular area of competence. An example can be found in the steps Roosevelt took to improve the Navy.

Not bound by service traditions nor influenced by personal preference for the status quo, he had no difficulty perceiving that mobility and the capacity to hit targets are two of the principal requisites of a first-class Navy. Yet he found the Navy clinging to coal, while endlessly discussing the pros and cons of conversion to oil. Roosevelt ordered conversion to begin forthwith. He found the Navy persisting in gunnery practices that produced poor results. During the Spanish-American War, he had heard of a young lieutenant, Sims by name, who had the audacity to criticize naval gunnery and propose improvements. For a while it looked as if something might be done, for it was feared that the French had trained the Spanish Navy. When it was discovered that Spanish ships aimed no more accurately than American ships, the matter was dropped. But to Roosevelt, the layman, a navy seemed of little use if it could not hit the target. As soon as he was able to do so, he put Sims in charge of organizing a new system of naval gunnery and backed him to the fullest against the enemies of progress.

His interest in the Navy, indeed in the buildup of our military forces in general, was an outgrowth of his recognition, long before others, that our country stood at the crossroads. Up to the turn of the century we had gone about our domestic affairs showing little interest in the world outside, protected as we were by friendly oceans which the British Navy kept free. He realized that the time had come for us to look to our own defenses.

So, too, he saw earlier than most of his countrymen that we were approaching a crisis in natural resources. Our rapid industrial growth had cost us a fantastic price in needlessly wasteful exploitation of natural wealth. Unless restraints were put on the lavish use of this wealth, we would be leaving a sadly depleted heritage to future Americans. The "experts" in turning natural resources into industrial products—the lumbermen, the mine owners—might scoff at conservationists and call them impractical dreamers, asserting that they "knew" our riches were inexhaustible. But Roosevelt, the educated layman, was not impressed. He knew enough arithmetic to figure out that if you keep taking from a treasure house, you will eventually reach bottom, no matter how large the original hoard might have been. In his time, this simple truth was a novel idea in America. Even today there are people who find it so distasteful they simply ignore it.

To Roosevelt must go much of the credit for whatever progress we have made in the last 50 years in conservation, in wild life preservation, in land, water and forest management through public channels. While he had the power to influence policies in Washington, several important national parks were established and 100 million acres set aside as national forests.

Roosevelt loved his country intensely but not blindly. If he saw defects, he pointed them out and called upon everyone to help eliminate them. He is best known for his battle with the "malefactors of great wealth," which began when he was Governor of New York and continued unabated during the years of his Presidency. He sensed the growing cynicism among ordinary Americans towards a government that permitted one law to exist for powerful corporations and another for individual citizens. Though he was bitterly attacked by them, he had no wish to harm corporations except when they violated the law. But this he could not tolerate. He understood better than most men of his background that corporate lawlessness undermined the very foundation of democracy, which rests upon the great principle of equal justice for all. Years later, the *New York World* remarked that "the United States was never closer to a social revolution than at the time when Roosevelt became President." The danger was averted when Roosevelt ordered suits brought against corporate giants (which proved successful) and initiated legislation protecting the public against injurious corporate practices.

He was a man of principle. Moral issues that many people today find confusing were plain to him. He saw no need to compromise with the Ten Commandments. To him, a thief was a criminal, whatever his social position and irrespective of whether he stole a loaf of bread, a thousand acres of public land, the Nation's mineral wealth, or the wages he owed to his employees in fair payment for their work. He was a kindly man, yet he seldom pardoned men who had committed serious crimes. For him, the right of law-abiding citizens to be protected against criminals outweighed the compassion he felt for the kinfolk of these wrongdoers when they came to plead with him for mercy.

During his chairmanship of the police board of New York City, he bent every effort towards eradicating police corruption and upgrading the quality of the police force. Like Harun-al-Rashid, he was wont to stalk the streets at night to see if his policemen were on the job. Out of a similar wish to improve the quality of government in general came his hatred of the "spoils system" which he branded inimical to American institutions. While he chaired the Civil Service Commission, 20,000 public offices were withdrawn from patronage and placed on a basis of merit, both as to appointment and as to promotion.

Though he was proud of the size and wealth of our country, he emphasized that what counted most was not our affluence but "the way in which we use what we have." He considered it more important that we be honest, brave, truthful and intelligent, "than that we should own all the railways and grain elevators in the world." He never tired of reminding Americans that in final analysis it was the individual citizen who was responsible for the quality of our society. "The art of successful self-government," he warned, "is not an easy art for people or for individuals. It comes to our people . . . as the inheritance of ages of effort. It can be thrown away; it can be unlearned." Freedom is not made secure by popular institutions alone; it calls for "great and masterful qualities": "above all, the combination of two qualities—individual self-reliance and the power of combining for the common good." He wanted us never to succumb to the "fear of living," but always to face our destiny with high and resolute courage.

USS WOODROW WILSON (SSBN 624)

NAMED FOR Thomas Woodrow Wilson (1856–1924), scholar and statesman, a student of political science who, as 28th President of the United States, was able to put into practice his own academic formulations of good government. More than any other man who has held the office (with the possible exception of Jefferson) Wilson had a coherent philosophy of the Presidency; in his view it should be a partnership between the occupant of the White House and the great mass of the people, whose confidence and support would make the President the most powerful political force in the Government. It may have been Wilson's greatest achievement that he was able to emerge from the academic world to become the hero of the common man. With the people behind him, Wilson achieved an extraordinary record of domestic reform; when he lost their support at the end of his Presidency, his career ended in failure.

He was one of those rare men who pursue two professions and reach the top in both. As a scholar and educator, Wilson became the leading political scientist of his day and the president of Princeton University; in government, he rode the wave of moral indignation to the governorship of New Jersey before serving two terms as President of the United States. And yet, although he was a spellbinding orator, Wilson's personality was more suited to the scholar than to the politician. An introvert – aloof, quiet, he was more at home immersed in thought than addressing the multitudes. "It is not men that interest or disturb me primarily," he said. "It is ideas. Ideas live; men die."

He believed in the persuasive force of logic. This, combined with his devotion to principle (his critics called it "stubbornness"), made him resistant to compromise. A trait understandable in a scholar, it was disastrous for the administrator and leader and led eventually to failure in each of his two presidencies – at Princeton and in Washington.

Wilson's belief in, and adherence to, a set of general principles can be traced to his youth. As he described it later, he was raised in the "stern Covenanter tradition" of his Scotch-Irish mother and father. Born in Virginia, he grew up in the vestry of the First Presbyterian Church of Augusta, Ga., where his father served first as pastor and later as Stated Clerk of the Southern Division of the Presbyterian Church. The stern Presbyterianism of his father left an indelible mark upon Wilson's character. He tended to treat his professional battles in later years almost as if they were holy crusades; in political speeches he would not infrequently identify his programs as "the Right" or "the Righteous Way."

His boyhood, spent in Georgia and South Carolina, caused him to be deeply affected by the sufferings of the South during the Reconstruction period. Throughout his life he modeled his conduct on what he described as the "Southern life and manners." In what was then still accurately described as the "Solid South," he developed his lifelong connection with the Democratic Party. In the tradition of Calhoun and generations of other Southern statesmen, he held a strong aversion to protective tariffs. This conviction was to provide the fuel for the first successful political battle of his Presidency – the fight over the Underwood Tariff Act in 1913.

In 1875, Wilson enrolled at Princeton, where he began the study of political science which was to be the focus of his life for the next quarter century. He read the Greek and Latin theorists and the works of Burke, Hamilton, and Madison; he was familiar with the writings of Walter Bagehot, the English critic whose work was to be the model for Wilson's first book, *Congressional Government*, published in 1885.

After graduating from Princeton in 1879, Wilson entered the University of Virginia law school. But neither the study of law nor its practice interested him. By 1883, he was again studying government and history, now at Johns Hopkins University where he received the degree of Ph. D. in 1886. After teaching history and political economy at Bryn Mawr and at Wesleyan, he accepted a chair of jurisprudence and political economy at Princeton. His lectures were models of clarity, brilliance of phrasing and persuasiveness. He had the facility for tracing the development of ideas and putting a complex body of thoughts into coherent form and relating them to each other.

271

He also had moral imagination—the power of ethical perception which strives beyond the barriers of private experience and events of the moment. Later published as essays, these lectures, as well as his addresses, displayed keen critical capacity. Though not remarkable for erudition or for striking creative power, they aroused considerable political interest and won him national reputation.

Throughout his academic career, Wilson was a productive and widely read author. His writings on political science and history constitute a comprehensive study of American government and politics. Before entering politics, he had published eight major works; these have stood the test of time to the extent that six are still in print, although his major work, the five-volume *History of the American People* (1902), is available only in the larger libraries. His political ideas as President can be traced to his writings as a professor. His distrust of Congress as an irresponsible and negative body—later reflected in his rebuke of the "little group of willful men" who blocked his war legislation in the Senate in 1917—is a recurring theme in his books. In *Congressional Government* (1885), he suggested the adoption of a parliamentary system to restore responsibility and accountability to the legislative branch. Wilson's view of the Presidency is expressed in *Constitutional Government in the United States* (1908): The President is "the political leader of the Nation. . . . The Nation as a whole has chosen him, and is conscious that it has no other political spokesman. Let him once win the admiration and confidence of the country, and no other single force can withstand him, no combination of forces will easily overpower him." Yet, while appreciating the power of the people to force reform, he was wary of revolutionary change. In *The State* (1889), he observed that revolutions frequently are followed by undesired reactions. "Political growth refuses to be forced."

Wilson's prolific writings and brilliant academic reputation caused him to be proposed for a number of distinguished chairs; he was also offered the presidency of several universities. But he relished the atmosphere of Princeton and the company of his colleagues and students. In 1902, after 12 years on the faculty, Wilson was elected president of the university. His academic reforms, together with the call for a "Princeton for the Nation's Service," brought him national recognition. But his efforts to democratize the social life of the university and to build a graduate school at the heart of the undergraduate college aroused controversy among alumni, faculty, and students. His single-mindedness was exemplified by the story of a woman whose son had just been expelled for cheating. She appealed to Wilson, pleading that she had to have an operation and would die if her son were not reinstated. "Madam," he replied, ". . . you force me to say a hard thing, but, if I had to choose between your life or my life or anybody's life and the good of this college, I should choose the good of the college." His refusal to compromise what he considered to be fundamental principles culminated in 1910 in the trustees' request for his resignation.

If ever a man lost a job to his profit, it was Wilson in 1910. Accepting the Democratic nomination for Governor of New Jersey, he was elected 2 months after leaving Princeton. Progressivism was now stirring New Jersey and other Eastern States in the same way that it had swept the Middle West. Supported by the progressive elements of the State, he carried through a series of reform measures such as a Direct Primaries Law, a Corrupt Practices Act, the Employer's Liability Act, and the creation of a Public Utilities Commission. These reform measures gave him national prominence and were indicative of the attitude he would later have as President of the United States, a position he attained 2 years after leaving Princeton.

Wilson's mercurial rise was the result of a conjunction of events which so often marked fundamental changes in the American political scene. One was agrarian unrest, particularly in the South and in the States just west of the Mississippi. The Populist Party sought agrarian and currency reforms. After a severe agricultural depression the party grew rapidly and sent colorful leaders such as Jerry Simpson (the "Sockless Socrates"), and Georgia's Tom Watson to Congress. Fervent and emotional, the Populists of the West and South could not stay united, and the great days of the party were over by the turn of the century. Yet the popular discontent and the desire and need for reform remained.

But the tides of public attitudes were moving. A new group arose, the progressives, concerned with urban reform, control of corporations, and better State government. Such writers as Lincoln Steffens, Ida Tarbell, and Upton Sinclair all brought home the abuses of the political-industrial-financial combination that had run the country since Reconstruction. Progressives were to be found in both parties: Robert La Follette of Wisconsin and Hiram Johnson of California were Republicans; Joseph Folk of Missouri was a Democrat. All were Governors fighting for effective State government. Each represented a congeries of the discontented seeking change in the frozen structure of the political system.

When Theodore Roosevelt and William H. Taft fought over the Republican nomination in 1912, their party split: the regulars going with Taft, the progressive Republicans with Roosevelt. The Democrats, united under Wilson, faced a badly divided Republican Party.

Wilson was a powerful candidate. He was a progressive, but also a "liberal conservative," reluctant to adopt the radicalism of the extreme Populists, yet deeply concerned over the excesses of political bosses and corporate leaders. He knew that many Americans had subordinated their intelligence to dominant political interests and purposes. As early as 1902, in his *History of the American People*, he warned that the new economic arrangement known as the "trust" could "give to a few men a control over the economic life of the country which they might abuse to the undoing of millions of men." In 1908 he observed that, whereas the Founding Fathers feared arbitrary power of Government, Americans in the 20th century had come to fear the power of accumulated capital. "For the first time in the history of America, there is a general feeling that the issue is now joined, or about to be joined, between the power of accumulated capital and the privileges and opportunities of the masses of the people." This power must be reduced or it would take over the national idea.

In his campaign Wilson had no historic choice except to be the instrument of change. He voiced the popular discontent with the Republican administration which he believed to be too closely allied with "privileged big business." His purpose was: "To square every process of our national life again with the standards we so proudly set up at the beginning and have always carried in our hearts." The country was treated to the most instructive and fundamental political debates since the Lincoln-Douglas debates of 1858. His campaign speeches were remarkable for their high moral tone. Rooted in religion and in historical consciousness, and against the indifference of irresponsibility, they appealed to the true principles of democracy. He stirred "mystic chords of memory." Like Theodore Roosevelt, he asked for a national renaissance of ideals for the "rule of justice and right" to prevent special interests from frustrating the democratic process. He asserted that great opportunities had been lost through the interlacing of privileges and private advantage within the framework of existing laws: "We must effect a great readjustment and get the forces of the whole people once more into play . . . we need no revolution, we need no excited change; we need only a new point of view, and a new method and spirit of counsel." Although the popular feeling was responsive to his views, he would not have been elected except for the division of the Republicans because of Roosevelt's candidacy as a Progressive.

Wilson's election in 1912 and the reforms enacted during his first term resulted from the confluence of the two conditions he had recognized as essential for effective American Government: an aroused people anxious for fundamental change, and a President willing to channel these sentiments into specific measures of reform. Circumstances permitted him virtually to form a new Democratic Party. Between Reconstruction and Wilson's inauguration, that party had not been much more than a Southern organization with strong allies in the big city machines of the East and Middle West. By exercising his personal influence, and with a Democratic majority in both Houses (nearly half the Democratic Congressmen in 1913 had been elected for the first time), Wilson was able, despite strong opposition from vested interests, to carry through his campaign promises. What made him usually irresistible was his fusion of the powers of the Presidency with those of party leader, along with intense moral purpose.

The prospects for success of his reforms were increased when the Senate Finance Committee was enlarged by Wilson's supporters so as to outvote the opposition. His legislative program, which he called "The New Freedom," remains today the basic governmental control over banking and corporate activity. The Underwood Tariff Act, which established lower duties and also introduced an income tax under the authorization of the newly ratified 16th amendment; the Federal Reserve Act; the Clayton Anti-Trust Act; and the Federal Trade Commission Act—these were all products of his first 2 years in office. His administration continued Theodore Roosevelt and President Taft's battle against the trusts by instituting actions against major corporations, notably American Telephone and Telegraph and J. P. Morgan's New Haven Railroad.

This is not to say that his legislative program was entirely effective in checking private corporate power. Although the Wilson reforms gave the Government some measure of control, the financial and political power of the great corporations continued to grow. When Franklin Roosevelt became President in 1933, he, too, faced the problem of corporate power in American life. He, too, forged a battery of new legislation to deal with these "private governments." Because men, being endowed with free will, continually alter the conditions of life, this pattern has repeated itself in the present era as large corporations have grown beyond the limits of control established in the New Deal legislation. Thus, as in 1913 and 1933, one of the most important issues facing the country today is concentration of economic power and the need for governmental control over corporate giganticism. Faced once more with the interlacing of public power and private advantage, we must again effect a great readjustment. We must find workable answers between the extremes—to limit concentrations of corporate power and at the same time increase corporate efficiency.

Basic to Wilson's "New Freedom" was a determined isolationism. With the ascendancy in Mexico of the military dictator Huerta in 1913, his caution in international affairs was given its first test. Many observers felt that the struggle between Huerta and the Constitutionalists under Carranza to control the country would force the United States to intervene. Wilson, however, believing in the moral approach to foreign affairs, refused to recognize a government he was convinced did not represent its people. His stand brought him into diplomatic difficulties, but although the crisis dragged on for several years, he managed, with patient diplomacy and a minor naval action at Vera Cruz, to weather the Mexican storm.

His foreign policy was characterized by a desire to avoid stressing the power of the United States for the material advantage of its citizens. He took steps to prepare the Filipinos for self-government, and he repudiated the "dollar diplomacy" of the preceding administration. Nevertheless, as had been the case with Presidents who preceded him, when confronted with actual cases, he had to temper his beliefs to the realities of the situation. Thus, in 1915, customs in Nicaragua and Haiti were taken over by U.S. officials, and a virtual protectorate was established over Haiti. In 1916, marines were landed in Santo Domingo followed by proclamation of a military government under American auspices.

Wilson's response to the outbreak of war in Europe in July 1914, was one of "watchful waiting." A week after start of the fighting, he formally declared American neutrality, and in an address to the American people adjured them, in view of the mixture of nationalities in the United States, to be impartial in thought and action. In the main, these actions reflected the view of the American people. Most, by reason of history and descendancy, were disposed to favor the Allies. Yet few felt strongly enough to advocate active intervention. The majority, motivated in part by pacifism, felt that America's best position was to stay out of the war.

The period of American limbo—from the outbreak of hostilities to American intervention in 1917—was a trying test of Wilson's leadership. It was not easy to practice a neutral foreign policy or to achieve one's goals when dangerous emotions and vital interests were involved. He was torn between his deep commitment to isolationism and his sense of moral obligation to the French and British—between Senator La Follette and the pacifists on the one hand, and Theodore Roosevelt and the interventionists on the other. The growing German submarine campaign eroded what pro-German sentiment there was among the American people, thus making it more and more difficult for America to hold to her stated neutrality. In response to the U-boat warfare, he informed the German Government on February 10, 1915, that the United States would hold it "to a strict accountability for property endangered or lives lost." Thereby he took a stand that would lead inevitably to war, unless he or the German Government backed down.

While no single event can be said to have tipped the balance of public opinion from isolation to intervention, the shock created by the sinking of the passenger liner *Lusitania* on May 7, 1915, with the death of 1,195 civilians, including 128 Americans, must not be underestimated. The outrage of the American press and public over this "illegal and immoral" act was great. Yet the incident itself should not have been completely unexpected. The *Lusitania* typified the problem of civilian rights in the advancing technological warfare. This accounts for the tremendous outrage over the unrestricted submarine warfare in 1915 and later, which was absent during World War II. Further, before the war, on June 10, 1913, Winston Churchill, then First Lord of the Admiralty, had stated in the House of Commons:

> "Merchant vessels carrying guns may belong to one or other of two totally different classes. The first class is that of the armed merchant cruisers, which in the outbreak of war would be commissioned under the white ensign and would then be undistinguishable in status and control from men-of-war. In this class belong the *Mauretania* and *Lusitania*."

This statement no doubt gave Germany, in her view, some justification for her action. Although the fact was little noted by the American press, the *Lusitania* was carrying contraband munitions when she was sunk.

Wilson still wished to remain neutral. In an address to the American people on the *Lusitania* incident, he used an unfortunate phrase he lived to regret: "There is such a thing as a man being too proud to fight." But the prospect of American intervention was growing more and more probable by the end of his first term; the issue with Germany was brought to a head by the attack on the unarmed liner *Sussex* in March 1916. Wilson's formal note of protest was couched in the form of an ultimatum: unless Germany immediately abandoned its present methods of submarine warfare the United States would sever diplomatic relations. The German reply was, in effect, a promise no longer to sink merchant ships without warning and without saving lives. This diplomatic victory was used during Wilson's 1916 presidential campaign. Officially at least, the United States was still a neutral; Wilson was able to run for reelection on a slogan of "Peace, Prosperity, Progressiveness." The slogan that dominated his campaign was "He kept us out of war with honor."

His reelection enabled Wilson to make peace proposals to the belligerents. He had authorized his emissary Colonel House to propose to the British that the President "on hearing from France and Britain that the moment was opportune" should propose a conference to end the war. "Should the Allies accept this proposal and should Germany refuse it, the United States would probably enter the war against Germany." These proposals, centering on his principle that no European settlement would lead to stability except a "peace without victory" for either side, seemed sensible to neutral Americans. But the man who "kept us out of war" was unable to contend with the animosities that had brought the war about; his proposals were satisfactory to neither side.

Events of the first month of 1917 finally made entry into the war inevitable. The "Zimmerman Note," an intercepted dispatch from the German foreign minister, revealed the extent of German espionage within the United States, and the German diplomatic attempt to offer American territory to Mexico in exchange for Mexican intervention on the German side. The Allies came face to face with a supply and manpower crisis as they entered their fourth year of war. The most serious provocation was the decision of the German High Command in January 1917 to launch unlimited submarine warfare against belligerents and neutrals alike. This decision was based on detailed analyses by experts in the German General Staff. But, as is often true of their modern-day counterparts, the German "systems analysts" made the fatal mistake of treating an expectation as if it were a certainty. The German submarine decision was based on the analysts' prediction, as stated in a memorandum to Hindenburg, that shipping losses would be so large that Britain would be forced to sue for peace within 5 months. As for American entry into the war: "As far as shipping capacity is concerned, the effect could only be small . . . One should attribute just as little effect to American troops, which could not be transported in large numbers for lack of shipping." The determination of the British people and the success of Allied convoy tactics negated the basic foundation of the German strategy. The fateful submarine decision, therefore, failed to achieve the goals it was designed for and succeeded only in galvanizing American opinion in favor of intervention on behalf of the Allies.

Thus on April 2, 1917, Wilson was forced to take the step he had hoped to avoid. He requested a congressional Declaration of War in a message of spirited eloquence that inspired the Nation:

> "It is a fearful thing to lead this great peaceful people into war, into the most terrible and disastrous of all wars, civilization itself seeming to be in the balance. But the Right is more precious than peace, and we shall fight for the things that we have always carried nearest our heart—for democracy, for the right of those who submit to authority to have a voice in their own Government, for the rights and liberties of small nations, for universal dominion of right by such a concert of free people as shall bring peace and safety to all nations and make the world itself at last free."

What made belligerency acceptable was Wilson's conviction that if the German submarine warfare was thwarted, the war could not last beyond the summer of 1917. American intervention would therefore shorten the war and give him a seat at the peace table where he could work for a peace of reconciliation.

Once war was declared, he was determined that it should be waged efficiently. Much has been written about the effectiveness of Wilson's administration of the American war effort; the Selective Service Act; the grant of executive powers to various boards and the power of the War Industries Board (copied in World War II); the disregard of party lines in his war appointments; the transition from peacetime to wartime production; the mobilization that enabled the United States to send 1,300,000 troops to Europe within 18 months; and the unprecedented governmental propaganda campaign to arouse public opinion against Germany. This effort was unique in American history in that for the first time our Government, to justify its actions, undertook the task (previously the province of the press, as in 1898) of molding public opinion – an activity it has followed in subsequent wars and which has since spilled over into its peacetime domestic activities.

But if the war was the acme of Wilson's Presidency, the peace that followed was its nadir. Long before America's entry into the war, Wilson had been devoting much of his time toward planning the peace that would follow. For him, peace was the only legitimate reason for American entry into the war. This was to be "a war to end wars," the war by which the world would be "made safe for democracy." Even at the height of American involvement, Wilson appeared more concerned with his peace plan than with progress of the war. In January 1918, he stated his basic design for a just and lasting peace. This was summarized in his "Fourteen Points," which called for "open convenants, openly arrived at," freedom of the seas, readjustment of European frontiers, and the creation of a League of Nations as a permanent world peacekeeping force. The effect on the Central Powers was not evident until their defeat, but Wilson's peace plan did act as a corroding factor, weakening their determination to fight. When they faced defeat, they offered to accept the "Fourteen Points" as the basis for peace.

Believing that his presence was necessary if the Peace Conference was not to be dominated by old-style diplomatic practices, Wilson announced, within days after the Armistice, his decision to lead the American delegation in person. He believed – and with considerable basis – that he would be the only man at the conference whose sole interest was a just peace among the nations.

Wilson knew before leaving for Paris that he might expect opposition from nationalistic elements among the Allies and at home where his political opponents were calling for a "strong peace" that would annihilate Germany (the official propaganda of the U.S. Government had borne fruit). Further, now that the war was over, the traditional isolationism of the American people was returning.

Many of our people, unfamiliar with European history and culture, considered that continent decadent – inferior to us in idealism and in democracy. As a result there was little enthusiasm for a League of Nations which would have required common international action – the agency Wilson regarded as essential to a just and lasting peace.

He had weakened his position at home by an appeal immediately before the congressional election of November 1918, asking the voters to cast their ballots for Democratic candidates because a Republican Congress would divide our leadership at a moment of crisis. As the proclaimed war leader of the Nation, he could not likewise play the party leader. The Republicans won the election and Wilson lost control of the Senate.

Returning to Paris in March 1919, he was able to obtain a number of amendments to the League Covenant — as required by American sentiment — and unanimous approval of its final draft.

He was confronted by demands for territorial and economic concessions by the French, Italians, and Japanese, which he was forced to accept — concessions contrary to his own principles and which aroused opposition in England and the United States. But he considered that in securing the League of Nations he had won the major victory, since the League afforded the means to redress the inequities contained in the treaties. These, so he believed, would ultimately be corrected.

In June 1919, Wilson brought the Treaty of Versailles and the Charter of the League of Nations home to the American people and to the Senate for ratification. In the Senate, the treaty immediately became a bitter, tangled controversy. The "irreconcilables," led by Senator Henry Cabot Lodge, were determined to reject the treaty outright unless Wilson would accept reservations on American obligations. Some of the opposition was motivated by politics or personality; but there was legitimate basis for many Senators' concern. For example, Article X of the League Charter could be read to obligate United States involvement in every border skirmish between members of the League.

The Senate's fighting mood was matched by Wilson's stony determination to have his treaty without alteration. Friends, advisors, and journalists who urged him to compromise were reminded of the President's remark during his first battle with Congress over the Underwood Tariff Act in 1913: "I am not the kind that considers compromise when once I take my position."

Wilson saw this battle with an obstinate Congress as the ultimate test of his partnership theory of the Presidency. Accordingly, in the summer of 1919, he took his fight to the people. In 22 days he delivered 40 speeches on the League throughout the Midwestern and Western States. But his health failed midway through his tour and he returned to the White House to spend his last year as President a virtual recluse. The Senate, in March 1920, refused to ratify the treaty by 16 votes (57–39). In the presidential election of 1920, in which approval of the League was the inevitable issue, Wilson once more appealed to the people. The Republican victory sealed his defeat, and Wilson retired from public life.

In reviewing Woodrow Wilson's failure, it is profitable to examine the reason. Simply stated, it was his feeling—which seems to have run through his life—of righteousness and his belief that he could set standards for others to follow. His view of Congress was a manifestation of this attitude. He wanted the Executive to be, like a parliamentary prime minister, the leader of the legislature rather than head of a separate and equal branch of government. Although ratification of the treaty was the Senate's constitutional responsibility, he refused to invite any of its members to take part in the negotiations; he neglected even to inform the Senate of the negotiations as they proceeded. For this imprudence he paid dearly. It is a lesson that should not be lost on future Presidents who would try to ignore Congress' proper role in the formulation of foreign policy.

To the day of his death, February 3, 1924, he believed that his principles would triumph. His last writing was an article *The Road Away from Revolution* published in 1923. Removed from daily affairs of life he was writing as a philosopher, epitomizing the thoughts and actions of his life. He warned the American people that their society, unless it was redeemed by being permeated with the spirit of Christ, could not survive. This meant a social and economic order based on "sympathy and helpfulness and a willingness to forego self-interest in order to promote the welfare, happiness, and contentment of others and of the community as a whole."

Woodrow Wilson's legacy is one of shattered aspirations. The impact of Wilsonian idealism and of the First World War produced a belief that the shackles of the past—secret diplomacy and sacrifice of the common good to narrow interests—had been ended; that Americans, indeed all mankind, conscious of the identity of their interests in all parts of the Nation and the world, would rally to a new social integration. Today we know how deceptive were these hopes.

USS HENRY L. STIMSON (SSBN 655)

NAMED FOR Henry L. Stimson (1867–1950), a man of notable achievements both in his vocation, the private practice of the law, and in his avocation which was public service of the appointive kind.

Born in New York City, son of a distinguished surgeon, Stimson received his education at Andover, Yale, and Harvard Law School. He was only 25 when Elihu Root took him into partnership. The young lawyer learned much from association with this commanding figure in the legal profession of whom it was said that he had been connected with every important case in New York since 1880. Root, who became a lifelong friend and mentor, taught him not only a highly effective trial technique emphasizing painstaking preparation, close reasoning and systematic ordering of arguments—intellectual habits that proved useful to Stimson in the varied positions he later filled with great distinction—but living and working in Root's office, as he later remarked, also made him aware of "the importance of the active performance of his public duties by a citizen of New York." Though his steadily expanding practice kept him busy Stimson found time to participate energetically in local and State politics, his chief interest being better government.

In 1906 Theodore Roosevelt appointed him to his first public office, that of U.S. Attorney for the Southern District of New York. Thereafter and until he finally retired in 1945 at 78, Stimson took frequent leave of absence from his lucrative private practice to assume public duties, serving under every President except Woodrow Wilson and Warren G. Harding. He was the first to sit in the Cabinet of *four* Presidents (two Republicans and two Democrats): as Secretary of War under

283

William H. Taft, Franklin D. Roosevelt, and Harry S. Truman, and as Secretary of State under Herbert Hoover. He served Calvin Coolidge as adviser on Latin American affairs, peace-maker in Nicaragua and Governor General of the Philippine Islands.

All his public offices, except one, were appointive and came to him unsought. Stimson had no flair for politics of the elective kind. He lost his bid for Governor of New York in 1909. The only election he won was for delegate at large to the New York Constitutional Convention of 1915. There he worked tirelessly for reforms that would give the State a more honest and efficient government. Although in that year's election the voters rejected the revised constitution, by 1926 almost 80 percent of the proposed amendments had become part of New York's fundamental law and 30 other States had followed suit.

Politically, Stimson was identified with the reform or pro-gressive element in the Republican Party. His views on govern-ment were formed early in life and changed very little. They are set forth in the autobiographical book, *On Active Service in Peace and War*, written conjointly with McGeorge Bundy and published shortly before Stimson's death at 83. "His basic convictions were two—first that the primary and overriding requirement of all government was that it should not infringe the essential liberties of the individual, and second, that within this limitation government could and must be made a powerful instrument of positive action." The restraint imposed by law on government in the interest of "the primary and essential liberties of the individual" was, to Stimson, "a funda-mental principle of any decent society. But to construe this respect for personal freedom into an assertion that all govern-ment was evil seemed to him absurd." He felt that "in the industrial civilization of the 20th century it was the duty of government to provide for the general welfare wherever no private agency could do the job."

Given this point of view, Stimson could serve Theodore Roosevelt loyally as U.S. Attorney and Franklin D. Roosevelt equally loyally as Secretary of War. Under the Republican Roosevelt, his task was enforcement of Federal laws which had been enacted to protect our society against harmful actions of large and powerful private organizations; under the Demo-cratic Roosevelt, his task was mobilization of the country's industrial potential in support of a war we fought against powerful nations threatening our free society. He accomplished both tasks extremely well.

Stimson's private work made him rich (he remained throughout his active life a member of the firm which originally had been headed by Root), but he derived his deepest satisfaction from the public services which supplemented and at frequent intervals replaced his private activities. He once told friends that the life of an "ordinary New York lawyer" could never wholly satisfy him since it was "primarily and essentially devoted to the making of money." Stimson shared with his father a desire to serve some larger cause than his own well-being.

The elder Stimson was a first-rate surgeon but had little interest in building the profitable private practice his talents could so easily have won him. Instead, he gave all his time to hospital work, much of it devoted to the charity cases that came to him as attending surgeon at the Chambers Street House of Relief, the emergency unit of New York Hospital. He liked to quote a famous French surgeon who said he preferred the poor for his patients since God was their paymaster.

Henry L. Stimson, the son, found that when he became U.S. Attorney, thus defender of the public interest and of the people, his work had an ethical content that enormously increased the satisfaction he derived in his professional life. Now he could do something to help redress a deplorable situation he found all too common; whenever private interests came into legal conflict with public interests, whenever great public issues put "a rich corporation on one side and only the people on the other," the side of the people usually "went by default," since so few successful lawyers were "putting their shoulders to the public wheel."

There can be little doubt that ancestry had something to do with Stimson's strong sense of civic responsibility. Nearly all his forebears were of New England stock, having arrived before 1650. After the Revolution they migrated westward and took up land in upper New York State. Hardworking, thrifty, self-reliant and strongly identified with their community, they fought in every war in which the country was embroiled (even as Stimson volunteered in the Spanish-American War and World War I) and produced, as he put it, "enough clergymen and deacons to keep up fairly well the moral standards of the stock."

In a more direct sense, Stimson's devotion to public service was an outgrowth of his concept of the function of law and advocacy in a democratic society. This comes out clearly in his autobiography where he describes how he came "to learn and understand the noble history of the profession of the law," and "to realize that without a bar trained in the tradition of courage and loyalty our constitutional theories of individual

USS WILL ROGERS (SSBN 659)

NAMED FOR Will Rogers (1879–1935), the Oklahoma cowboy who became one of America's most popular folk humorists. He was born and raised near Oolagah, Indian Territory, in what is now Rogers County, so named for his father, a prosperous rancher prominent in the councils of the Cherokee Nation and member of the convention that drafted the first constitution of the State of Oklahoma. Both parents were part Cherokee, and Will was named for William Penn Adair, an Indian Chief who was his father's friend.

The only son of a well-to-do family, he was offered every educational advantage but never got beyond the fourth grade. As told in Will's autobiography, his father "tried terribly hard to make something" of him, sending him to "about every school in that part of the country." Will, who hated school and loved the outdoor life on the ranch, seldom lasted more than 4 months at any one of them before deciding that the teachers weren't "running the school right, and rather than have the school stop," he would leave. Though he joked about the tricks he used to avoid schooling, Will did not recommend them to others. "I have regretted all my life," he would say, "that I did not at least take a chance on the fifth grade." When he left home at 19, to make his own way, he had little formal education but was an expert cowpuncher and lariat thrower. Neither he nor anyone else could have foreseen that these skills would open the door to a highly successful career.

He began modestly enough as a cowhand on ranches in Texas and Oklahoma. Wanting to see the world, he worked his way on cattle boats, roped mules in Argentina, and broke horses for the British army in South Africa. It was there, in Johannesburg, that he got his start in show business. He joined Texas Jack's Wild West Show as a rope artist and trick rider.

Calling himself "The Cherokee Kid," he toured South Africa, Australia, and New Zealand for 3 years. On his return to the United States in 1905, he appeared regularly in Wild West circuses and on the vaudeville circuit.

Quite by accident, Will discovered he had a gift for making witty impromptu remarks which kept his audience in paroxysms of laughter and greatly enhanced the popularity of his rope tricks. When he joined the Ziegfeld Follies in 1915, he was an instantaneous success though, to hear him tell it, he "was the least known member of the entire aggregation," doing his "little specialty with a rope and telling jokes on national affairs, just a very ordinary little vaudeville act by chance sandwiched in among this great array."

From the stage Will moved to screen and radio, becoming one of the highest paid performers of his time. His rope tricks had given him a start but what made him a success was his talent as a humorist.

He was a humorist, not merely a comedian. He wrote his own lines and it was their content no less than his inimitable delivery that appealed to the public. This is why he could progress from showmanship to authorship. In 1922 he became a newspaper columnist for the McNaught Syndicate, his column eventually being printed in 350 papers and reaching an audience of 35 million. He was the only syndicated columnist of his time whose daily comment was printed on the front page of metropolitan papers. In addition to his column, he wrote many magazine articles and was in great demand as a radiobroadcaster, platform lecturer, and after-dinner speaker. His popularity was not restricted to the United States. He traveled extensively and met many of the world's greats, but fame never changed his innate modesty, his natural and unassuming bearing. "I am just an old country boy in a big town trying to get along," he once said. "I have been eating pretty regular and the reason I have been is because I have stayed an old country boy."

He wrote for what he called "the big Honest Majority" and felt himself a part of this majority—the people who believed in doing right, in tending to their business, and in letting other fellows alone. He shared with them a certain skepticism toward the men elected to public office, a suspicion that these were not always doing what the voters wanted nor telling them the whole truth about the country's position in the world. Will appointed himself reporter to the American people on the doings of the Government. His comments were sometimes sharp but usually fair and never wounding. Perhaps because he never met a man he didn't like, Will was more lenient toward individuals in public office than towards groups such as the Congress or the bureaucracy. He shared with "the big Honest Majority" a tendency to deprecate the Congress, seemingly not realizing that it is the great bulwark of the people's rights and closer to the electorate than any other branch of Government.

Will got the material for his comments from the newspapers, from personal observation, and from contact with people. He traveled the length and breadth of this country, taking its pulse, watching its foibles and follies, joshing it gently, and sometimes telling it disagreeable homely truths. Since he dealt mostly with contemporary events, much of what he said has a slightly archaic flavor now but some of his remarks remain relevant. Here are a few samples, just as he wrote them, with spelling and grammar unchanged: "We are going at top speed, because we are using all our natural resources as fast as we can. If we want to build something out of wood, all we got to do is go cut down a tree and build it. We dident have to plant the tree. Nature did that before we come. Suppose we couldent build some thing out of wood till we found a tree that we had purposely planted for that use. Say, we never would get it built. If we want anything made from Steam, all we do is go dig up the coal and make the steam . . . . If we need any more Gold or Silver, we go out and dig it; want any oil, bore a well and get some. We are certainly setting pretty right now. But when our resources run out, if we can still be ahead of other nations then will be the time to brag; then we can show whether we are really superior." He returns to this thought time and again. "The Lord has sure been good to us," he wrote. "Now what are we doing to warrant that good luck any more than any other Nation?" These ideas cannot have been overly popular in isolationist America of the 1920's and 30's.

Then, as now, Americans found it hard to understand why they were not as popular abroad as they thought they should be. "It will take America 15 years steady taking care of our own business and letting everybody else's alone to get us back to where everybody speaks to us again," was Will's comment.

Another time he said: "You don't know what a Country we have got till you start prowling around it. Personally I like the small places and sparsely populated States. A place looks better before it gets houses on it than it does afterwards." And here are a few shorties: "Humanity is not yet ready for either real truth or real harmony." "A remark generally hurts in proportion to its truth." "You must judge a man's greatness by how much he will be missed."

Charles Collins said of Will Rogers that he was "the average American, as that theoretical figure likes to imagine himself." His humor was in the tradition of Mark Twain, Artemus Ward, and Finley Peter Dunne's "Mr. Dooley." It was typically American in its determination to see things as they are and in its lack of reverence for established pomposities and pretensions. In his homely way Will made sense out of life as it is lived by ordinary men and women. And he made them laugh. He once wrote: "I have been over 20 years trying to kid the great American public out of a few loose giggles now and again. Somebody had to act the fool, and I happened to be one of the many that picked out *that unfunny business of trying to be funny.*"

The sense of loss so widely felt at his untimely death in an airplane accident showed that Will Rogers had done far more than entertain his public; he had touched their hearts, too.

USS GEORGE C. MARSHALL
(SSBN 654)

NAMED FOR a distinguished soldier-statesman, General of the Army George C. Marshall (1880–1959). Born and raised in Uniontown, Pa., the son of an operator of coal and coke industries who had left Kentucky after the Civil War, Marshall grew up with an unusual understanding of Northern and Southern viewpoints. His family, of Scotch-Irish origin, were among the earliest settlers in Virginia. Moving to Kentucky around 1780 when this was still frontier country, they became prominent in local and State politics and as planters and professional men. In his boyhood, Marshall got tired of hearing about his famous collateral relative, Chief Justice John Marshall, and felt it was about time someone else in the family made a name for himself. As it turned out, he took the first step in this direction when, after graduation from Virginia Military Institute, he applied for and received a commission as second lieutenant in the Army. His retirement to private life at 71 brought to an end a half century of public service which, for sheer competence and devotion to duty, has rarely been surpassed.

Yet, outside the military, he was known only during his last 12 years as a public servant. The early careers of nearly all great war commanders seem drab and in no way predictive of their wartime achievements. The reason, of course, is that a career officer *normally*, that is in peacetime, does not practice his profession but remains a student, eternally preparing himself for an eventuality that he and everyone else hopes will never occur. This peculiarity of the military profession accounts for the fact that the special competence of career officers tends to be undervalued by outsiders, although without it no war is won. This competence can be acquired only by practical experience over a long career span. No layman, however brilliant he may be, has it; intellect alone, pure ratiocination alone will not produce it, just as it will not produce the surgeon's operating skill.

It was a measure of President Roosevelt's greatness as a war leader that he fully understood this. He was very much his own Commander in Chief, he ran the war, made the broad policy decisions, but in the execution of these policies, in matters of strategy, tactics and operations, he nearly always deferred to the professional judgment of his military top command, especially that of General Marshall.

Marshall's unusually long tenure as Army Chief of Staff contributed to his effectiveness, for able men grow abler when they see a task through from beginning to end. He became Chief of Staff on the day Germany attacked Poland—"by a favor of Providence," as President Truman was later to remark. Heading the military establishment during the entire 6-year war period, he was responsible for the rapid and orderly expansion of the Nation's military forces from 175,000 men, 13,000 officers and some 1,000 planes to over eight million men, 764,000 officers and 69,000 planes. In an incredibly brief time, a peacetime army ranking 17th among the world's national armies, had become a vast, flexible, superbly equipped and trained force—"mobilized as if from nowhere," to quote Secretary of War Stimson—with which a difficult six-front war was won. Once the initiative was ours, there were "practically no serious setbacks." Marshall's "timetables of the successive operations" proved accurate. To an astonishing extent, the war went "according to plan." His estimates of the number of combat divisions required for victory were "adequate and yet not excessive." No combat division was left in this country when Germany surrendered; all were overseas in the theaters of war. It took every man the Nation had mobilized, wrote Marshall in his Final War Report, "to do our part of the job in Europe and at the same time keep the Japanese enemy under control in the Pacific."

Not the least of his achievements was Marshall's completion of a good part of the military buildup during the 27 months of peace that were granted us while Europe and the Far East were embroiled in war. The Army had grown to eight times its peacetime strength when Japan attacked Pearl Harbor on December 7, 1941. We were much better prepared than we had been in 1917, and this despite widespread opposition to military preparations, reflecting in its emotional intensity the passionate determination of the American people not to become involved in *this* war.

Marshall worked hard to dispel the popular confusion of preparedness with warmongering and to dispel the dangerous illusion that our unrealized power potential would deter an aggressor, our mere wish to avoid war would secure us peace. He tried to make clear to the public that much time must elapse between deciding to arm and being armed and that we could not safely count on being granted this time if war were thrust upon us. He said once in a speech that "perhaps the most important task of the Army is to plan and scheme and work to the end that this time factor will be kept to a minimum." Our past experience worked against him. We had never yet had to pay the price of defeat for failure to prepare in time for war. Although the war was manifestly moving closer, the bill extending selective service passed by but a single vote — just 4 months before we were at war. It was an election year and public opinion had made itself heard.

World War II was a coalition war of global dimensions in which 93 million men and women were mobilized. For the Allies to win, it was as essential that they prosecute the war in the closest accord, as that they exert themselves to the utmost. Never before was a coalition war fought with such unity of purpose and effort by so disparate a group of allies; never had such prodigious exertions been required of each member state. Decisive for the success of the alliance was the fact that the two members who jointly accounted for the larger part of its total military and economic strength fought the war, from the start, under a unified high command. In Stimson's judgment there were two main reasons why the United States and Great Britain were able to use their land, sea and air forces as if they were a single military unit: Roosevelt's and Churchill's determination to wage the war as a team, and General Marshall's organizing genius and diplomatic skill. He was the dominant member of the joint command organization — the combined Chiefs of Staff — of whom Churchill said that "there was never a more serviceable war machinery established among allies."

Upon his retirement from active military service at the end of the war, Marshall was summoned to important civilian posts: Ambassador to China (1945–46), Secretary of State (1947–49) and Secretary of Defense (1950–51). He was the first military leader ever to hold the two highest ranking Cabinet positions, the first to serve in one war as the military head of the Army and in another (Korea) as the civilian head of all our land, sea, and air forces. Momentous changes took place in American foreign policy while he was Secretary of State and in these he played an active part—rescue of Greece and Turkey from communist conquest, rehabilitation of Europe through the Marshall Plan, initiation of discussions leading to establishment of NATO. For his contributions to the generous and imaginative aid program which bears his name, Marshall received the Nobel Peace Prize (1953), the first military man ever to have been so honored.

A reticent man who shunned publicity, Marshall once remarked, "I think I prize my privacy more than anything else." This, and the fact that his life story could not be told honestly and completely without hurting the feelings of many people, decided him not to write his memoirs. Marshall resisted pressures from friends and lavish offers from publishers. The closest he came to an autobiographical record was his Final War Report, covering the years 1943–45. This brief (153 pages of lucid and factual description of the buildup, the logistics, the strategy, the steps on the way to victory) was, as his biographer Robert Payne remarks, "a history of the war which could only be written at a time of triumph by the man most responsible for the triumph." Through it "there shines the peculiar quality of the man at his best: complex and unyielding, stripped like a runner for the race." In carrying out his duties, Marshall stood up for what he thought was right. For example, in 1941 there arose the issue whether Army officers should be college-trained, and commissioned after a short period of military training, or whether candidates should be selected from among qualified men outside the service who would volunteer for officers' school after completing training. Marshall considered the latter method the superior; he felt so strongly about this that he even went to the point of declaring he would resign if Secretary Stimson insisted on holding civilian military camps.

Those who most directly depended on Marshall are best qualified to add to our understanding of this man. When President Roosevelt could not make up his mind to appoint Marshall Chief Allied Commander in Europe—even though he was so obviously the logical choice that the appointment was taken for granted—he left the decision to the general. The war was too big for personal feelings or desires to enter such a decision, replied Marshall, whereupon the President said, "I feel now that I will not be able to sleep at night with you out of the country," and kept him by his side.

Marshall knew as well as the President that field commanders rather than Chiefs of Staff are remembered in history, but this counted for nothing with him. As with all men who render great public service, his sense of duty always took precedence over personal concerns. Dean Acheson tells of an interview he had with him shortly after Marshall became Secretary of State. In reply to Acheson's query as to what was expected of him as chief aide, Marshall said: "First, the most unvarnished truth, particularly about myself. I have no feelings except those which I reserve for Mrs. Marshall." Churchill called him "a magnificent organizer and builder of armies—the American Carnot"; Truman wrote that "to him, as much as to any individual, the United States owes its future"; but Robert Payne came perhaps closest to the essence of Marshall in this passage: "It can be said of him, as it can be said of few others, that he lived for an idea, and the idea was America."

USS SAM RAYBURN (SSBN 635)

NAMED FOR one of the Nation's foremost legislators and parliamentary technicians, Sam Rayburn of Texas (1882–1961). A public servant during his entire adult life, a politician in the best sense of the word, Rayburn served in the House of Representatives longer than anyone before him: almost half a century, or more than one-fourth the life span of the United States. During the last 24 years of his life, he was either majority or minority leader or Speaker of the House. He held the speakership for 17 years—the longest record and double the one previously held by Henry Clay.

His tenure in the House coincided with a period of tremendous change in the fortunes of our country, of innumerable crises and as many triumphs; a period which saw the United States rise from relative obscurity to the pinnacle of world power, its population more than doubling, its affluence multiplying many times over. Government grew accordingly, as reflected in the Federal budget which rose from $1 billion to $84 billion.

Rayburn's name is connected with many important pieces of legislation, particularly after he became chairman of the Committee on Interstate and Foreign Commerce in 1931. He was the author of the Federal Communications Act, the Securities Exchange Act, the Rayburn-Wheeler Holding Company Act, and the Rural Electrification Act. He has been called principal architect of the legislative program of the Roosevelt era. In August 1941, he persuaded the House to extend the draft act. The vote was 203 to 202. Only thus narrowly was dissipation of our military manpower averted just 4 months prior to Pearl Harbor.

Rayburn's reputation as a statesman and skilled parliamentarian, however, rests chiefly on his handling of the speakership. To quote the late Clarence Cannon: "The foundations of the growing power of the speakership were laid under Speaker Thomas Reed, flowered under Speaker Joseph Cannon, and have culminated under Speaker Rayburn . . . in all the long and stately procession of illustrious men who have occupied that exalted position he is the greatest and the most powerful."

The speakership is an ancient and venerable institution going back to 14th century England. Congress took it over from the colonial legislatures. Curiously, the office now puts its incumbent next in succession after the Vice President. If Rayburn's life did not quite follow the tradition of log cabin to White House, it came close; for the speakership is held to be the second most important public office in the land.

Sam Rayburn was born in Tennessee, one of 11 children of a Confederate cavalryman. The family moved to a 40-acre cotton farm in Texas when he was 5. There he attended a one-room schoolhouse and did the usual chores expected of farm children. When he wasn't farming he read voraciously. As he later remarked, "By the time I was 9 or 10 I had read every history book I could find . . . everything I could get hold of about Washington, Hamilton, Jefferson, the Adamses, Monroe, Madison, and all I could about the men then in public life." By the time he was 13, he had decided on a public career. He didn't lose time reaching his goal.

At 17 he entered college, working his way through by sweeping floors and milking cows. Upon graduation he taught school. At 24 he was elected to the State legislature, serving 6 years, the last 2 as Speaker of the House. He studied law between sessions and was admitted to the bar. He was 30 when first elected to Congress.

Despite his rise to positions of power and influence, Rayburn remained a plain, homespun man. President Johnson said of him that there wasn't anyone in the United States who couldn't see him "if they were willing to sit a spell. To the dismay of his staff, he made his own appointments—often on the back of an old envelope in his hip pocket. And he read his own mail. 'When someone writes me on tablet paper with a lead pencil,' he once told me, 'I figure what he's writing me about is pretty important to him.'" And once, in talking of Flag Springs, the little town where he attended school, Rayburn said: "All of us are just a little way from Flag Springs. You know I just missed being a tenant farmer by a gnat's heel."

There is hardly a name in our history so bound up with our democratic traditions and ideals as that of the man for whom this ship is named.

"He was the last tie between the frontier concepts and ideals of Thomas Jefferson, Andrew Jackson, Davy Crockett, Sam Houston, and Abraham Lincoln and the new Frontier of Science."

Firing of a Polaris A–3 missile off Cape Kennedy, Florida.

APPENDIX

Polaris Fleet Ballistic Missile Submarine Shipbuilding Program

Name	Authorized by Congress	Shipbuilder	Keel laid	Launched	Commissioned
USS GEORGE WASHINGTON (SSBN 598)	1958	Electric Boat Company, Groton, Conn.	Nov. 1, 1957	June 9, 1959	Dec. 30, 1959
USS PATRICK HENRY (SSBN 599)	1958	Electric Boat..........	May 26, 1958	Sept. 22, 1959	Apr. 9, 1960
USS THEODORE ROOSEVELT (SSBN 600)	1958	Mare Island Naval Shipyard, Vallejo, California.	May 28, 1958	Oct. 3, 1959	Feb. 13, 1961
USS ROBERT E. LEE (SSBN 601)	1959	Newport News Shipbuilding & Dry Dock Co., Newport News, Va.	Aug. 25, 1958	Dec. 18, 1959	Sept. 16, 1960
USS ABRAHAM LINCOLN (SSBN 602)	1959	Portsmouth Naval Shipyard, Portsmouth, New Hampshire.	Nov. 1, 1958	May 14, 1960	Mar. 8, 1961
USS ETHAN ALLEN (SSBN 608)..........	1959	Electric Boat..........	Sept. 14, 1959	Nov. 22, 1960	Aug. 8, 1961
USS SAM HOUSTON (SSBN 609)..........	1959	Newport News..........	Dec. 28, 1959	Feb. 2, 1961	Mar. 6, 1962
USS THOMAS A. EDISON (SSBN 610)..........	1959	Electric Boat..........	Mar. 15, 1960	June 15, 1961	Mar. 10, 1962
USS JOHN MARSHALL (SSBN 611)	1959	Newport News..........	Apr. 4, 1960	July 15, 1961	May 21, 1962
USS LAFAYETTE (SSBN 616)	1961	Electric Boat..........	Jan. 17, 1961	May 8, 1962	Apr. 23, 1963
USS ALEXANDER HAMILTON (SSBN 617)..........	1961	Electric Boat..........	June 26, 1961	Aug. 18, 1962	June 27, 1963
USS THOMAS JEFFERSON (SSBN 618)..........	1961	Newport News..........	Feb. 3, 1961	Feb. 24, 1962	Jan. 4, 1963
USS ANDREW JACKSON (SSBN 619)..........	1961	Mare Island	Apr. 26, 1961	Sept. 15, 1962	July 3, 1963

Name	Authorized by Congress	Shipbuilder	Keel laid	Launched	Commissioned
USS John Adams (SSBN 620)	1961	Portsmouth	May 19, 1961	Jan. 12, 1963	May 12, 1964
USS James Monroe (SSBN 622)	1961	Newport News	July 31, 1961	Aug. 4, 1962	Dec. 7, 1963
USS Nathan Hale (SSBN 623)	1961	Electric Boat	Oct. 2, 1961	Jan. 12, 1963	Nov. 23, 1963
USS Woodrow Wilson (SSBN 624)	1961	Mare Island	Sept. 13, 1961	Feb. 22, 1963	Dec. 27, 1963
USS Henry Clay (SSBN 625)	1961	Newport News	Oct. 23, 1961	Nov. 30, 1962	Feb. 20, 1964
USS Daniel Webster (SSBN 626)	1961	Electric Boat	Dec. 28, 1961	Apr. 27, 1963	Apr. 9, 1964
USS James Madison (SSBN 627)	1962	Newport News	Mar. 5, 1962	Mar. 15, 1963	July 28, 1964
USS Tecumseh (SSBN 628)	1962	Electric Boat	June 1, 1962	June 22, 1963	May 29, 1964
USS Daniel Boone (SSBN 629)	1962	Mare Island	Feb. 6, 1962	June 22, 1963	Apr. 23, 1964
USS John C. Calhoun (SSBN 630)	1962	Newport News	June 4, 1962	June 22, 1963	Sept. 15, 1964
USS Ulysses S. Grant (SSBN 631)	1962	Electric Boat	Aug. 18, 1962	Nov. 2, 1963	July 17, 1964
USS Von Steuben (SSBN 632)	1962	Newport News	Sept. 4, 1962	Oct. 18, 1963	Sept. 30, 1964
USS Casimir Pulaski (SSBN 633)	1962	Electric Boat	Jan. 12, 1963	Feb. 1, 1964	Aug. 14, 1964
USS Stonewall Jackson (SSBN 634)	1962	Mare Island	July 4, 1962	Nov. 30, 1963	Aug. 26, 1964
USS Sam Rayburn (SSBN 635)	1962	Newport News	Dec. 3, 1962	Dec. 20, 1963	Dec. 2, 1964
USS Nathanael Greene (SSBN 636)	1962	Portsmouth	May 12, 1962	May 12, 1964	Dec. 19, 1964
USS Benjamin Franklin (SSBN 640)	1963	Electric Boat	May 25, 1963	Dec. 5, 1964	Oct. 22, 1965
USS Simon Bolivar (SSBN 641)	1963	Newport News	Apr. 17, 1963	Aug. 22, 1964	Oct. 29, 1965
USS Kamehameha (SSBN 642)	1963	Mare Island	May 2, 1963	Jan. 16, 1965	Dec. 10, 1965
USS George Bancroft (SSBN 643)	1963	Electric Boat	Aug. 24, 1963	Mar. 20, 1965	Jan. 22, 1966
USS Lewis and Clark (SSBN 644)	1963	Newport News	July 29, 1963	Nov. 21, 1964	Dec. 22, 1965
USS James K. Polk (SSBN 645)	1963	Electric Boat	Nov. 23, 1963	May 22, 1965	Apr. 16, 1966
USS George C. Marshall (SSBN 654)	1964	Newport News	Feb. 19, 1964	May 21, 1965	Apr. 29, 1966
USS Henry L. Stimson (SSBN 655)	1964	Electric Boat	Apr. 4, 1964	Nov. 13, 1965	Aug. 20, 1966
USS George Washington Carver (SSBN 656)	1964	Newport News	Aug. 24, 1964	Aug. 14, 1965	June 15, 1966
USS Francis Scott Key (SSBN 657)	1964	Electric Boat	Dec. 5, 1964	Apr. 23, 1966	Dec. 3, 1966
USS Mariano G. Vallejo (SSBN 658)	1964	Mare Island	July 7, 1964	Oct. 23, 1965	Dec. 16, 1966
USS Will Rogers (SSBN 659)	1964	Electric Boat	Mar. 20, 1965	July 21, 1966	Apr. 1, 1967

SS—Attack Submarine   SSN—Attack Submarine (Nuclear)   SSBN—Ballistic Missile Submarine (Nuclear)

INDEX

303

306

313

☆ U. S. GOVERNMENT PRINTING OFFICE : 1972 O - 82-336